BILLY BISHOP
Canadian Hero

Second Edition

BILLY BISHOP
Canadian Hero

Second Edition

Dan McCaffery

James Lorimer & Company, Publishers
Toronto, 2002

This book is dedicated to my father, the late James Cyril McCaffery, who served as an air gunner with Bomber Command during the Second World War.

Copyright © 2002 by James Lorimer & Company, Publishers.
Published 1988, Second Edition 2002.

James Lorimer & Company Ltd. acknowledges the support of the Ontario Arts Council. We acknowledge the financial support of the Government of Canada through the Book Publishing Industry Development Program (BPIDP) for our publishing activities. We acknowledge the support of the Canada Council for the Arts for our publishing program.

National Library of Canada Cataloguing in Publication
McCaffery, Dan

        Billy Bishop, Canadian hero / Dan McCaffery. — 2nd ed.
Includes bibliographical references.
ISBN 1-55028-768-0
        1. Bishop, William A., 1894-1956. 2. Fighter pilots—Canada—Biography.
3. Great Britain. Royal Flying Corps—Biography. 4. World War, 1914-1918—
Aerial operations, British. I. Title.

UG626.2.B5M33 2002   940.4'4941'092   C2002-904269-0

James Lorimer & Company
35 Britain Street
Toronto, Ontario M5A 1R7
www.lorimer.ca

Printed and bound in Canada

TABLE OF CONTENTS

ACKNOWLEDGEMENTS

F irst and foremost, my thanks go out to the First World War veterans who served with Bishop on the Western Front eighty-four years ago and who took the time to write to me or to sit down for interviews. These marvellous gentlemen, now all deceased, were extremely generous with their time and energy. Their recall of minute details was, frankly, astonishing. I could not have written the book without them or their countless fresh new stories about this famous figure in history. They include (ranks given at the time that they knew Bishop):

Corporal George Stirrett, who trained with the future ace in the 7th Canadian Mounted Rifles and who went overseas with him in 1915 aboard the troop ship *Caledonia*;

Captain Roger Neville, who was the pilot of Bishop's two-seater during the Canadian's eight months as a gunner/observer in 21 Squadron, Royal Flying Corps, 1916;

Captain Harold Balfour, who taught Bishop how to fly at the Central Flying School, Upavon;

Lieutenant Hamilton "Tim" Hervey, who took pilot training at Upavon with Bishop and who later flew combat sorties with him when both were members of 60 Squadron's fabled "C" flight in the spring of 1917;

Lieutenant William Fry, who was Bishop's Deputy Flight Leader and constant flying companion during Billy's heyday at 60 Squadron; and Captain Tommy Williams, himself a twelve-victory ace, who knew Bishop during 1917–18.

Special thanks are also owing to Lieutenant Phil B. Townsend, 12 Squadron, RAF, who visited the vicinity of Bishop's famous solo raid on a German airfield shortly after it happened, and who provided the author with vital new evidence on this controversial event.

Thanks also to Robert Percival, whose late brother, Edgar, flew with Bishop at 60 Squadron.

On the German side, I would like to thank Otto Roosen, a Rumpler two-seater pilot who fought against Bishop.

Others who were of invaluable assistance were members of the International Cross and Cockade Society of World War One Aero Historians. They provided me with a wealth of material, bringing to my attention letters and memoirs (some never before published) of 60 Squadron Bishop contemporaries Jack Scott, William Molesworth, Keith Caldwell, Spencer Horn and Harold Lewis, as well as the diaries of John Grider, who served with the ace in 85 Squadron, and of John Brophy, who, like Billy Bishop, was in 21 Squadron in 1916.

I am very grateful to *Cross and Cockade* editor Paul Leaman, to Dennis Hylands, and to 60 Squadron historian Joe Wane. These three British gentlemen put up with the endless inquiries of a Canadian writer for years.

In the United States, I would like to thank air historians George Cooke and Ed Ferko, both noted experts on World War One.

In Canada, my thanks go out to Group Captain Arnie Bauer, chairman of Billy Bishop Heritage in Owen Sound, and Mrs. Horace Vick, who was secretary of that organization. Mrs. Vick put me on the track of material dealing with Bishop's early years in Owen Sound. Thanks also to Steven Dieter for giving me a tour of Bishop's boyhood home.

Others who helped in various ways include Stewart Taylor, official historian of Canada's World War One flyers; W.A.B. Douglas, former Director, Directorate of History, Department of National Defence, Ottawa; Professor S.F. Wise, Carleton University, Ottawa; Paul Cowan of the National Film Board; Clifford Chadderton, chief executive officer of the War Amputees of Canada; and Marc Haslip.

Steve Harron, an old newspaper pal, brought to my attention some valuable newspaper clippings from 1917 editions of the *Owen Sound Sun*.

The staffs of the following institutions were extremely helpful: the

Public Archives of Canada, the Department of National Defence, the Toronto Public Library, the University of Western Ontario library and the Imperial War Museum, London, England.

Thanks also to Curtis Fahey and Margaret Doane at James Lorimer and Company, for helping me "fine-tune" the manuscript, and to Diane Young.

Last, but not least, heartfelt thanks to my wife, Val, whose loyalty and love has meant more than she will ever know, and to my dear friend Mary-Jane Egan, whose support has been greatly appreciated.

INTRODUCTION TO
SECOND EDITION

T he need to revise and reissue this book became obvious on the morning of April 16, 2002. On that date, the Canadian Press (CP) reported a soon-to-be published book by author Breteron Greenhous would make the claim that legendary Canadian war hero Billy Bishop was a liar and a fraud. The book, entitled *The Making of Billy Bishop*, would also argue that the First World War flying ace had won the Victoria Cross, Canada's highest gallantry award, by making up a story about a single-handed attack on a German airfield.

Greenhous's claims were not new. In fact, the same charges had been levelled twenty years earlier in a controversial National Film Board documentary called *The Kid Who Couldn't Miss*. Nevertheless, they created a firestorm of publicity from coast to coast. The CP story was much longer than most newspaper articles, quoting a number of historians and other interested parties. And that was just the beginning: the subject was debated on television, radio and in the newspapers. Historians quickly waded in with their opinions. This was clearly an issue that had struck a public nerve. Perhaps that shouldn't be too surprising — people seem to enjoy reading about heroes with clay feet. Besides that, as *Legion* magazine columnist Douglas Fisher noted as far back as 1988, "the Billy Bishop legend has endured almost beyond belief." Generations of Canadians have been taught about Bishop in school, making him one of our few truly well-known historical figures. In addition, the controversy is easy to grasp. Either Bishop was a brave and skilful pilot or a manufactured hero blown up by a government desperate to sell a cruel and unpopular war to a weary public.

Nevertheless, the uproar took me off guard because I felt my book, *Billy Bishop: Canadian Hero*, had settled the issue when it was published fourteen years ago. The book, which was the result of eight years of research, contained new information that I thought had exonerated Bishop from the principal charges against him. I had found a number of First World War veterans who had made a convincing case that the ace was a legitimate hero. Others agreed. The *Vancouver Sun* described my book as "a solid work that lays the Bishop controversy to rest." Historian Gwynne Dyer noted the book contained "new evidence that pretty well closes that debate." As recently as two years ago, historian David Bashow had written "McCaffery's extensive research and frequently unique, highly valuable offerings need to be treated with respect and accorded serious consideration."

The critics seemed to accept that I was no hero worshipper. Although I had concluded the Bishop legend was basically true, I had argued that about one-third of his aerial victories should be subtracted from his total, that his poor leadership had cost men their lives, that he was a womanizer and a heavy drinker. A review of *Billy Bishop: Canadian Hero* in the *Ottawa Citizen* included a headline that read: "Bishop was brilliant in the air but a boor in real life, says author."

Even Greenhous, writing in 1989 in the *Canadian Historical Review*, said I had "taken a somewhat harder look at Bishop's record" than previous biographers.

I certainly had not accepted stories that backed up the Bishop legend without first putting them under the microscope. For example, I chose not to include in my book a story supporting the VC raid told as far back as 1917 by a British balloon observer named Louis Alexander Weirter. Weirter, who served on the same section of the front as Bishop, claimed to have witnessed the Canadian's attack on the German airfield. But he made the claim as he attempted to sell a painting of the episode to a British museum. The museum commissioned his work, and Weirter produced a painting that showed a lone British aircraft fighting four German fighters at about 5,000 feet. Had he actually seen the raid, I concluded, his painting would have depicted a single Nieuport attacking a German Albatros flying at treetop level as it struggled to get airborne.

In some ways, I may have been too harsh on Weirter. Bishop, after all, had climbed to 5,000 feet on his way home. And he reported being briefly trailed by four German fighters as he made his way toward the Allied lines. Perhaps that's what Weirter saw. Realizing that wasn't dramatic enough for a painting, he may have embellished the scene by painting a picture of Bishop fighting off the four enemies. In the end, I decided to leave out the story altogether because I didn't believe Weirter was a reliable witness. Put simply, his story just didn't ring true to me.

Nevertheless, I felt the evidence I did present was solid. But over the years, it seemed to have been forgotten. Few people made reference to my findings when the debate erupted again in spring 2002. Many were apparently willing to believe that Bishop really was a charlatan. I tried to rectify this by writing a letter to the *Globe and Mail,* but it soon became obvious that much more was needed. It simply wasn't possible to make the case for Bishop in a few paragraphs. So when my publisher suggested *Billy Bishop: Canadian Hero* should be revised and reissued, I jumped at the chance.

Greenhous was subjected to a number of personal attacks in the media, but I will not resort to such tactics here. Instead, I will concentrate on dismantling his arguments. I believe that, because of his background as a professional historian, he tended to give too much weight to official records while not paying enough attention to the oral histories passed down by airmen who were on the scene. For example, writing in the *Canadian Historical Review* in 1989, he accused me of relying at least partially on "the unsupported recollections of old men" to make my case that Bishop had attacked the airfield. At the same time, he pointed out that German casualty records do not mention the raid, suggesting that lack of confirmation could be seen "as specific documentary evidence against Bishop." He went on to say that the Canadian's own combat reports claiming victories "are positive evidence" in his favour. Here was clearly a man who placed a good deal of faith in the printed record.

Readers will have to judge for themselves whether the recollections of the veterans can be dismissed so easily. They might also ask why some Bishop critics have been quick to reject the memories of old men who supported the ace while, at the same time, embracing the stories of aging veterans who criticized him. They might also want to question whether what's left in the surviving official records from the First World War is all that reliable.

Reading Greenhous's book, I felt that, like an overly aggressive Crown attorney, he sometimes tried a little too hard to prove his case. That's a perfectly legitimate strategy for a defence lawyer, whose sole objective is to win. But a good prosecutor should be dedicated to uncovering the truth, even if that means conceding some points to the other side. If, in the course of the trial, it becomes clear that the accused is innocent, the good Crown attorney will go to the judge and ask that the charges be dismissed.

An example of where I thought Greenhous tried too hard to convict Bishop came when he argued that the ace could not have raided Estourmel Aerodrome because, while he claimed to have attacked Albatros D-2s, the German airforce unit stationed there flew Albatros D-3s. The D-3, he noted, had curved back wings and V-shaped struts, while the D-2 had square wingtips and vertical struts. What he didn't say was that aircraft misidentification has been a problem in every air war ever fought. Even the great Red Baron, Manfred von Richthofen, frequently wrongly identified "several of the aircraft types he claimed," according to biographers H.J. Nowarra and Kimbrough Brown. Indeed, all thirteen of the Vickers two-seaters he claimed to have shot down were actually FE2Bs! In fairness to Bishop, Greenhous might just as easily have noted that both the Albatros D-2 and the D-3 were single-seater tractor biplanes of about the same size, built by the same company, with the same torpedo-shaped fuselages, similar landing gear and almost identical tails. He might have cut Bishop a little slack in this instance, conceding that a pilot zooming over an enemy camp at 100 miles per hour in the half-light of dawn while dodging withering machine-gun fire could perhaps be forgiven if he mistook an Albatros D-3 for an Albatros D-2.

I also formed the impression that Greenhous had made up his mind that Bishop was a fraud long before his book was published. In his 1989 article in the *Canadian Historical Review*, which was entitled "The Sad Case of Billy Bishop, VC," he wrote, "The argument for Bishop being everything he claimed to be — and which others have claimed him to be — is weak." In the same article, he listed ten points about the VC raid, concluding that "fundamentally at least six, and arguably eight, of the ten points go against Bishop and, taken together, they create a pattern which does nothing to inspire confidence in his official record." While he may not have gone into his research with his mind made up, at least thirteen years before *The Making of Billy Bishop* appeared, Greenhous was expressing grave doubts about his subject's record.

With this new edition, I have taken the opportunity to add information that I have collected since my book was first published. Most notably, I have included important new evidence provided to me by Otto Roosen, who was the last surviving German pilot of the 1914–18 war. I have also explained in detail where I received the confirmations of Bishop victories contained in this book.

I have also corrected some mistakes, including a few that were pointed out by Greenhous. In the end, I am confident that my book will stand the test of time much better than will the Greenhous book. That's because I am convinced that Bishop was an authentic hero. I have read his private letters, in which he expressed anguish for the loss of friends, and remorse at having killed people. In one, writing to his fiancée, he said, "Sometimes all this awful fighting in the air makes you wonder if you have the right to call yourself human. My honey, I am so sick of it all, the killing, the war. All I want is home and you." Somehow, I can't believe a man who was inventing stories about killing people would have penned those emotional words. There is a ring of genuine remorse in them.

I have looked into the eyes of men who served with Bishop as they told me their stories about him. I have heard the tone in their voices and observed their body language. I have read their private letters. Anyone who had done the same could not help but be struck by the reverence in which they held Bishop. Such devotion, I suspect, would not be given away easily by grizzled combat veterans. In a word, it would have to have been *earned.* I should add that this same respect was shown by Roosen, who told me Bishop was greatly admired by the pilots and gunners of the Imperial German Air Service.

At the same time, I did not ignore the official records. Indeed, I delved deeply into them in a bid to find out what Bishop did or didn't do. First World War records are piecemeal at best, making it difficult to prove Bishop did everything he claimed to have done. Many German airforce records for the 1914–18 era were lost during the Second World War fire bombing of Dresden, making it impossible to prove much of anything from those that remain. For example, some surviving records for German airforce units only mention the loss of a plane if the pilot was killed. If he was wounded, or if he walked away from the wreckage unhurt, there would be no record that the fight ever took place. Even records of dead German pilots can be deceiving because they often only list the date and place of the man's death, not where he was shot down. If, for example, a pilot was shot down and wounded over Vitry on April 3, 1917, and died three days later in a hospital at Arras, the records might simply say he had died on April 6, 1917, at Arras. Anyone looking to match up an Allied victory claimed over Vitry on April 3 with names found in German casualty records for that date would be out of luck.

Likewise, British records dealing with Bishop's Victoria Cross exploit have disappeared, either destroyed by German bombers in the Second World War or culled by bureaucrats looking to make space for new documents. Still, it would be a mistake to think that the records that do survive are totally unsupportive of his claims. Historian Stewart Taylor, for instance, told the Canadian Senate that he found twenty-two confirmations of Bishop victories in German records.

Still, there's no doubt that the authorities used Bishop in a bid to help sell the war. The British flying services, anxious to promote heroes for propaganda and morale purposes, were far too generous when it came to awarding victories to pilots. In other words, there are cracks around the edges of the Bishop legend. But the same could be said for virtually every Allied ace of the war, including the top-scoring British,

French and American pilots. At its core, however, the Bishop story is true. Of that I have no doubt.

Perhaps the most amazing thing about Bishop is that even if we take the word of his harshest critics he remains an undeniable hero. Greenhous believes he shot down about twenty-seven planes, which would make him an ace five times over; an ace was a pilot who shot down five or more enemy planes. Although the figure seems modest enough, it's important to keep in mind that only five per cent of all fighter pilots became aces. It's also important to note that Greenhous's calculations would give Bishop one more victory than was achieved by the leading American pilot of the First World War, the fabled Captain Eddie Rickenbacker. It would also give him seven more victories than German pilots needed to win their nation's highest gallantry award, the legendary Blue Max.

Regardless of how many planes he shot down (and I believe his true score was closer to fifty), Bishop was a man of unmatched bravery. Those of us who have not flown combat missions cannot know the courage it takes to sail into enemy territory time and again. As a boy, I can remember asking my father, who was a Second World War airman, whether he was afraid prior to the first of his twenty-two raids over Germany. "It didn't take any courage at all to go the first time," he replied. "It was going back the second time that took courage." Bishop went back an astonishing 207 times after his first heart-stopping patrol as a fighter pilot. During one two-day period in April 1917, he flew no fewer than ten flights over enemy lines! His squadron commander, Major Jack Scott, wrote a report that month "recommending Captain Bishop for some recognition or award." He added:

> I beg now to suggest to you that the subsequent conduct of this officer merits further distinction. On different dates between the 6th and 30th April he has destroyed 10 hostile aeroplanes and two balloons, while he has driven down 10 other German machines. In the same period he has 34 times engaged enemy machines. He often flies six or seven

hours a day, two or three hours by himself looking for hostile aircraft. Comment is, I think, needless on this record of 24 days work, as the figures speak for themselves.

On top of his 208 fighter missions, he flew about two dozen operations as a gunner aboard a lumbering two-seater. And he flew a number of combat patrols over England as well, dodging his own anti-aircraft fire as he searched for Zeppelins in the dark and dangerous skies over London in the days before night fighters had radar or even radios. In all, he went hunting for enemy aircraft about 250 times during three different tours of duty in 1916, 1917 and 1918. Many famous or wealthy men have used their influence to duck combat, but Bishop, after he became a national hero, used his celebrity to get back onto the firing line.

Besides all that, Bishop played a major role in helping to defeat the Nazis in the Second World War. Put in charge of recruitment, he attacked the job with determination, helping to build the tiny Royal Canadian Air Force (RCAF) into one of the strongest airforces in the world. In many ways, his recruitment effort was his finest hour. His exploits in the First World War had demanded great courage, but the conflict itself was seen by many as a needless exercise that could easily have been avoided had a handful of men of vision been in the halls of power in 1914. But history shows that the 1939–45 war was essential. The Nazis could only be stopped by brute force, and Bishop, by helping to build up the RCAF, played an honourable role in their defeat. He had aged beyond his years and was in poor health, but he drove himself tirelessly. In a fitting tribute, Minister of Air C.G. Power told the old ace, "Your magnificent record in the First Great War fired the imagination of our Canadian aircrews in this war and has inspired them to deeds of courage to rival your own."

History is not an exact science. But solid general conclusions can be drawn by examining all the information available, whether it's to be found in fragmented official records, interviews with eyewitnesses or by reading the letters and diaries of the people who were there. After looking closely at all of these sources, my conclusion is that Billy Bishop deserves all the accolades he received. And I should point out that I am by no means alone in that regard. Many respected historians have said the same thing. S.F. Wise, the former Directorate of History for the Department of National Defence, told a Canadian Senate committee hearing in 1985 that: "A very high proportion of Bishop's kills, so-called, were in fact verified as a result of corroborative testimony. The allegation that there is fraudulence in the Bishop record I find without foundation whatsoever, and I believe I can say that authoritatively, having examined the whole record."

Historian David Bashow, who spent three years investigating Bishop's record for his book *Knights of the Air*, said, "I went into it being a strong believer that there were some discrepancies in Billy Bishop's wartime career, but I became a total believer after going through all the material. I started out being very dubious about his Great War record but in the end, I am absolutely convinced he did everything he claimed to have done under the rules of the day."

For all his faults, Bishop was a likeable rascal who survived the countless perils, beat the odds and became a giant in Canadian history. He was, in other words, a hero Canadians should not be quick to discard.

Dan McCaffery
Sarnia, Ontario
July 2002

This book is about the leading Allied air ace of both world wars and the most controversial combat hero Canada has ever produced. Like so many others of his generation, Billy Bishop quickly signed up when the First World War broke out in August 1914, eager for a taste of fame and glory. But unlike so many of his contemporaries, he actually found what he was looking for. Anxious to escape the mud and slime of the rat-infested trenches, he joined Britain's fledgling Royal Flying Corps, where he immediately excelled at the dangerous new art of aerial fighting. Driven by blind ambition, a fiercely competitive spirit and an undisguised hatred for his enemies, he shot down German planes at an almost unbelievable pace, quickly becoming the "top gun" of the Allied air forces. He won two Distinguished Service Orders, the Military Cross, the Distinguished Flying Cross and the coveted Victoria Cross (not to mention an array of foreign decorations). And he did it all in just seven months of front line duty as a fighter pilot. Moreover, he captured the public imagination like no soldier has done before or since.

Until Bishop came along, the military giants of Canada's history books had always been the generals — Brock, Wolfe and Montcalm — and not the men who actually did the fighting. But the Western Front discredited the generals. They seemed totally incapable of coming up with solutions to break a hopeless stalemate that dragged on for year after bloody year. It was a barbarous, filthy war of attrition in which artillery fire, poison gas and machine guns combined to dehumanize the fighting. Amid this mechanized slaughter of literally millions of men emerged Bishop, the lone warrior flying above the clouds in a little, open cockpit biplane with scarf flapping rakishly in the wind. For all appearances he was the modern knight in shining armour — a rugged individualist who took on swarms of opponents and always triumphed. Other aces were well-known, but none were as popular as the man they called the Lone Hawk. He usually operated by himself, far behind the enemy lines, while his peers fought from the safety of large formations, relying on teamwork to get the job done.

Bishop won the accolades he sought, but soon found himself becoming important to the Allied cause more as a propaganda symbol than as a pilot. This turn of events disturbed him greatly. Taken out of action with fifty victories to his credit, he was sent across North America on a speaking tour designed to drum up enlistment. Now he was being used not to fight the war, but rather to "sell" it. He played this new role rather well until he realized that active fighter pilots were catching up to his victory total. Before long, he was dethroned as the ace of aces.

Desperate to regain his title, he rushed back to the Front. In a frenzied killing spree unmatched in the annals of aerial warfare, he shot down twenty-five opponents in a scant twelve days, including five in one mission. Single-handed, he wiped out two enemy squadrons in less than a fortnight. It put him comfortably back into the lead in the scoring sweepstakes. But he was again yanked from the battle zone, this time for good, by a High Command fearful that his death would have an unsettling impact on public morale. More to give him something to do than anything else, the Canadian government asked him to work on the formation of an independent Canadian Air Force. He worked at this for the last few months of the war, but the armistice came before Bishop finished his task and it wasn't until 1924 that the Royal Canadian Air Force came into existence.

With peace Bishop found new challenges. He went on the lecture circuit, giving speeches about his war experience for huge sums of money. And when that petered out, he got back into flying, as a barnstorming stunt pilot at Toronto's Canadian National Exhibition and as an airline operator. Later, he worked as an oil company executive and became a highly successful businessman.

When the Second World War broke out, Bishop was back in uniform, again as a propaganda tool. This time he held the honorary rank of Air

Marshal. Too old for the cockpit, he settled into the job with relish, helping to build the tiny Royal Canadian Air Force into one of the most powerful fighting machines in the world. He again stumped the country, giving speeches, pinning wings on new pilots (including his own son) and rallying public support for the war effort. No hero, not even George Beurling, the leading Canadian ace of the Second World War, could even begin to match the spell Bishop had on the public.

But when the war ended in 1945, the joy seemed to go out of Bishop's life. He tried to keep occupied, taking up hobbies, reading history books and dabbling in a few money-making ventures. But it was never the same. In 1950, when Canadian troops were sent to Korea, he again volunteered his services. This time, he was rejected. Ottawa was ready to meet its United Nations obligations by sending a small force to the Asian battleground, but the last thing it wanted was to turn Korea into a full-scale Canadian conflict. Bishop faded quietly away after that, spending his last years in semi-retirement before dying peacefully in his sleep at age sixty-two, on September 10, 1956.

Despite his fame and undeniable popularity with the public, Bishop was a controversial figure in his own lifetime. Some of the men who flew with him believed he was an overly ambitious pilot and ruthless killer. They thought he cared more about personal glory than the safety of squadron mates, that he occasionally falsified combat reports and, most disturbing of all, that he won the Victoria Cross by making up a story of a lone raid on a German aerodrome. He was, some said, determined that absolutely nothing would stand in the way of his quest to become the war's leading ace.

Bishop's peers had trouble understanding him. They found him to be fun-loving — the life of the party, in fact — but unwilling to form warm personal relationships. All of them were awed by the ferocity he displayed in dogfights, but such combat aggressiveness only served to cement the impression that he was cold-hearted.

All of this was unknown to me — and to the rest of the Canadian public — when I first heard of Billy Bishop. My dad had been an airman in the Second World War and, because of that, I had developed an early fascination with military aviation. I read everything I could find about the subject and, naturally, it wasn't long before I came across the Bishop legend.

Bishop seemed larger than life to me. There was nothing of the bland Canadian stereotype about him. He was something right out of an Errol Flynn movie.

But as I grew older, I found the various accounts of his career to be strangely incomplete. It was easy enough to find out what he had done, but there was little to indicate why he had been so successful or how he felt about it. Was he really the bloodthirsty killer that his own wartime writings made him appear, or was that just the false bravado of youth? How did a kid from rural Ontario cope with the fame and glory that was so quickly thrust upon him? What was his reaction when close friends were killed? What did he think when he realized he was becoming more valuable as a propaganda symbol than as a pilot? What were his hopes and dreams? In other words, what made the man tick? And just what was it about him that made him a hero in the first place? One Canadian machine gunner at Vimy Ridge, beating back a German counterattack, must surely have mowed down more of his nation's ene-mies in one afternoon than Bishop had killed during the whole war. Why, then, was Bishop a legendary hero while the machine gunner remained anonymous?

The answers to these questions were not to be found in the literature available when I began my research.

Among the hundreds of books about First World War aviation there were just two solely about Bishop. His autobiography, *Winged Warfare*, appeared in 1917 and was published under the watchful eye of wartime censors. It contained virtually nothing about his prewar life and made no mention of the twenty-five kills he registered in 1918. It also tended to leave the reader with the impression that all of Bishop's victims were destroyed when, in actual fact, many were simply damaged or driven off. Although a useful book in that it tells us what Bishop was thinking during some of the more crucial moments of his life, it is far from a complete look at his remarkable combat career.

His biographer was his son, William Arthur Bishop, who in 1965 published *The Courage of the Early Morning.* It was as objective a piece of work as a son could write about a father, but it, too, left the reader with the impression that all of Bishop's victories were decisive. Also, it contained nothing about the identities of his victims or comments from German airmen who had fought against him. It made no mention, either, about the tension between Bishop and some of his squadron mates, or the doubts that some had about his record.

By the mid-1970s my appetite to know more about Bishop was whetted when a gallant old cavalryman named George Stirrett walked into my newspaper office for a Remembrance Day interview. Stirrett, it turned out, had known the ace personally. And his stories painted a picture of a vulnerable, sometimes gentle man who bore little resemblance to the hard-nosed killer in the history books. I began gathering as much information about Bishop as I could lay my hands on, with the vague notion that some day I would write a book about him. By 1980 my reporter's instincts had taken over and I started to work on the project seriously.

I spent countless hours poring over logbooks, combat reports, letters, diaries, memoirs, official records and faded newspaper and magazine articles from a bygone era. Soon, I had a file bulging with data. From there it was on to interviewing or corresponding with as many of Bishop's contemporaries as I could find. (This was no easy task because most of his flying mates were long dead and, among those still living, many lived an ocean away in Great Britain.) Next, I began contacting aviation historians across Canada and around the world.

Before long I began hearing rumours about Bishop that had never been aired in public. That Bishop was a glory seeker I had no doubt. He made constant reference to his victory score, even in letters home, forever comparing it to the leading British and French flyers. But was his whole legend a lie? I was determined to find out.

In the midst of my research the National Film Board of Canada released its highly controversial documentary *The Kid Who Couldn't Miss.* The 1982 production tackled publicly what had only been whispered for decades. It openly suggested that Bishop was a monumental fraud who didn't deserve his Victoria Cross. The film was attacked savagely by critics and near-hysterical veterans groups but, the truth is, no one seemed able to prove that Bishop really had done the things for which he had been credited for so long. In the minds of many, the Bishop legend lay in tatters.

I spent the next few years investigating his record, examining each of his seventy-five victories in detail. I searched for confirmations in German records and in Allied documents. And I paid special attention to the controversial raid for which he won the Victoria Cross, determined to get to the bottom of the issue.

It was a tedious chore, because few of Bishop's contemporaries were willing to be quoted on such a sensitive issue. There were times when I despaired that I would ever finish but, with the help of many people and no small measure of luck, I was able to come up with startling new evidence that I was confident would lay the whole controversy to rest.

Along the way I also uncovered a wealth of new information that tells much about Bishop's character and destroys some long-held public misconceptions in the process.

This book is not a complete look at Bishop's life. I decided before I ever sat down at a keyboard that I would concentrate on his career as a fighter pilot. That, to me, was what made him famous. The fact is that his battles in the skies over France were the most eventful days of his life, and I have investigated them in detail. I have also included a chapter on his youth because there are clues in his childhood that explain why he became such a successful fighter pilot.

Since each passing year reduces the number of people who knew Bishop during the Great War — most, if not all of them are now dead — friends told me I waited until the eleventh hour before getting to work on this book. Actually, it was closer to thirty seconds to midnight. But fortunately, it was also just in time. I have, I believe, produced a work that should allow Canadians to understand just what type of person Bishop was and to appreciate what he really did.

Dan McCaffery
Sarnia, Ontario
June 1988

CHAPTER ONE

William Avery Bishop, one of the most colourful swashbucklers of the twentieth century, was born in Owen Sound, Ontario, Canada, on February 8, 1894. Before he was twenty-five years of age, he would claim to have defeated 100 men in mortal combat He loved, some say, at least that many women. He was the quintessential adventurer-roughneck who somehow survived the perils of a thousand ordinary lifetimes to become a fabulous national hero.

To the mythmakers at the War Department and in the newsrooms of the Allied nations, Bishop was a godsend. As one historian has so aptly noted, Billy "epitomized everything that the public demanded of a Knight of the Air. Young, dashing and handsome, he exuded an appealing mixture of gentlemanly manners and schoolboy devilry."[1] To generations of Canadians, he was the very symbol of the invincible air ace.

Yet Bishop was also a complicated, even paradoxical, man. He espoused the virtues of chivalry, treating even prisoners of war with sympathy and respect. But in combat he was utterly ruthless. To German pilots, who nicknamed him "Hell's Handmaiden,"[2] he was the adversary who laughed as he sent them down in flames. On at least two occasions he admitted to strafing downed airmen, and he once slaughtered the crew of a two-seater from point-blank range after the observer's gun had jammed.

Millions who never knew him idolized him but, among his fellow pilots, the reaction was decidedly mixed. Some swore by him, insisting that he was a fearless aviator and a charming companion. But others harboured animosities toward him that did not fade with the passage of the decades.

Was he a homicidal maniac or a hero? Did he, as the commander of the Royal Flying Corps once said, execute "the greatest single show of the war"?[3] Or was he just an adroit storyteller who won the Victoria Cross by pulling off the most sensational hoax in military history? To get to the bottom of the Billy Bishop legend, it is essential to understand just how complex a person Bishop was. And to understand the forces that shaped his personality, we must go back to the beginning.

The Bishops were a typical middle class family. Billy's father, Will Bishop, was an articulate, well-educated man who had gone to law school before setting up practice in Owen Sound. He was appointed to the plum job of county registrar as a political favour after backing the winning candidate in the national elections of 1896. As a result, Will, his wife, Margaret Louise, and their four children (Billy was the second youngest) were never in financial difficulty, although they were by no means rich.

Few Canadian schoolboys lived far from the great outdoors during the Gay Nineties, and Billy was no exception. Then, as it remains today, Owen Sound was a small community nestled among the rolling hills of Western Ontario, overlooking the windswept waters of Georgian Bay. In such surroundings, Billy had every opportunity to hunt small game. There were dozens of squirrels infesting the family orchard. One Christmas morning, his father presented Billy with a .22 calibre rifle and offered the boy twenty-five cents for every squirrel that he bagged. A quarter of a dollar went a long way in those days, but the senior Bishop didn't expect to make substantial payments.

He was wrong. Within a week his son was collecting a dollar or more per day. Billy soon boasted that he could bring down a squirrel with a single shot. Fortunately for his father, the lad virtually wiped out the local squirrel population before the elder Bishop was forced to renege on the deal. Although no one realized it at the time, there could have been no better training for aerial combat than hunting.

His mother certainly hadn't reared him to be a killer. Indeed, she dressed him in a suit and tie before packing Billy off to school each morning. Looking like a perfect little gentleman, he was soon the object of much schoolyard torment. Other boys were fearful that his example might lead to *them* being outfitted in such stiff, formal attire. Life soon became an endless round of brawls between Billy and his classmates. They were certain that if they could only soil his suit and tear off his tie, the whole problem would simply evaporate. Besides, it was reasoned, a fellow who took piano lessons and who preferred the company of girls would be easy to manhandle.

They were sadly mistaken. Billy may have been dressed like a timorous mommy's boy but, beneath that suit, there lurked a little tiger. He slammed heads together on more than one occasion to prove that he "couldn't be pushed around by anybody."[4] Once he made the point when the odds were seven to one against him.

Yet, although he was soon very good with his fists, Billy was by no means a schoolyard bully. One of his former classmates remembered him many decades later as "someone who often went to the rescue of the smaller boys when they were being picked on by the older lads. Billy was in a lot of fights and, although he never started them, he sure finished 'em! He could hold his own in fights with bigger fellows because he didn't show any fear. And because he would attack like a wild man. But you shouldn't get the wrong impression. I always found him to be a very good-natured boy. Exceptionally so. He was the class clown at Owen Sound Collegiate you know."[5]

Scholastically, Billy was a complete disaster. His report cards were consistently poor. Those early failures were to have a profound influence on his future behaviour. Racked by self-doubt, he quickly abandoned any pursuit that he could not immediately master. He had to be the best at whatever he did or he just wasn't interested in pursuing it. In extra-curricular activities he was also a failure. He had no interest in contact sports such as football, hockey or lacrosse. He entered a race once, but gave up on running after finishing second. Still, if he was skilled at a thing, he drove himself tirelessly until he had completely mastered it.

Often, during school hours he could be found downtown in the local pool hall. Billy had by now developed his legendary charm to a noteworthy degree and could easily explain his absence to teachers with a convincing series of lies. When the truant officer finally caught up with him, Billy was hauled before the principal and warned that, if he didn't mend his ways, he would end up as a derelict To his worried parents, the schoolmaster added that Billy was proficient at nothing but fighting.

Besides his restless spirit, Billy had a good deal of spunk. When, as a 15-year-old, he read a newspaper account about a new flying machine called the aeroplane, he decided to build his own craft. He quickly slapped together a rickety contraption made of cardboard, wood crates and strings and hauled it to the roof of the family's three-storey home. There, some thirty feet off the ground, he took off on his first solo flight. When his sister dug him out of the wreckage he was, miraculously, unhurt. His only fear seems to have been that his parents would find out about the episode.

As he entered his teens, Billy was developing into an undeniably handsome youngster. He was of average height, slim, with a firm jaw, full mouth, straight nose, sparkling blue eyes and a head of bushy blond hair. Later, he added a pencil moustache, which somehow gave him an even more youthful appearance.

He had no trouble attracting female company. His younger sister often paid Billy to take out her friends. Once, he charged an astonishing five dollars to escort a young lady named Margaret Burden. He required that much, he claimed, because the girl was such an eyesore.

In reality, Billy loved her at first glance. Writer Alan Hynd, who conducted extensive interviews with Bishop for *Liberty* magazine, described young Margaret this way: "She was a picture of white organdy, with laughing dark eyes and raven hair." The granddaughter of department store magnate Timothy Eaton, Margaret lived in Toronto. Her parents sent her to the family summer home on Georgian Bay at the end of each school year. It was here that she met Billy.

Hynd paints a picture of tender "puppy love" between the rough-and-tumble lad from the hick town and the big city rich girl. He writes: "Billy was an outdoor boy, and he used to point out to her gaily coloured birds that a little girl never saw in the city. She talked about him so much that the two families eventually became acquainted. Fall came, and she went away. But she didn't forget, and neither did Billy."

The relationship produced mixed reactions from the parents of the two young lovers. The Bishops were amused when Billy boldly announced that he would make Miss Burden his bride one day. The Burdens, on the other hand, found no humour in the situation. Mr. Burden, who had married into wealth, took an immediate dislike to Billy. He would make several attempts to scuttle the budding romance.

While Billy was becoming known around Owen Sound as a ruffian and a poor student, his older brother, Worth, was upholding the family honour by doing well at Kingston's Royal Military College.

It was sad, people said, that Billy wasn't more like his older brother.

So, as might well be imagined, when Billy decided at age seventeen to join RMC, his parents were openly relieved. They were hopeful that a strong dose of military discipline would make a gentleman out of him.

Billy had other reasons for choosing the cadet school. He had no idea what he was going to do with the rest of his life, but be did realize that his mediocre high school marks would make it impossible to enroll in a more traditional university. He was off to RMC and his life would never be the same again.

Bishop quickly discovered that his decision to enroll at Royal Military College was a mistake. First of all, the place was old, uncomfortable and overcrowded. Billy and the rest of the class of 1912 were housed in a barracks that had been built exactly a century before, during the War of 1812. Originally, their quarters had been part of a shipping yard for Britain's Royal Navy. Like the rest of the historic limestone buildings and ancient Martello towers that made up the school, it was damp and cold. Less than half a mile away, just across Navy Bay, Fort Henry stood silently, looking down from green hills.

But much worse than the surroundings was the treatment meted out to new cadets. The motto of RMC was *Truth, Duty, Valour*, but in fact it was a place in which senior cadets, operating with the tacit approval of the commandant, subjected newcomers to sadistic and dangerous treatment. Billy got a taste of it soon after he arrived when he was ordered to clean out a turret. An upperclassman conducting an inspection of his work discovered a spider in the turret and forced Bishop to eat it in front of his peers.

But that was just the beginning. What had started out many years earlier as a good natured, one-day initiation process had by now developed into a cruel, year-long practice of torturing first year men. Whole classes were "licked" with rifle slings, cadets were forced to sleep with windows open, even in sub-zero temperatures, and beatings were routine. Juniors were forced to run everywhere. Anyone caught walking was immediately thrashed. One young cadet, the *Ottawa Citizen* reported, had to be hospitalized after being whipped by seniors.

And there was an almost unbelievable ritual, so outrageous that the upperclassmen hid it even from the Commandant. It took place at the beginning of a new school year, when seniors would burst into the rooms of juniors after dark wearing masks, hoods and heavy, dark coats. Disguising their voices, they ordered the juniors to enact love scenes with one another. The first year men were assembled in a line and one was forced to go up and down the column kissing and hugging everyone present. Others were forced to roll on the floor from one end of the line to the other, in a very rapid fashion.

But the worst was yet to come.

The cadets were taken to a darkened section of Fort Frederick where they were grabbed by invisible hands and slammed heavily against a wall before being blinded by a brilliant flashlight. Those who tried to keep their eyes shut were beaten with a hickory stick. Each man was then forced to swear that be would serve the seniors "above all."

That was followed by a series of a dozen or more sharp blows on the buttocks. Following that each cadet was forced to walk slowly down a tunnel lined on each side by seniors armed with clubs. Anyone deemed to be moving too quickly was called back and forced to walk the gauntlet again.

One cadet who went through this ordeal wrote afterward:

> "After coming out of the tunnel we were left to ourselves for
> a minute or so. Our backs and legs were covered with welts

and bruises from the beating. Some had lumps like eggs on
their legs to remind them of the tunnel."[6] The recruit, clearly upset by the treatment, added "when it comes to getting
a blow on the leg which leaves a bruise about four inches in
diameter and which swells up as big as an orange the affair
goes beyond a joke."[7]

Still the seniors were not finished. Some junior cadets were ordered to
start marching into the water. Many were not given the command
to stop until they were up to their waists in frigid water.

Bishop himself reported being beaten every Friday night for no
apparent reason. And he was assigned to a senior cadet who forced Billy
to kiss him goodnight every evening. It was little wonder, then, that
Bishop wrote home declaring that new cadets were treated like the lowest form of life on the planet.

Under such brutal conditions, a free spirit such as Billy was bound
to wilt. He failed his first year. The lad was so ashamed that he did not
return to Owen Sound to face his parents, deciding instead to spend the
summer working in Kingston.

Year two was more fruitful. Billy buckled down to his studies and
managed a passing grade. But his third term at RMC was marred by
one disciplinary problem after another. He was late for parade. He
failed to pass inspection. He snuck out of barracks after dark.

Billy was not overly popular with his classmates, apparently because
they were jealous of the success he enjoyed with the young women of
Kingston. He was forever sneaking into town for late-night encounters
with girls. While he was away, his personal belongings often disappeared. He could ill afford to lose them because cadets were only paid
300 dollars per year. And part of that money was needed to buy a uniform.

One evening, he talked another cadet, E.J. Townesend, into coming
along with him for a late evening rendezvous with two local ladies.
After dark, the pair crept down to the harbour and stole a boat. Both
bad been drinking heavily and, as they stumbled down to the water,

hiding in the shadows of the round Martello towers, the two made enough racket to wake the dead.

Somehow, they managed to avoid detection long enough to launch their craft.

Townesend was not especially skilled with paddles and, as they shoved off, they spun wildly around for a few anxious moments before straightening out. The harbour was pitch black and the dark water was as smooth as glass. It was so silent that the smack of paddles against the bull of the canoe echoed across the surface, creating great clunking sounds. They were loud, boisterous and giggling almost uncontrollably when the inevitable happened — the boat capsized.

The water in early spring was near-freezing, but the junior cadets both made it safely to shore. However, young Townesend was badly chilled and required immediate medical attention.

Billy himself went back to bed after helping his friend to the infirmary. Later that night he was hauled before the Commandant and charged with theft, drinking and leaving the grounds without permission. Unaware that the authorities had forced all the details out of poor Townesend, Billy denied everything, even when it became clear that he bad been caught red-handed.

Suddenly, his superior exploded. "Bishop! You're a liar!"[8]

Billy was very nearly expelled on the spot. As it was, he was confined to barracks for a month (the stiffest penalty in RMC history to date).

Although allowed to continue his education, be found himself unprepared to write May exams. In a desperate move, be cheated and was caught. For the second time in two months he was brought before a smoldering commandant. Dismissal was the only course of action possible but, in order to let him brood about it longer, it was decided that his formal discharge would not be made official until the beginning of the fall term in 1914.

At this low point in his life, disgraced cadet Billy Bishop was rescued from his personal predicament by the outbreak of the First World War. Not one to ignore such an opportunity, Billy had a simple goal — he would enlist and be overseas by autumn. His misadventures at RMC would be forgotten.

His only fear now was that the war would be over before he could get into action. That phobia was intensified in coming days as newspapers confidently predicted Germany would be crushed by Christmas.

If he could somehow get into battle before it all ended, Billy was certain he'd have the time of his life. From what he could gather from Canada's Boer War veterans, war was a picnic: you simply went off, whipped a cowardly foe and returned home with a wheelbarrow full of medals. Indeed, less than ninety Canadians had been killed in the South African conflict and, as a result, Canada's military establishment had no concept of the terrors of total war. They remembered only the Boer campaign, which had been over quickly and — for the most part — rather painlessly.

Billy was not alone in this line of thinking. All thirty-eight members of the RMC class of 1914 were terribly anxious to get to the Front. They could not know that thirteen of them would never come home again, nor that most of the rest would suffer serious wounds.

As for the school Commandant, he thought the record of the class of 1914 in battle was "outstanding." The college was as proud of its losses as it was of the awards that would be won by the graduating cadets.

It was a nervous young man who strode up to the front entrance of the Burden household in Toronto on a warm evening in September 1914. Billy had come to see Margaret. She put on a brave front when he told her his news, but years later she confessed that she was worried. "Of course you're going to enlist, Billy," she whispered. "I would expect it of you and I know it's what you want to do anyway. I just pray that the war will not last too long."[10]

After his visit to Margaret, Billy proceeded to the nearest recruiting station. Barging in, he demanded to be taken into "whatever outfit is going over first."[11]

The recruiting officer, after giving a double glance at this brash young man, signed Billy up. He was immediately inducted as a lieutenant of the Mississauga Horse, a cavalry regiment.

How had Billy Bishop, an RMC reject, been able to secure a position of authority in any military unit? In peacetime, such an appointment would have been unthinkable. But Canada was in need of officers to command the thousands of volunteers who were pouring in from farms, schools and factories from coast to coast. There was a serious shortage of brass in the regular army and most of the newcomers had no military background whatever. Billy's limited military training and his ability to ride a horse and shoot put him several notches above the other recruits. The war truly had come to his rescue.

CHAPTER TWO

Corporal George Stirrett was a compact man of average height with a friendly face that had been tanned brown by the sun of rural Ontario. He had been playing football in his hometown of Petrolia only a few months earlier when someone suggested that the whole team enlist. Nine of them did.

Stirrett had thought he would be going overseas immediately, but he was mistaken. After joining the 7th Canadian Mounted Rifles he was posted to a cavalry camp outside London, Ontario. There, he had undergone intense training under the direction of a stern-faced colonel named Ibbotson Leonard.

On a morning in February 1915, Stirrett made his rounds of the barracks and stables soon after reveille signalled the start of another day's activities. It was cold. Plumes of frozen white breath could be seen climbing from both men and beasts. The whole camp smelled of sour horses, oiled saddlebags, straw and manure. There was the grinding clatter of hoofs moving across the scarred earth, the familiar tinkling of bits and the creaking of saddles.

Completing his inspection, Stirrett reported to his immediate superior, Lieutenant Billy Bishop. Bishop was standing outside an old barn that served as a barracks, stomping his feet in an effort to keep warm. He barely noticed Stirrett's salute, returning it with a casual wave of his hand.

"How's everything, Georgie?"

"Good, sir. That is, everything seems to be in order."

"Fine. Didn't see any medics about did you?"

"No, sir."

"Keep an eye out for 'em, George. They're roaming around trying to vaccinate everybody with those damned needles."

Stirrett, recalling the conversation more than sixty years later, said: "Bish was a nice fellow for an officer! He treated us more like buddies than subordinates, if you know what I mean. He'd laugh and joke with us. We slept in a drafty barn and, one night, he reached into the straw and pulled out a bottle of brandy and shared it with us. He'd smuggled it out of Leonard's headquarters! Maybe it was because he was the youngest officer in the camp, but he was well liked by the fellows who had to take orders from him.

"You could just see he didn't get along as well with other officers, especially if they were of a higher rank than him. Then he became withdrawn and reserved. He would never let his guard down around people he didn't trust. But with the ordinary fellows, he was great. You couldn't ask for a better comrade."[1]

Everyone in camp was fearful that the war was about to end. Whenever a neighbouring unit received word it was going overseas, there was much sulking among those left behind.

The 19th and 20th Battalions were the first to be told they were headed for France. That night, much excited, they paraded around the grounds, led by a fife and drum band. One jealous major in the Mounted Rifles, kept awake by the carryings-on, leapt out of his bed, buckled his sword and Sam Browne belt to his pyjamas and confronted the procession.

"Get t' hell out o' here!" he cried, brandishing his sword menacingly in the night air.

When the band continued forward, pushed by men to the rear, the major attacked, slashing a bass drum and routing the bandsmen in every direction. One musician was seen retreating with a piece of his instrument in either hand sobbing, "The son-of-a-bitch, he cut my piccolo in two!"[2] Such was the mood in London that winter.

Bishop was especially concerned about the delay in getting into action. He had been slated to go to England in October 1914. But when the Mississauga Horse left for Europe, he found himself left behind. He was languishing in a Toronto hospital bed, recovering from pneumonia and a mysterious allergy. His doctors blamed it on his diet but Billy was sure that parade ground dust was the culprit.

Released from hospital, he was posted to the 7th Mounted Rifles in London in January 1915. There he found himself continuously cold, wet, tired and fearful that he would be caught by the doctors — who were vaccinating everyone in camp against every disease known to man.

Weather conditions were appalling. In a letter to Margaret he wrote: "We slept here last night and cold, oh darling, cold isn't the word for it. Although wrapped up in three blankets, we were all nearly frozen. It was so cold that we couldn't sleep at times and lay there telling each other just how cold we were. I'm lying on a tick full of straw that felt as if it grew in bunches like bananas and a little pillow of the same period."[3]

To take their minds off conditions, the Mounted Rifles often ventured into London. The following story by George Stirrett gives a good example of how they tried to amuse themselves.

"It was kind of a dull place back then," Stirrett said. "But we did have one notable adventure there that winter, and it nearly got poor Bish kicked out of the cavalry. What happened was that some of us got to drinking pretty heavily when we decided to go into town to have supper in the dining room of a local hotel. When we finished, we got the idea that it might be fun to sneak out without paying. It was more for a gag than anything ... we weren't out to save money, although Lord knows we never had much .... I guess you could say we were looking for something to break the boredom.

"So into the bathroom we went, one at a time, trying to squeeze through a very small window! Bish was the last one. He was still out in the dining room flirting with the waitress. She was a good-looking blonde girl and she'd been showing him special treatment all night."

"We were all already outside by the time he comes in [to the washroom]. In fact, everybody else had taken off except men ... I was crazy enough to wait for him. Bish tries to get through a window and — without a word of lie — he got stuck half way out! By this time the manager comes looking for us. He sees Bish dangling half out of the window and grabs him by the leg and tries hauling him back in. I'm on the other side of the wall pulling for all I'm worth on his arms ... it's a small miracle we didn't pull the poor devil limb from limb. Finally, I won the tug-of-war and Bish comes tumbling out, right on top of me. He had a window frame around his waist and one shoe missing. And when he fell on me he twisted my ankle so bad that I could barely walk."

The two young horse-soldiers scrambled to their feet and began hobbling down the road. The proprietor, meantime, was alerting police.

"There we were," Stirrett continued, "limping along, both drunk, Bish with a window frame around his waist and with one shoe missing — and half the town after us! We only got away because Bish 'borrowed' a car that, as it turned out, belong to a local judge. We left the car just outside of camp and then snuck into our bunks, freezing wet and banged up."

Next morning, a small army of policemen, city councillors, the hotel owner, the judge and the waitress showed up demanding that the colonel turn the guilty culprits over to authorities. Bishop was the prime suspect because he was known as the camp's practical joker. But he was ready for them. "He just denied everything," Stirrett remembered. "He put on that angel face of his and they must have believed him because we weren't charged."

"They couldn't say anything because the hotel owner had never seen his face — just his backside poking out a window. They brought the waitress along but she was no help at all. She looked right at Bish, he winked at her, and she told the police chief, 'No, sir, this isn't the man.'"

Bishop later made good his debt to the hotel owner. Just before the Mounted Rifles moved out, he won some money in a card game, went into town, apologized and paid the man off. "And I think he saw the waitress too," Stirrett added, "because when he came back the front of his tunic smelled like a perfume shop!"[4] In the spring of 1915, Bishop was readmitted to hospital after a riding accident. He explained what happened in a letter to Margaret on April 6th: "One of my new horses reared and fell back on me yesterday morning and by pure good luck didn't hurt me very badly as it is really a wonder it didn't crush me to death. It made rather a mess of my head and face, as it shoved my head right into the ground. My nose is of course broken and quite swollen and I can't see out of one eye, face is scraped a bit and my head a series of bumps and bruises. My body is pretty well bruised too, and I have two broken ribs. I'm all stuck up in plasters and bandages and my right hand is sprained. I shall probably be able to move around by Monday."[5]

To George Stirrett he exclaimed: "There's something vindictive about that animal. Do you notice the look in its eye whenever I'm around? I think it's trying to kill me."[6]

He was back in action April 20th, setting a division record when he led his men through a four-mile march in forty-two minutes flat But more calamities awaited him. In a letter a week later, he told Margaret: "By the way, I didn't tell you I had another close shave yesterday. A rifle I was firing backfired and the bolt flew back and hit me on the point of the cheekbone about one-and-a-half inches from my right eye. It is cut a bit and bruised but okay otherwise. I am lucky, am I not? It might have blinded me."[7]

Bishop was quickly gaining a reputation as an accident-prone clod. The next day, weakened by his inoculation (the doctors had finally cornered him) he fell off his horse and came within inches of being trampled to death.

About the only place he excelled was on the firing range. The Owen Sound squirrel hunter was a crack shot on the machine gun. The man who taught Bishop how to operate a machine gun was Lieutenant Walter Moorhouse. In an interview sixty years later, he still beamed with pride as he explained that his star pupil could take a Lewis gun apart and put it back together again, blindfolded, after only a few minutes of tinkering with it.

Stirrett recalled that Bishop often put an entire drum of bullets right on target from 300 yards range. "It was uncanny! Bish would just riddle a target that the rest of us could barely see. The instructors would keep putting it further back, until it was just a tiny black dot, and still he'd shoot it to ribbons! And I'm not talking about scoring with ninety per cent accuracy like the odd marksman achieved. I mean he put every damn bullet on target. He never missed. I distinctly recall the instructor shaking his head and saying, 'If Bishop doesn't kill himself in training, he'll win the war by himself."[8] It wasn't long before Billy was put in charge of the whole machine gun section.

Undoubtedly, Bishop had a natural ability with a gun. But even more important was his eyesight. It was almost superhuman. Stirrett recalled: "We were out in the field one day. We were supposed to be doing drills but Bish let us dismount and rest for awhile. After a few minutes he turned to us and said, 'Better mount up boys, a major and two captains are coming.' We looked in the direction he was pointing but couldn't see a thing. A few minutes later three black specks came into view several hundred yards off. A while after that, three officers rode up. One was a bloody major and the other two were captains!"[9]

Meanwhile, in France, the war was grinding along. It hadn't ended that first Christmas after all, although more than 400,000 Allied and German soldiers had perished in the first four months of fighting.

Some of those dead men belonged to the Mississauga Horse. Unknown to Billy, his incredibly bad luck in training was probably a lifesaver. Had he been on the Western Front with his original unit, he may well have been mowed down in one of the war's early, and completely insane, charges into the teeth of German machine guns.

But eventually, Bishop too got his chance to taste some real action. In June 1915 came orders for the 7th Mounted Rifles to report to Montreal. From there, they were to board a ship for the journey to Europe. Before they left London, the men gathered for the mandatory picture-taking ceremony. Bishop immediately began hamming it up for the photographers. Stirrett never forgot the scene.

"Everyone else was trying to appear as stern and warlike as possible but Bishop jabbed his fist into his chest and asked if he was demonstrating the proper Napoleon pose! Well that broke everybody up and we all had a hard time trying to look serious for our picture."[10]

Much different was the departure from Montreal on June 6. There the men experienced a sendoff that brimmed with patriotic sentiment. A Salvation Army band played stirring music and there were speeches from politicians and a clergyman. The minister urged the lads to do their duty "in this holiest of crusades."[11] Colourful Union Jacks fluttered from every pole.

Billy was deeply moved by the scene as he looked on from the deck of the troop ship, *S.S. Caledonia*. He would write home: "As we pulled out of Montreal the crowds cheered and waved like mad. Every whistle within miles blew furiously and our men sang *God Save the King* and cheered back. It was very impressive."[12] But there was a bit of sadness in it for Bishop as well. He admitted: "My heart swells when I think in a few hours we will see the last of Canada."

No one seemed to notice that the convoy was without any kind of escort. There wasn't a battleship, cruiser or even a destroyer anywhere in sight.

The fifteen-day voyage quickly became an ordeal. The *Caledonia* was a stinking, overcrowded, leaky old cattleboat that had been pressed into service as a troop carrier. Men passed the time playing cards in the smoker or by practising ship evacuation drills. The food, which they were assured was stew, was barely fit for human consumption.

High seas made matters worse. As the ship was buffeted by waves, most of the 240 men and all 600 horses aboard *Caledonia* became hopelessly seasick. And the men had difficulty sleeping in their hammocks. "To say they were packed in like sardines is only half expressing it,"[13] Billy commented. After a few days he wrote: "This ship certainly knows how to pitch and roll. We are running diagonally across the swell and we get motion every which-way. Two horses died in the night and we tossed them overboard. The men started to get sick and went down by the dozens. I felt a little squirm at times; especially as I was on duty in the stables below deck. The stench was horrible there."[14]

The whole convoy was on alert for U-boats. Extraordinary precautions were taken. Everyone, for example, was ordered to wear his cumbersome lifejacket at all times; a regular U-boat watch was posted; and smoking was strictly prohibited on deck after dark. George Stirrett thought that order was absurd because the *Caledonia* was equipped with green and red navigation lights that shone brightly from both masts.

Sub-watch, he remembered, was tedious work. It put a great deal of strain on everyone involved. You were expected to scan the ocean for hours on end, looking for seagulls! "It was claimed," Stirrett said, "that the gulls would follow in the wake of U-boats. We were also told to be on the lookout for periscopes. But for all the precautions — they still caught us with our pants down."[15]

When the submarines attacked, off the Irish coast on June 21, they did so with devastating force.

"We didn't even know they were there until the first ship was hit. A bright orange flame jumped fifty feet into the air, sending huge chunks of metal into the water," Stirrett recalled. "It [the metal] hissed when it hit the water and hot air came rushing across the surface, hitting the *Caledonia* with shockwaves."[16]

The deck of the *Caledonia* was instantly swarming with men. They could do nothing more than watch, as ships all around them came under fire. In horror, they looked on as a second vessel went into a watery grave. Stirrett remembered: "You can't begin to imagine the noise and light. The whole sky was lit up. It was terrifying and, I'm telling you, it made us feel stark naked."[17]

Bishop, who actually spotted one of the raiders on the surface, acknowledged similar feelings. He was choked with tension. For the first time in his life he was in real danger of dying — of never seeing his family, home or Margaret again. The water was brutally cold. A man couldn't survive in it long. A third ship sagged over on one side. It, too, was sucked under, leaving behind only a trail of air bubbles. Bodies of dead men bobbed in the oily sea. The water itself was ablaze. More than 300 young Canadians died in a matter of minutes.

Somehow, the attack ended with the *Caledonia* still afloat. But a shaken Billy wrote Margaret: "I wonder if I shall ever come home to you."[18] The lieutenant had had his first taste of warfare — twentieth century style.

The convoy pulled into Plymouth Harbour on June 23rd, and within a few days the troop had arrived on the clay plains of Shorncliffe Cavalry Camp. It was, the men agreed, the muddiest place they had every seen. Billy described it as "an incredible mass of mud, muck and mire, with the special unpleasantness that only horses in large quantity can contribute."[19]

Lieutenant Walter Moorhouse, the man who taught Billy how to operate a machine gun, said the mud was not only unpleasant — it could be downright unsanitary. "I saw the cook-house orderly carrying a side of beef slip on the duckboards and in saving himself shot the carcass off his shoulder into the mud where it disappeared. However, it was soon hauled out, hosed down and put into the stew."[20]

Rain fell day after dreary day. And when it stopped, it became sizzling hot and windy. Sandstorms cut the faces and bled the eyes. Still, training continued at a torrid pace, eight hours of drilling each day, rain or shine. The men even slept outdoors in the rain. "This place," Billy moaned, "is unbelievable."[21]

If the weather was bad, the leadership was worse. Upon arrival, the 7th had been issued more than 160 riding and light draught horses, brand new Lee-Enfield rifles and several hundred swords. Clearly, the High Command was still living in the nineteenth century, despite the terrible truth that had been presented to it on a daily basis for almost a year in France. The generals continued to dream of a dramatic breakthrough in the trench warfare in which cavalrymen, with sabres flashing in the sun, would lead the way to victory.

Even on the rainiest days, the men were ordered to leave their dry tents and to carry out useless inspections of the horse lines. One such inspection changed history. Stirrett recalled:

"Bish and I were sent out into a cesspool of black muck. It was stupid, but orders were orders and we had to do it. As we slopped about in the slime, Bish sank up to his knees in mud. It clung to his wet clothes and made a really pathetic sucking sound as he tried to extract himself. I tried to free him, lost my balance and fell face first into the muck!" At that moment, out of the mist, a Royal Flying Corps aeroplane appeared overhead. Bishop and Stirrett watched as it cut its motor and glided in for a gentle landing in a nearby field.

Billy stared at the flying machine for a long time. Raindrops dripped from the bridge of his nose. Finally, he turned to Stirrett and said, "George, it's clean up there! I'll bet you don't get any mud or horseshit on you up there. If you died, at least it would be a clean death." [22]

Stirrett recalled: "Both of us decided right then and there to join the Flying Corps. I never was accepted but Bish, after he became a famous ace, didn't lose touch with us. Whenever we were anywhere near his aerodrome, he would come and visit the Mounted Rifles. He'd tell us all kinds of tales about his life in the Flying Corps." [23]

Yet Bishop's transfer to the RFC wouldn't be as easy as he thought. Several days after making his decision, he still hadn't applied. He had no idea how to go about requesting a transfer, and was afraid to ask his CO the procedure.

But he found out in the most unlikely place — on the dance floor of the glassed-in hall at the Grand Hotel in Folkestone, near Shorncliffe. It was a popular tourist resort that attracted soldiers and civilians from across the region. Canadians from the Mounted Rifles attended at every opportunity, attracted by fine wine, food and the pretty English girls.

It was in this setting that Billy stumbled upon a man who could help him.

One evening, as the dance orchestra played, he spotted an officer wearing a double-breasted jacket, white-corded trousers and the distinctive cap of the RFC. Deserting the company of a redhead he was wooing, Billy darted across the room and introduced himself to the startled flyer. The aviator told him that, if he were serious about flying, he would have to go to the War Office in London to see a certain Lord Hugh Cecil.

And that is what he did. In July he went to London on leave and, after a week of dithering, decided to visit the War Office. Coming off the bridge in St. James Park, he turned east and took in a breathtaking sight. The War Office, the Home Guard and the black, pyramid-shaped roofs of Whitehall all loomed massively before his eyes. The three structures appeared as one building from this view, with towers, stone sculptures and roofs all mingling together like some fairytale castle.

He advanced tentatively, feeling, he admitted later, as frightened as a kitten. For the first time he began to question his decision to become a pilot. The whole business of taking a machine off the ground was suddenly very scary. But there was no turning back now. He screwed up his courage and marched into the War Office.

Bishop's first sight was a great set of stairs that were downright intimidating. At the top of the stairway was a stern-faced commissionaire who demanded that he fill out several forms.

The room was painted pale green and it smelled of varnish. It was filled with filing cabinets, wooden desks and bureaucrats dressed in blue uniforms. Bishop was led up a whole series of staircases and down a maze of hallways. Suddenly, he was there, outside room 613A. He was ordered to take a seat.

Bishop was astonished to find the waiting room packed with other eager applicants. He began to have doubts, for the first time, that he would be accepted. He waited patiently for the best part of the afternoon. Finally, he was ushered in to see Lord Hugh Cecil.

Cecil turned out to be a mild-mannered man of about forty-five with a balding head. He was leaning back in his chair, clutching a pen and notepad. The office was incredibly small and smelled of stale tobacco.

"Looking back from here," Bishop wrote in 1944, "the conversation had qualities of divine comedy."

Cecil looked him in the eye and asked, "Can you ride a horse?"

Bishop was quickly taken aback. What on earth did horseback riding have to do with aeroplanes? He replied in the affirmative, drawing attention to the fact that he was a cavalry officer.

"Can you she?"

Billy nearly fell out of his chair. "I had no idea what he meant, unless it had something to do with sex. I played safe and simply answered, 'Yes sir,'" he recounted later.

It dawned on Billy that Cecil's English accent was responsible for making the word 'ski' come out sounding like 'she.' That had to be it, but what the devil did skiing have to do with the Royal Flying Corps?

The next question was, "How well can you drive a motor car?"

Never having owned a car in his life, the young lieutenant answered, "Very well."

How well can you skate?"

Billy was relieved by the question. Here was one he could answer truthfully!

"Very well."

Next Cecil inquired about his experience on the track.

Billy paused for a moment, his mind working overtime. He quickly reasoned that the War Office wasn't about to take the time and effort to check out his Owen Sound Collegiate sports record. He told the Englishman his room back home was filled with cups and awards he had won for his athletic prowess.

By this point in the interview Billy was badly rattled. "I was wondering," he said later, "what sort of game is this flying anyway? Am I going to land on the lakes of Switzerland, or high in the Alps? Am I going to be chased by battalions of German infantry? Where does the flying come in?"[24]

Actually the queries were not as bizarre as they sounded. There was a theory making the rounds in 1915 that people with good balance made fabulous flyers. An accomplished horseman was believed to be superlative pilot material. If such a man could ski and skate, all the better!

Cecil had saved the bombshell for last. He explained that there were two classes of airmen, pilots and observers. There was a long line-up for flight school and it might take Billy the better part of a year to become a pilot. In the meantime he would have to go to France with the Mounted Rifles.

The lieutenant was crestfallen. The newspapers were saying the war would be over by Christmas. They had said the same thing in 1914, of course, but he was sure the Germans couldn't possibly hold on for another twelve months. Still, he didn't exactly relish the thought of being an observer either. That was the fellow who went along for the ride. He took pictures, observed enemy troop movements, dropped bombs and directed artillery fire. Piloting the plane was the glamour job. Observing was all work.

But, Cecil pointed out, there was a shortage of observers and it was a way out of the trenches.

That was all there was to it. Billy Bishop was in the RFC.

The RFC had been formed in 1912 and, by the time war broke out two years later it was still in its infancy. In fact, the Corps could only put five squadrons and about fifty planes into action in August 1914. Four years later, it had 3,300 aircraft carrying out bombing raids, directing artillery fire and taking photographs of enemy positions. It had become the 'eyes' of the army and included in its ranks more than 200,000 men, including 20,000 Canadians. Without national air forces of their own, men from Canada, New Zealand and Australia were forced to join the RFC if they wanted to fly. Squadrons were stationed all up and down the front lines, usually only ten miles or so from the trenches. The airmen were right in the thick of the action and that's exactly where Bishop was headed.

Posted to Salisbury Plain flying school, Bishop fell in love with flying the moment he bounced into the air in the rear cockpit of an Avro 504 two-seater. Below him, he could make out turquoise hillsides, green valleys, miniature automobiles, thatched-roof cottages, a crumbling English castle and the tiny specks that were people. In a letter home he described the aeroplane as the "most wonderful invention. A man ceases to be a human up there. He feels nothing is impossible."[25]

Billy spent the next several months training to be an observer with 21 Squadron at Netheravon Flight School. Conditions were primitive. Communications between the aircrew and ground control was laughable.

"We had small Morse transmitting sets in our machines with which we could send to the ground for a very short distance while carrying out artillery observation and directing on their targets," Billy recalled. "The only answer we could receive upstairs from the gunners was given by means of strips of cotton laid on the ground, each of which had a cryptic meaning of its own."[26]

There was culture shock to overcome as well. Billy had left an all-Canadian cavalry unit made up mostly of country boys or lads like himself from the small towns, to join a service comprised mainly of upper-class Englishmen from the great cities of Britain. Soon he began faking a British accent in the hope that that would help him win acceptance from his comrades.

His pilot was Captain Roger Neville, a good-natured individual who was destined to win the Military Cross for gallantry. Neville hit it off very well with his junior officer. Sixty-eight years later, he remembered: "Bish was a good-looking, personable young man. His voice was pleasant and he had none of the Canadian accent which we got accustomed to later in the war. Indeed, when I first took him to my family's home in London they all thought he was British-born and probably educated in a Scotch public school. The family liked him and especially my young sister." Neville added that the future ace "got along very well with his comrades in 21 Squadron."[27]

Bishop spent much time goofing off, sleeping behind haystacks while he was supposed to be in training, and paying no attention to the technical side of his duties. That Christmas he was to be found in London's plush Regent Palace Hotel. It was, he said, "full of people on weekend honeymoons, and the grill and the restaurant are full of love-girls and men intent on picking them up."[28] Billy, no doubt, did his share of womanizing at the Regent that holiday season.

Curiously enough, the war did not end on December 25. The Germans were, however, clearly on the defensive. They had launched only one major attack on the Western Front during the entire year, employing poison gas for the first time in the history of war during a surprise thrust that fell with sledgehammer force in April. The attack was aimed at Canadian and French troops defending Ypres. The French bolted in terror but the Canadian Corps held like a rock, repelling the onslaught.

For the balance of the year the Germans themselves beat back a series of British and French offensives, inflicting heavy casualties on the Allies at Lens and Vimy Ridge. As 1915 came to a bloody close, both sides counted their dead in the hundreds of thousands. Peace was nowhere in sight.

But Billy was happy. Indeed, for all his failings as a cadet and cavalry officer, he now seemed to have found his calling. He was a first-class aerial photographer. By the time he left Netheravon he had been put in charge of training new observers with the camera. His photographs were being used as models for others to study.

There was a great deal of excitement in the squadron when word finally came through that they were going to the Front. The crews had been told that once they got to France, they would receive an extra pound per day in "flying pay." Neville was ecstatic. He noted, "This was indeed riches in those days."[29]

And so, in January 1916, Bishop, Neville and their 21 Squadron mates left for France and their first look at the real war.

CHAPTER THREE

The first combat mission of the future leading RFC air ace of World War One had all the earmarks of a Laurel and Hardy movie. A new German howitzer battery was tearing British infantry units to shreds in the Boisdinghem sector of Northern France, and 21 Squadron had been given the task of knocking it out. The RE7 crew of Roger Neville and Billy Bishop would undertake the mission at dawn.

Billy awoke that morning filled with nervous anticipation. He didn't want to admit it, not even to himself, but he was afraid. This was the real thing, not just another test flight. He knew that the Germans would have the battery well protected. A ring of anti-aircraft guns would be surrounding it and there might even be Fokker Eindekkers prowling in the vicinity. The little monoplanes were the first flying machines of the war to be equipped with a forward firing machine gun. A new synchronization gear allowed the pilot to fire directly through his own whirling propeller blade. It gave the enemy an enormous advantage in a dogfight. Already aviators such as Max Immelmann and Oswald Boelcke were becoming known across the Front for their phenomenal success in shooting down Allied planes.

It was a bitterly cold morning. In fact, Northern France was locked in the coldest winter in memory. 21 Squadron was carrying out patrols in sub-zero temperatures. Take-offs and landings often had to be attempted with several inches of snow on the ground, and there were more casualties being attributed to the weather than to enemy action.

Billy bundled himself in sweaters, a heavy coat and scarf. His pre-flight preparation was complicated by regulations that called on airmen to bring along an extra pair of goggles, tool kit, binoculars, cooking stove, biscuits, cans of corned beef, chocolate bars, a pistol and a canteen filled with scalding hot water. He probably felt more like a grocery store attendant than a combat flying man.

Before leaving the barracks he reached down and grabbed a heavy iron frying pan from under his cot. He had stolen it from the cookhouse and intended to sit on it during the mission. The idea had occurred to him after hearing tales of a pilot whose testicles had been shot off by anti-aircraft shrapnel. Others were known to be carrying metal mirrors in front pockets to guard the heart.

About the only form of protective equipment not being used was the parachute. The top brass at RFC had refused to issue the life-saving devices to air crews because it feared that some men might bail out rather than attempt to bring a crippled aircraft home for repairs. It was a blockheaded decision that would cost thousands of young men their lives. About the only consolation for British flyers was the knowledge that the French and German high commands had handed down the same insane orders.

A fresh snowfall had come down during the night and the white stuff crunched loudly under foot. Climbing into the observer's seat, Billy placed the frying pan under his cushion and settled in. The plane was armed to the teeth. Bishop and Neville had four machine guns at their disposal. On top of that, they were carrying a 500-pound bomb and several twenty-pounders. All that firepower was reassuring but, for the life of him, Billy could not figure out how he was supposed to fire the guns without hitting his own machine. His cockpit was located in front of the pilot, amid a maze of struts and flying wires that held the wings together. It was a near-impossible arrangement that made it difficult to see behind or below. Only later, with development of the RE8, was the observer's seat moved behind the pilot's, giving him a vastly improved field of vision.

Neville said that Bishop "had no means of communications with his pilot, who was seated a long way behind him, other than by hand signals similar to those used by tic-tac men on the race course. I might add that after a couple of hours of flying, most observers were in such a cold condition that they could not wave anything! No heat was available from the slow-running, water-cooled Beadmore engine, except in very hot weather when one did not need it."[1]

The plane, besides presenting insurmountable headaches for an observer, was extremely difficult to fly. Neville called it "a hopeless aeroplane, outdated before it arrived in France." He added, "The letters RE stood for Reconnaissance Experimental and the 7 meant, according to cynics, that the previous six had failed to get off the ground."[2] The machine was also extremely dangerous. It could manage a top speed of only sixty miles per hour and had a tendency to stall at forty-five. Once in a spin, it usually crashed before a pilot could regain control. 21 Squadron pilot Don Brophy said that when a new RE7 was destroyed just after being delivered, "a cheer went up and down all the sheds. The goodwill in which the RE7 is held by the boys was plainly shown by the vicious kicks and heavy rocks directed against what was left of it. Everyone hates them."

Neville gunned the motor and turned the old bus into the wind. Billy crouched lower in his cockpit as frigid air swept over him. With painstaking slowness the aeroplane taxied down the field. The two men waited for the inevitable liftoff as the flying wires grew taut and the landing wires relaxed. Nothing happened. The machine kept rolling at a tortoise pace as the end of the runway approached.

Neville shook the controls, almost begging the machine to leave the ground. His pleas were ignored by the RE7. With the tree line moving rapidly toward them, the exasperated pilot was forced to turn his machine around and taxi back the way he had come. Again and again they "roared" across the field in a vain, almost comical attempt to get airborne. Finally, after a dozen fruitless attempts, Neville called it quits.

After a brief huddle with his commanding officer, he came back announcing they would have to lighten the plane. The 500-pound bomb would have to go. Minus the huge bomb, (and the frying pan, which Neville insisted Billy leave behind) the two intrepid birdmen rolled down the field again.

"The wheels bounced a few times but we still weren't in the air at the point on the runway where we would have to throttle down and turn to avoid running off the field,"[3] Bishop said later.

Finally, after stripping the plane of two of its machine guns and the smaller bombs, Neville was able to coax the reluctant machine into the sky. It struggled for altitude, gasping and wheezing like a locomotive. The landing gear only cleared the treetops with a few feet to spare. As they climbed in a wide circle above the drome, Billy rigged up the wireless and sent off a few test signals. After receiving the correct responses, he arranged his maps, fed plates into his Williamson LB camera and sat back as the machine made for German-held territory.

As the RE7 lumbered along below layers of wet clouds, crimson flashes from the muzzles of cannons showed the way to the Front. Billy experienced an eerie foreboding as he heard the thumping of the big guns for the first time.

Below him, the countryside became more and more desolate as the plane neared the battle zone. For more than a year now, both sides had been locked in a hopeless stalemate all along the Western Front. Both armies dug in and established trenches that cut an ugly swath across the land from the North Sea to Switzerland. It was an elaborate setup with numerous parallel lines of intercommunicating trenches. A narrow strip of ground separating the belligerents was known as "No Man's Land."

At some places the Allied and German positions were only yards apart. The ruins of shattered towns and villages passed under their wings and, as they approached the Front, Billy became aware of an apocryphal lack of trees. There were no farms, fences, roads, villages — no signs of life of any kind. Craters filled with snow dotted the landscape as far as the eye could see. The snow was stained here and there with a light yellow colouring — a reminder of places where the Germans had launched poison gas attacks.

Battered earthworks and rows of coiled barbed wire materialized. In a moment they were over No Man's Land and, seconds later, had crossed into German country. Billy felt a flush of excitement as he realized he was flying over the heads of the enemy. He scanned the sky intently in search of Fokkers. Resting on his lap was a map of the sector and photos of enemy positions taken twenty-four hours earlier. It was his task to check the terrain, find the German battery, and direct artillery fire onto it.

The RE7 had to fight howling winds and sleet as it made its way to the German rear areas. Despite his layers of clothing, Billy was soon suffering from an indescribable chill. The cold burrowed straight through his coat. He was worried that his exposed cheeks would become frostbitten. Such a fear was not unfounded. Historian Alan Morris, in his book *The First of the Many*, graphically outlined the hazards of winter flying in an open cockpit: "Air becomes one Fahrenheit degree colder for every 365 feet climbed." After some high altitude patrols, faces and extremities were "transformed into fungoid horror by brawny swellings and sloughed black skin. Unusual merely in severity was the misery of the observer whose cheeks bulged until they were in line with the tops of his shoulders. It was a strong heart that did not run wild from the panic." Billy's canteen of hot water (RFC men called it a "winter warmer") was of little use. It did nothing more than blister his thigh.

Two bursts of black smoke suddenly appeared 100 yards in front of the plane. Another anti-aircraft shell exploded only yards behind them. The blast all but lifted Billy and his maps right out of his seat The RE was thrown violently upward but, after a moment, was back on level course. A stinking toxic odour pervaded both cockpits. Roger Neville banked casually to throw off the aim of the gunners and continued on his way as if nothing had happened.

Bishop, under fire for the first time, was not quite so calm. He was, however, alert enough to see two red flashes as he glanced at the ground below. A pair of angry puff-balls appeared far to the left of the two-seater, indicating that Neville's maneuver had worked. After a time, as its pilot made periodic course changes to confuse the enemy, the machine was being trailed by a whole series of exploding shells. Occasionally one would erupt nearby, but none of the deadly shrapnel found its mark.

Neville, for his part, seemed totally unconcerned. Once, he even looked up and flashed a broad grin at Billy. Soon, the Canadian realized that the chances of a direct hit were millions to one. Even damage from a chunk of flying shrapnel was unlikely, as long as Neville made regular course adjustments. After a time Billy was actually thankful to the Germans for taking his mind off the cold. He'd discovered what all front line veterans knew — "Archie" fire seldom brought down a machine in 1916, although it was a frightening experience when encountered for the first time.

Off to one side Billy made out four huge mounds that gave away the enemy howitzer position. He tapped Neville on the shoulder and pointed in the direction of the target. The Germans scrambled for cover. They knew full well that, once an artillery plane started circling overhead, an enemy barrage would soon follow.

Billy transmitted the coordinates and sat back to watch the results. Behind the British lines he could just make out the flash of a cannon muzzle. For what seemed like an eternity afterward, nothing happened. Then, without warning, a great mound of gray earth shot skyward fifty yards in front of the battery. Billy didn't hear anything. The roar of the RE7's engine muffled the sound of the explosion out. It was like watching a silent movie. He signalled a correction and watched as another volley followed. This time, the shell went off fifty yards behind the target.

Billy fired off a second correction on his wireless, instructing the gunners to lob the next round at a point directly between the first two shots. The third blast went off right in the middle of the gun pit.

"Good shooting,"[4] he signalled the English battery.

Back at the aerodrome, Billy had to be helped from his seat. The cold air had nearly frozen him solid. His eyes were bloodshot and he feared that his cheeks were frostbitten. A British flyer who served with Bishop recorded the trauma of landing after a cold-weather patrol this way: "My recollection is that one's finger tips were the parts to feel the cold most, and the pain in them when one came down into warmer air was excruciating, so much so that we sometimes climbed back into the cold again to get relief and descended gradually in order to restore circulation."[5]

After post-flight deafness (caused by listening to the engine for two hours) had subsided, Neville approached him with an outstretched hand.

"Congratulations, Lieutenant, you didn't get the wind up."[6] Getting the "wind up" was the RFC's term for outright cowardice. Billy beamed with pride. Everyone was afraid, but no one in the service would admit it. Hiding your fear — being thought by your peers to be fearless — was almost as important as staying alive.

When the effects of the cold had left him, Billy found himself deeply depressed. The strain of the mission had taken a heavy toll. After one flight, he wrote Margaret: "In the air you feel only intense excitement. You cheer and laugh and keep your spirits up. You are all right just after you have landed as you search your machine for bullet and shrapnel holes. But two hours later when you are quietly sitting in your billet you feel a sudden loneliness. You want to lie down and cry."[7]

The balance of Lieutenant Bishop's career as an observer was a trying experience for him.

Said Neville: "After we had been on operations in France for a time, he became noticeably more moody and frustrated, the limitations of the RE7 as a combat machine became more and more apparent, whereas Bish's one object in life was to shoot down enemy aircraft and not just drop bombs or make out 'art recce' reports."[8] Bishop, in his autobiography, admits that he never once fired his gun at a German plane during this period. On one mission he watched as a marauding Fokker pilot attacked and shot down an Allied two-seater but he was unable to bring his own gun to bear.

Neville kept a close eye on his gunner's performance. "I do not think he could be said to be 'cool under fire,' as the saying goes. On the contrary, he was boiling with rage because he could not fire back without danger of shooting off the RE7's tailplane or his pilot's head. He was a very fine shot; spent hours on the range where armament was tested near the airfield on the ground, adjusting and firing his Lewis gun. Yet inevitably all this keenness made pilots wonder when his enthusiasm was going to overcome his judgement."[9] Neville added, "Bish was by no means the best observer in the squadron but he was by far the best air gunner. When one's attention is concentrated on spotting enemy aircraft in the attack, one cannot count railroad tracks in junctions below."[10]

Bishop soon discovered that, while observation work wasn't any more glamorous than slopping around in the mud of a cavalry camp in England, it was considerably more risky. On one flight he was lightly wounded in the head by "Archie" fire. "Although I was not only his pilot but also his flight commander," Neville recalled, "he had no hesitation in blaming me for not dodging the missile. But we remained good friends."[11]

On another occasion the two men were ordered stripped of their guns so that they could carry more bombs. The entire squadron was sent twenty miles behind enemy lines, completely unarmed, to carry out a raid on a railroad station. The scheme had been dreamed up by some paper-pusher at headquarters. Fortunately, they attacked the station without being intercepted. Had a flight of Fokkers happened upon the scene, it would have been a massacre.

Another foolish assignment came up when the group was ordered to fly cover over General Haig's headquarters. The RE7s droned in a circle above the General's head all day, returning home only for more fuel. The planes were totally unsuited for aerial combat and would have been extremely hard-pressed to drive off any German aircraft. Luckily, none showed.

It was a small wonder that the crews began referring to Number 21 as the "Suicide Squadron."[12]

With the type of leadership they were receiving, casualties were inevitable. When the first man died, Bishop wept. He followed that up, noted Neville, with a period of "gloom, and an increased determination to hit back at the enemy as hard as possible. As the RE7 was no fighter, this meant with bombing."[13]

Despite the ever-present threat of sudden death, the airmen found time for humour. They even composed a Squadron "alphabet" which took a good-natured poke at each man. Bishop's went like this:

B is for Bishop
Who likes a good moan

Though he lives on his pay
He has piles of his own

Neville found the rhyme to be "scurrilous, but true at that point of time."[14]

On one severely cold day, the chimney in the mess collapsed and Bishop and Neville were ordered to the rear to fetch a new stove pipe. What happened next is perhaps the best example of Bishop's ingenuity and aplomb under pressure.

On their way back to the base a Fokker appeared, skidding sideways across a porcelain sky as it strained to slip in behind them. The pipe encumbered Billy, but he instantly took up his Lewis and fired off a test burst. Nothing happened. The gun was frozen solid. The quick-thinking Lieutenant aimed the metallic stove pipe at the Fokker and fired a bright red signal flare through it. The startled German turned and fled, Billy recalled later, "like a chicken with its head cut off! I'm sure he thought I had my own cannon."[15]

Just as was the case during cavalry training in Canada, Bishop was again struck with a rash of nagging injuries and illnesses that kept him out of action periodically, for up to a week at a time. The worst of the mishaps occurred in April, after the squadron had left the line to have its planes fitted with new 12-cylinder air-cooled engines.

"With this engine the RE seemed like a scout to us, but it was utterly unreliable from the start, developing all sorts of unexpected teething problems and a great number of forced landings," explained Neville. "It was one of these forced landings which eventually freed Bish from the frustrations of 21. What actually occurred was an engine failure, just as we were about to take off, causing us to run through a hedge on the perimeter of the airfield and finish "tail-up" in the neighbouring ploughed field. We had three 112-pound bombs on board but they did not explode .... Bish was much more concerned about his damaged knee, which probably would not have been so damaged if he had obeyed regulations and been properly strapped in at take-off. But characteristically Bish was never one to take more notice of regulations than Horatio Nelson did."[16]

Billy's knee was seriously damaged, but he refused to seek medical attention, deciding instead to limp about and remain on active service.

The injury was aggravated that May while he was on leave in London. Dizzy from too much champagne, he fell from a gangplank filled with drunken soldiers going ashore in England. Nevertheless, he caroused around London for a week and did not land in a hospital bed until the day he was scheduled to return to the Front. He was not about to let a trifle thing like a smashed knee keep him from enjoying the pleasures of London's wartime night life — not after four months at the Front!

What finally put him in hospital was an incident described by former RFC pilot Cecil Knight, in a 1981 interview:

"Shortly after he'd finished his first months at 21 Squadron, Bishop on leave, coming out at night from the Savoy Hotel, fell down the steps and broke his arm. He was immediately taken to this wonderful hospital in London, in Bryanston Square, run by society ladies for the Royal Flying Corps and a few days later a nurse came around and said, 'The king is going to visit us. Now we certainly can't have you here and when the king comes to your bed you say "I fell down the steps at the Savoy." We must put a bandage around your head and then you must use your own inventive genius to tell him how you were wounded in the head."[17]

Doctors who examined him found that, in addition to his other injuries, the young Canadian was suffering from a strained heart. He was ordered hospitalized, much to his own relief, for an indefinite period.

Billy Bishop came out of a drugged sleep to find himself in a hospital bed. An elderly, thin little lady with white hair tied behind her head in a stern bun, revealing absolutely massive ears, was standing over him. The room had that telltale antiseptic smell.

She smiled at him and he noticed at once that her eyes were much younger than the rest of her face.

The old woman introduced herself as a certain Lady St. Helier.

The name, renowned throughout London's high society, meant nothing to Bishop.

"I saw your name on the register, and I was sure that someone named

William Bishop from Canada must be the son of my friend Will Bishop. And when I looked at you I was sure of it. You look very much like him."[18]

Billy didn't fully comprehend. The lady, sensing his lack of understanding, explained that she had met his father years earlier, on a trip to Ottawa.

In Lady St. Helier, Bishop had found himself a wealthy patroness who had influence in high places. Indeed, she was a personal friend of Sir Winston Churchill, the Secretary for Air, and Lord Hugh Cecil, the man who decided who could, or could not, apply for pilot training. Before long she would be pulling strings that would make his advancements embarrassingly easy.

The old woman was fiesty. A member of London City Council, she had become something of a legend in the capital for her battles to upgrade conditions for the city's poor. When she wasn't delivering stormy speeches in the council chamber, she was playing the role of angel of mercy, helping to care for wounded servicemen in hospital. She was a lady of boundless energy; although seventy years old, she enjoyed horseback riding, cycling and skating.

Lady St. Helier took an immediate liking to the charming young roughneck from Canada and insisted that he continue his recovery at her plush, four-storey mansion at 52 Portland Place, London.

At Portland Place, Billy could hardly have found a world more different from his native Owen Sound.

The nobility of London's west end lived in almost obscene splendour. Gentlemen of the district wore blue coats embroidered with gold, top hats and white britches. Their ladies pranced about with lengthy trains trailing in their wakes. They wore long dresses, sparkling jewels and, in their hair, ostrich feathers. At Lady St. Helier's residence, life was one endless party. Everyone who was anyone in British high society showed up at St. Helier's door sooner or later. Invitations to her home were cherished.

A special relationship quickly formed between Billy and the old woman. One day, choking back tears, she told him: "You are the kind of grandson my son would have given me, had he lived."[19]

Embarrassed, yet at the same time deeply touched, Billy replied "Yes, Granny."[20] The name stuck, and from that date forward she introduced him to everyone as "my grandson.'[21]

But despite the special treatment, his convalescence went slowly. Lady St. Helier decided he needed a complete rest and arranged for him to be granted home leave and a ticket aboard the next ship bound for Canada. His record most certainly did not warrant this privilege, but it was a hint of her considerable power.

Bishop stayed in Canada from July to September, and although his leave was restful, it was utterly uneventful. He spent some time in Toronto, visiting with Margaret. Back in Owen Sound, Billy was treated like a hero, simply because he had been in action. The attention embarrassed him. He was more than ready to return to the war when his leave finally expired.

His absence from the Front during these months could not have come at a better time. In France, both sides had wrestled fiercely for control of the skies and the German aces, in their deadly Fokker Eindeckkers, had won hands down. Number 21 Squadron was virtually annihilated during the bloodbath known as the Battle of the Somme; Billy's old pilot, Roger Neville, was one of the few to escape with his life, although he was wounded in action. On the German side, in contrast, Max Immelmann ran his victory score up to fifteen and Oswald Boelcke shot his twentieth victim down in flames. Others, including Kurt Wintgens, Wilhelm Frankl and Walter Hohndorf also became household names in Germany. The situation was so serious that a British Member of Parliament referred to RFC airmen as "Fokker Fodder."

Billy was back in England by September. He applied for pilot training and, with Lady St. Helier knocking down all obstacles, he was accepted.

The Flying Corps medical examination was a farce. Pilots were now badly needed at the Front and anyone who could get in and out of the RFC's medical room under his own steam was deemed fit to fly.

Bishop's doctor tapped him gently on the heart and lungs, made him walk a straight chalk line with his eyes closed and then motioned him to sit in a swivel chair. The medical man spun the chair wildly and, when it came to a halt, he ordered Billy to stand up. When the Canadian did so without falling flat on his face, he had passed a key test!

After he proved he could utter the words "ninety-nine" and "aah," he was judged ready for flight training. He was immediately posted to the big flight school at Netheravon on Salisbury Plain.

Captain Harold Balfour eyed the group of nervous young trainees as they assembled in front of a hangar, chatting excitedly among themselves. Balfour was only a year or two older than most of them, but he carried himself with the self-assurance of a seasoned professional. He was, in fact, a combat veteran who only recently had been posted to England to take up the duties of Flight Instructor. The posting, as he himself admitted, had come in the nick of time; his nerves had been on the verge of cracking under the terrible strain of daily fighting. Now, however, he had the almost equally thankless task of taking up clumsy young greenhorns in an old BE2.

One of the recruits, Lieutenant Billy Bishop, caught the captain's attention. There was something about the newcomer that attracted him at once. Decades later in a National Film Board interview, Balfour commented: "He was a very good, apt pupil and I would say he was really an outstanding personality. Even though twelve pupils were sitting in a row in front of a hangar waiting for their turn for myself or one of the other instructors to take him up, he was a figure and a personality that stood out amongst that twelve."[22]

Balfour took Bishop aloft in Avros and BEs, communicating with him through what was known as the "Gosport Tube." He found the Canadian to be a man who showed absolutely no fear. Perhaps it is just as well, because a student pilot needed all the courage he could muster. After just three hours of flight time, he was judged ready to solo. After twenty hours or so, he received his wings.

Such limited preparation seems preposterous today, and perhaps it explains why fatal crashes were an everyday occurrence at British flight schools. Indeed, while 6,000 aviators were killed in combat with the German Air Force between 1914 and 1918, a shocking 8,000 more were destined to die in England, while they learned how to fly. German training deaths, it is interesting to note, were only a fraction of active Jagdstaffel losses on the Western Front.

Another pilot-trainee at Upavon at this time was Hamilton "Tim" Hervey, a jovial young lieutenant from the south coast of England. He had served in France as a gunner-observer aboard a BE2C and was, in fact, one of the few airmen flying in that antiquated aircraft ever to shoot down an Albatros. Both Hervey and Bishop were extroverts and both had flown combat missions as lowly gunners. They quickly became fast friends.

Hervey recalled many years later: "I first met Bishop at Central Flying School, Upavon, where we were both in the same training squadron flying Sopwith 1¹ᐟ² Strutters and Sopwith Pups. I had -- returned after a long spell in France as an observer and Bishop was having a conversion to scouts from as far as I can remember, flying BE2Cs in England. He often talked to me about flying in France and my chief memory of him at that time was his burning ambition to be posted to a scout squadron." Billy was, he added, "always dead keen" about getting back into combat.

If he ever did get to France in a single seater, Bishop vowed to his comrades, he would return either with the Victoria Cross or in a pine box.

Strapping himself into a Farman Pusher (an aeroplane with the engine located behind the pilot) Billy prepared for his solo flight. He was extremely unsure of himself and had absolutely no confidence that he could fly the plane. And he gulped at the realization that, in the event of a crash, the Farman's engine, located directly behind him, would be driven straight through his head. Looking across the field he spotted an ambulance standing by. Its motor was running and the poker-faced driver was gazing back at him. Billy obviously wasn't the only one present who had doubts about his ability to get the Farman into the air — and back down again — in one piece. The sight caused a knot to form in his stomach.

He nervously opened the throttle and counted the revolutions on a dial in front of him. Throttling down, he motioned a mechanic to remove the wheel chocks. The Farman rolled forward. He swung the lumbering machine into the wind and started to pick up speed. The tail came up. Billy held the wheels down another moment, allowing the plane to gather more momentum. The landing gear bounced once, twice ... miraculously, the Farman was in the air! So far, so good!

He climbed as long as he dared before finally risking a slow turn. The Farman skidded shakily in a hideous pantomime of awkwardness. Onlookers below held their collective breath. Somehow, the plane managed to right itself and Billy continued on his way.

By now he was feeling rather pleased with himself, until he suddenly realized that he would have to put the big plane back down. It was, he said, an "awful thought."[23] Throttling back, he dropped the nose and began his descent. Not bearing to watch, he clamped his eyes shut for several agonizing moments. Risking a peek out of one eye, he decided he was diving too steeply and pulled up. "This maneuver I repeated again and again, giving the impression to the watchers below that my machine must be walking down an invisible staircase," he said.

Forty feet above the ground, he made a perfect three-point landing. Red-faced and grateful that no one could see him blushing, he circled back around and executed another flawless landing — this time eight feet off the runway. Finally, the old bus took matters into its own hands and set itself down with a sickening thump. Fortunately, there was no serious damage.

Balfour shook his head in disgust but, for Billy, the performance was the greatest moment of his flying career.

Eventually, after cracking up several airframes and busting more than a few tires with ham-fisted landings, he was given his wings in November 1916, and sent on his way. He had, his log book shows, just over eighteen hours flying time to his credit.

Transferred to Number 37 Squadron at Northholt, Bishop was assigned to zeppelin-hunting duties. The greatest danger here was not from an enemy airship but simply getting to and from home base in the dark. Taking off between two rows of yellow flares, he had only the stars and the shadows of a few local landmarks to guide him.

Billy hated the work, which was dangerous and unproductive. He cruised over London in the dark, dodging British Archie fire and straining to find the elusive airships in the dim searchlights that criss-crossed the sky.

The flight home was always terrifying. How he managed to find the aerodrome he did not know. Coming in for a landing, he saw trees and chimneys and rooftops where there were only black shadows. The whole experience, he found, was akin to being tossed into a lake at midnight.

As he had done so often elsewhere, he quickly ran afoul of the authorities because of reoccurring discipline problems.

His commanding officer was going to have him thrown out of the squadron until another officer, who saw some potential in Bishop, intervened on the Canadian's behalf. It was clear to those with a sharp eye that Billy had the mental make-up to be an outstanding combat pilot.

Still, his future in Home Defence did not appear bright and he was constantly applying for duty on the Western Front. In early March 1917, he was ordered to report to the War Office for a new assignment. While he was in the waiting room awaiting an audience with authorities, Billy had a chance meeting with a man who would give his career a major boost.

That man was Captain Albert Ball, the Royal Flying Corps leading ace with thirty officially confirmed victories to his credit. Ball, who was only nineteen at the time, was an incredibly youthful lad with short legs, wavy black hair, penetrating brown eyes and a snub nose. A shy individual noted for his good manners and "proper" Nottingham upbringing, he was the toast of Britain. His picture was on the front pages often, and he had already been presented with the Distinguished Service Order and the Military Cross by the King. He was deeply religious, and much troubled by his role as a killer. On the Front he was fond of spending his free time gardening or playing the violin. And he was forever eating homemade cake sent to him by his mother.

Although he usually kept to himself, Ball took an instant liking to

Bishop. As the two men passed the time awaiting an audience with the powers that be, it seems likely that Ball filled Billy with stories of the 60 Squadron and its various characters. What happened next isn't known for sure. But what is clear is that, after his interview, Billy was posted to 60 Squadron's base at Filescamp Farm near the French town of Izel-le-Hameau, just behind the front lines.

"These aerial duels are a waste of time and manpower!"[25]

The officer making the thunderous pronouncement was General Hugh Montague Trenchard, a bellicose, rugged Scotsman who was commander of the Royal Flying Corps. Trenchard, a tall, ungainly man with a thick moustache and a crop of disheveled brown hair, was known throughout the service as "Boom" because of his stentorian voice and no-nonsense approach to the business at hand. On this night, he was addressing a group of fighter pilots bound for France. One of those in attendance was Billy Bishop.

"It would be much simpler and more efficient to destroy the enemy's equipment long before it ever reaches a front line hangar. One strategic bomber, a trained bomber crew and the proper armament would do more in a week than all our multi-decorated aces can accomplish in a year. Aces are four-a-penny and are actually doing very little to win the war in the air," he stormed.[26]

The general was exaggerating, of course, but he was anxious to make his point. Fighter pilots were not on the Front for the purpose of making a name for themselves. Their role was to destroy German observation balloons, to drive away enemy reconnaissance ships and to provide protection to Allied bombers. Jousting with German fighters was a secondary function made necessary, he said, so that British two-seaters could operate safely behind enemy lines.

To Bishop, Trenchard was just another fool in a position of authority. Frightful losses in all three branches of the service had long since caused most fighting men to lose any respect for superiors. Turning to the man next to him, Bishop vowed, "Once I get to France I'm going to make a fool out of that General Trenchard."[27]

It would not be as easy as Bishop thought. The Germans, equipped with the deadly new Albatros and Halberstadt fighters, had taken control of the air for the second time in the war. Already the Imperial Air Service was taking a heavy toll of outdated British and French machines.

While the cocky Albert Ball had a low opinion of German aviators, he was virtually alone in that assessment among front line Allied flyers. The Germans, in truth, were better trained, better equipped, and every bit as brave as their counterparts. Already they were beginning to make mincemeat out of the old BEs, REs, and FEEs.

Good British aeroplanes, such as the Sopwith Pup and Sopwith triplane, were available but were not issued to front line units in significant numbers. The deadly triplane was more than a match for the Albatros but it had been assigned only to a few Royal Naval Air Service squadrons that were operating far from the main theatre of war. Sopwith products were not in favour with the High Command, which was anxious to showcase machines built by the state-owned Royal Aircraft Factory. When Albert Ball bluntly told authorities that RAF products were inferior, he was officially censured.

And so the best British pilots were being shot down in antiquated planes and their places were being filled by raw rookies. By March 1917, as Bishop headed across the English Channel, the Royal Flying Corps was slipping toward calamity. With spring weather, the aerial activity would be dramatically increased, and the German aces would be ready to mow down Allied pilots at a ratio of five to one.

By the time Bishop reported to his squadron, the life expectancy of an RFC pilot had been reduced to a scant three weeks. For a rookie, that figure was just eleven days. More than 1,200 British machines would be shot down during the months of March, April and May. In April, as fighting reached its bloody peak, a third of the entire Royal Flying Corps would be destroyed. Bishop did not know it, but he was about to enter a hell on earth that would be remembered for all time as Bloody April.

CHAPTER FOUR

It was bleak and forlorn in appearance. Three brown canvas tent hangars bordered one side of Filescamp Farm aerodrome. The big tents, nestled among a stand of pine trees, were located adjacent to a farmhouse and a quadrangle of barnyard buildings. Patches of snow lay among the trees and in ground depressions between the hangars. Bishop arrived at dusk on March 17th after a two-day train trip from the coast. The French countryside had been a sorry sight. Passing through the towns of Northern France, travellers were invariably struck by how many women were wearing black. In the fields, which spread brown to the horizon, mostly young lads and old men did work. As Bishop looked about for the squadron headquarters, a chilly wet wind swept in from the east, bringing with it a rush of cold air from the English Channel. The threat of still another snowfall in this, the bleakest winter in memory, hung ominously over the place.

It was a spacious farm by European standards, consisting of a picturesque but worn-looking old chateau, crumbling granaries, stock barns and a massive refuse heap, which occupied a full seventy-five yards and was surrounded by a wall of three-foot-high gray bricks. It was accessible only through two huge wooden doors. Manure and straw were piled high, giving the whole place an untidy appearance. There were familiar smells: straw, horses, mildew.

The squadron mess and headquarters were near the farm buildings, tucked away in an orchard. The whole place was altogether unmilitary in appearance. Buildings were arranged in no particular order, with barracks, cookhouses and storage sheds strung together. At one end, a fenced-in compound was stacked high with petrol drums. A dozen lorries were scattered about, mostly near the hangars.

The officers' mess was no more than a fifteen-second gallop to the flight lines. In an emergency, pilots could be airborne very quickly. There were tennis courts and even a makeshift theatre but, strangely, no firefighting equipment, nor any sign of a medical building. Anyone who limped home wounded would have to survive a trip in the back of a beat-up old lorry to the nearest field hospital.

Fortunately, there were no fences as far as the eye could see. That meant a man in difficulty could put his plane down wherever he pleased.

Number 60 shared Filescamp with Number 40 Squadron, which also flew Nieuports, and with Number 16, which fought its war in the short, stubby SPAD fighters. At full strength, each outfit had eighteen pilots, twenty mechanics, an armourer, several cooks, office clerks, batmen and chauffeurs. In all, about 150 men lived at Filescamp, along with a single French farm family.

The drome was located ten miles back of the trenches at Arras. It was far enough away to be out of the range of German artillery but close enough to hear the continuous rumble of guns in the distance. Its proximity to the fighting meant that only a few minutes flying time was required to reach enemy territory.

Filescamp was located adjacent to a depressing, half-deserted little rural village. Izel-le-Hameau's bland architecture and cobblestoned streets offered nothing of interest to the nearby Allied pilots. If the surroundings were grim, Bishop wasn't complaining. He was too excited to worry about appearances.

He got the first indication of what was in store for him when he asked where he could find the squadron commander. There was, he was told, no commander. Major Evelyn Graves, who had been 60 Squadron's leader, had been shot down in flames behind enemy lines just twenty-four hours earlier. Bishop was told to report to Captain Keith Caldwell, the commander of "C" Flight.

Caldwell's photographs suggest a lanky, perhaps slightly ungainly individual with dark hair, handsome features, a square jaw and pleasant brown eyes. There was nothing very warlike in his appearance. But photos can be deceiving. Before he was finished, Caldwell would be credited with twenty-four confirmed kills. When Bishop first met him he was already wearing the purple ribbon of the Military Cross. He had won the decoration by leading five Nieuports into an attack on a dozen Albatroses.

Just twenty-two years old, Caldwell had not planned on a career filled with adventure. Prior to the war he had worked in the Bank of New Zealand as a clerk, but it was a job that was ill-suited to his unique temperament. When fighting broke out, Caldwell was one of the first of his countrymen to join the RFC. Once in the Flying Corps, he was quickly dubbed "Grid" because he insisted on calling all aeroplanes "grids." The name stuck.

One of the men who knew him best was Tim Hervey. He remembered Caldwell as "a great chap, good fun to be with, a very good pilot, good all around athlete, rugby and tennis player and much liked by everyone. He was always dead keen — like Bishop — in getting a transfer to a scout squadron." When Caldwell arrived at 60, Hervey recalled, "He was a poor shot and, although he always scrapped with great determination against any odds, it was some time before he got over this trouble and was eventually very successful."

Bishop could not have come across a better man to see him through his perilous first days as a fighter pilot. Said Hervey:

> "Caldwell was particularly good with new and inexperienced arrivals in the squadron, nursing them during their early dangerous weeks, showing them the ropes and often giving them possibly more credit than was their due in scraps in which they were not involved. He was a great leader."

Caldwell must not have been impressed with Bishop's logbook. The newcomer, if his record were any indication, would be lucky to last a week or two. He had a long history of accidents and, worse than that, didn't seem to know how to follow orders. His record was sprinkled with offences unbecoming of an officer or a gentleman. On the positive side, he did have seventy-five hours flying time to his credit on Avros,

BE12s and Sopwith Pups. The average rookie was being sent into combat with only about twenty-five hours.

Caldwell warned the Canadian that he wouldn't be going into action immediately. There would be practice flights in the rear areas to give him some experience on Nieuports, and to familiarize him with the Arras sector. 60 Squadron was located, Caldwell pointed out to him, just across the line from Baron Manfred von Richthofen's Jagdstaffel 11.

Richthofen! The name alone was enough to produce a certain uneasiness in any RFC mess. Caldwell spoke of him almost with reverence. Like many Allied flyers, he half-suspected that the German ace was invincible.

Richthofen hunted in a blood-red Albatros. Already he had shot down nearly thirty British planes. Two of his victims had been aces and one of them, Major Lanone Hawker, had won England's highest award for valour, the Victoria Cross.

Allied pilots referred to Richthofen as the "Jolly Red Baron" or the "Pink Lady." The latter nickname arose from a fanciful French rumour that a beautiful young girl piloted the red German machine to avenge the death of her lover. Preposterous as the story may seem, it was not the only one of its kind circulating that year. In October, the *Vancouver Sun* ran a tale under the headline "German Girls Forced to Pilot Planes Under Penalty of Death." It read:

> *HELENA — A letter received here today from Dr. Philip G. Cole, of Helena, a surgeon with the American expeditionary force at the Front of France, says a German bombing plane recently forced to descend in the American sector proved to be piloted by a girl of sixteen, who said she was compelled under penalty of death, first to learn to fly and later to guide bombing planes over the Entente Front. She said many other girls were operating war planes under the same circumstances.*

It is hard to believe that anyone could take such a story seriously but rumours of German female flyers persisted throughout the war.

Richthofen's Jagdstaffel of brilliantly painted Albatroses was known as the "Flying Circus" or the "Head Hunters." The former title seemed especially appropriate to one 60 Squadron pilot who had a brush with Richthofen's unit. He wrote in a letter: "Talk about colours, you ought to see the Huns. They are just like butterflies, with bright red bodies, spotted wings and black and white squares on their tails, or else a wonderful mauve colour with green and brown patches."

The Baron himself was a stocky man of average height, with short blond hair and boyish features that made him look much younger than his twenty-four years. He was a crack shot and a courageous pilot who had molded Jasta 11 into the best front line squadron on either side of the trenches. And that isn't just so much empty rhetoric. When Richthofen assumed command in January 1917, Jasta 11 did not have a single victory to its credit, despite the fact that it had been on operations for several months. He immediately showed his pilots how it was done, shooting down an English fighter the first time he led the unit into action. Next day, as if to drive home the lesson, he bagged a two-seater. Within ninety days of his arrival, Jasta 11 had claimed 100 victories. By war's end it was credited with 350 kills against the loss of just fifteen pilots to enemy action.

Some writers claim that Richthofen was an uncommunicative, cold-blooded killer, disliked by his own men and possessing no warmth or personality. But they are wrong. In the air he always fought to win, but, said fellow pilot Gisbert Wilhelm Gross decades later: "On the ground, after duty, Richthofen was like a boy with a wonderful sense of humour."[1]

Bishop quickly felt right at home in 60 Squadron's mess. For one thing, he was delighted to find his old RMC buddy E. J. Townesend on the roster of active pilots. And a few days after he arrived, his pal from training school days, Lieutenant Tim Hervey, joined the unit.

Bishop was surprised by the informality of the group. Several men were not even in uniform half the time. They wore sweaters, overalls or whatever else pleased them.

The mess itself had a comfortable atmosphere about it. Along the far wall there was a collection of life-sized drawings of thinly-clad females. They had been copied, with painstaking care, from a French magazine. At Bishop's suggestion, garters wooed from Mesdemoiselles in Amiens would soon adorn the walls as trophies of the squadron's sexual conquests.

Combat momentos decorated the other walls. A propeller from a Fokker D-3 shot down by Captain Ball in 1916 hung above a huge red-brick fireplace. A circular padded seat surrounded the fireplace. Photos of aeroplanes were displayed prominently. Part of one wall was covered with souvenirs taken from German aircraft downed on the Allied side of the lines. There was something macabre about it all; each trophy represented a dead man.

Photographs of the squadron hung in clear view. In one, a brooding Albert Ball could be seen in the front row, sitting with Major Graves. The picture was only a few months old but, already, most of the men in it were dead. They looked, most of them, middle-aged, although few were over twenty-one.

But overall, Hervey said, it was "a very pleasant little station, nice to come back to after a patrol. The mess and Nissen huts for the officers were in a little orchard near the then still-occupied large and very old farm house. The mess was a very cheerful and comfortable place and we had an excellent band provided by other ranks which often played in the mess during or after the evening meal."[2]

Bishop and Hervey spent their first few days practice-flying in order to become familiar with the sector and to learn how to handle the tricky Nieuport.

Hervey remembered the Nieuport as a machine that was already past its time the moment that he and Bishop arrived at the Front. "Of French design, it was the outstanding machine of both sides during 1916, but I think its chief disadvantage by 1917 was its comparatively slow speed compared to the new Albatros, which had come into service on the German side," he said. "As nearly all the fighting was done on the German side of the lines, it was quite often difficult to break off a fight if it was necessary to do so, until the enemy decided to do so. Many pilots were taken prisoner through engine failure or damage of

one sort or another."[3] Another disadvantage, and this often proved crit-
ical, was the fact that the Nieuport had only one gun, whereas the
Albatros came equipped with two. Still, Hervey said, "the Nieuport had
quite a good climb and was quick on turns, but it was becoming out-
classed and started to be replaced with SE5s by July, 1917."[4]

Bishop found the training frustrating. He admitted later that his
heart beat a little faster each time he watched the veterans lifting off for
an Offensive Patrol. Looking on in awe, he watched as they left the
ground individually, circled the drome, formed up and headed east. In
the evenings, he sat in the mess and listened breathlessly to tales of
adventure and narrow escapes, told over wine and brandy.

By a curious twist of fate, he was given a mechanic named Walter
Bourne. Bourne was the same man who had served Albert Ball when he
was running up his score with Number 60. Finally, on the morning of
March 22, Bishop got his big chance. He was going on his first patrol,
after only five hours flying time in France.

Caldwell took him aside on the flight line for a final bit of advice.
The veteran warned him to keep a close eye behind and to avoid combat if at all possible. He was much too green to be of any use in a dogfight, he was told. If escape was impossible, the New Zealander told him
to keep his cool and fire in short bursts. Prolonged firing would only
alert an adversary to the fact that he was fighting a novice. If Billy did
get lucky and send a German spinning down, Caldwell said, he should
be sure to follow him, because the Hun might be faking.

But getting a victory was the least of Bishop's concerns. Just keeping
his battered old Nieuport in the sky was a task in itself. He had been
assigned a beat-up bus that had been in the RFC since the fall of 1916,
and it was exceedingly difficult to handle.

He was, because of his inexperience and the poor performance of his
machine, like a fish out of water on that first fighter mission. His
description of the patrol is brutally honest. He was totally confused and
unsure of himself, experiencing a great deal of difficulty even keeping
his place in formation. Whenever the leader changed direction Bishop

would fall several hundred yards behind. He would gun the motor to catch up and almost rammed one of his mates in the process.

He saw other aircraft in the distance, but had no idea whose side they were on. One of the far-off machines suddenly plunged to the ground, wrapped in flames from nose to rudder. One instant the plane was there and, a moment later, it was a mass of raging fire. Chunks of burning wreckage spilled out of the sky. Bishop, for the life of him, had no idea what had happened. Only later did he learn that it was a British plane that had fallen in a dogfight with an Albatros.

The flight came under heavy Archie fire. The Germans, with Krupp's new triangular ranging mechanism, were shooting much better than they had during Billy's early days with 21 Squadron. The gunners, he discovered, could get a fix on you in three seconds flat.

One shell exploded just under his tail, enveloping Bishop's Nieuport in smoke. The plane spun crazily downward for 300 feet before he could bring it under control. The blast had been so close that he could feel the heat from it, but the fighter sustained only minor shrapnel damage.

Once, Bishop glanced up and found himself completely alone. The sky was empty in every direction. He searched frantically about for several seconds before finally spotting the rest of the patrol several thousand feet below. Only in the mess that night did he learn that the others had exchanged shots with a large white Aviatik two-seater before driving it off. Bishop was mystified as to how he could possibly have failed to notice a plane that size.

Back at Filescamp Farm, Caldwell snarled at him, declaring "The Huns almost nailed you! You left formation and half a dozen V-strutters came out of the sun after you. They took off when they saw the flight turning back to help you."[5]

Bishop was shaken. He thought he had kept a sharp eye out, and yet five Albatroses had snuck up behind him and a huge German two-seater had passed directly beneath his Nieuport, without him seeing a thing! What he didn't realize was that even someone with his marvelous eyes had trouble, at first, spotting objects in the sky. The problem was that, when looking at a vast, empty area, the eye tends to focus only a few yards ahead. If he lived, the veterans told him, he would quickly overcome air blindness.

Major Jack Scott arrived to take command of 60 Squadron the day after Bishop appeared on the scene. And although he didn't realize it at the time, Billy was meeting another key figure in his life.

The major, who had previously commanded an observation squadron, was the most unlikely looking fighter pilot that the war produced. First of all, he was a cripple. Critically injured in a 1914 crash, he could barely walk, even with the aid of canes. He literally had to be lifted in and out of his Nieuport by his batmen. Headquarters had issued strict orders confining him to a desk, but he blatantly ignored them.

Secondly, Scott didn't look, sound or act like a pilot. He was too old, for one thing. At age thirty-five he was a dozen years older than most of his men. There were lines in his face and his head was sprinkled with gray. Combat flying was a young man's game. Anyone over the age of twenty-five, it was thought, did not have the reflexes needed for such work.

Finally, in terms of his personal make-up, Scott was nothing like his pilots. He was a mature, cultured, highly educated man who had been a successful lawyer before the war. Most of his pilots were young, brash, rough-and-tumble individuals with limited formal schooling.

Nevertheless, Scott was well suited for the job. For one thing, he had great physical courage. Mechanic A.A. Nicod and the rest of the squadron got a perfect example of that, just days after Scott arrived. Nicod, recalling the incident in 1934, wrote: "Whilst at target practice, a new pilot named Lieutenant Harris, for some unaccountable reason, failed to pull out of the dive, and he met a terrible death in full view of the horrified spectators. Realising the morale effect of this disaster on his pilots, Major Scott rushed from the Squadron office as fast as his disability would allow him and said quite calmly, 'Get my machine out, flight Sergeant.' Going up, he performed the most hair-raising stunts in diving that it has ever been my lot to witness. Diving on the same target again and again with engine full on, and pulling out of the dive with only a short distance from the ground, he had us with our 'hearts in our throats.' Landing safely, he quietly left his machine and walked back to the Squadron office."[6]

Tim Hervey remembered his commander as a man who would return from a day of fox hunting, sit down and "pull off his riding boots soaked with blood from his old flying injuries. He was a tough chap."[7]

But Scott was more than just courageous; he was also very ambitious. Willie Fry, another 60 Squadron pilot, remembered the major as a man with impressive connections. Those connections, it would later be claimed by some, allowed Scott to obtain decorations and victory credits for his pilots much more readily than was the case for other Royal Flying Corps commanders. Said Fry: "He was the third lame CO in succession, a man of character and presence, a barrister, Sussex squire and fox-hunting man with a host of friends, many in high places. He was obviously ambitious and determined that the squadron should be the best in France. He was the first commanding officer I had served under who was what today would be described as public relations-minded. All the others in my previous short experience had the old Regular Army outlook and shunned publicity of any sort. He was determined that his squadron's and his pilots' deeds should be known by all and sundry, and he was generous in recommending for honours pilots who did well."[8]

In Bishop, Scott sensed he had found a man who could help make the squadron number one. Unfortunately, Bishop had a problem — he couldn't seem to master the art of landing an aeroplane. That could result in serious trouble because, although pilots were seldom hurt in crackups on landing, the Squadron could ill afford to lose any of its Nieuports in such a useless manner. Already Bishop had had three mishaps —one burst tire, a cracked fuselage and a smashed prop.

Scott may have been thinking about those crashes on the morning of March 24 as he watched Bishop returning from a practice flight. Standing on the tarmac next to Scott was General John Higgins, who had arrived with an entourage of underlings to conduct an inspection tour.

The general, wearing a monocle and twitching a swagger stick, watched stiffly as the little fighter plane made its final approach. Its silver wings flashed in the morning sun as Bishop circled a stand of pines. Descending, he kept an eye on his air speed indicator, easing gently back on the joystick as he did so. He ignored the altimeter, which at low levels couldn't be trusted for an accurate reading. The Nieuport slowed almost to stalling speed. Its nose lifted and Bishop cut the throttle. He was too high! The wheels struck the earth with a teeth-jarring force. Bishop felt the plane bounce heavily and, the next instant, found himself staring up at the clouds. There was no time for fear. The machine suddenly flipped over on its back and tumbled violently across the field, its spinning prop churning up dirt for a split second before shattering to pieces. The Nieuport came to a crumbled rest almost at the feet of General Higgins.

Bishop was unhurt. Grinning sheepishly, he untangled himself from the wreckage. Although his reaction was not recorded, he must have gone pale when he spotted the man in a general's uniform standing sternly over him.

Higgins turned on his heels and stomped off toward the squadron headquarters, nodding Bishop to follow him. Billy trailed behind, looking for all the world like a disobedient schoolboy being led to the woodshed by a schoolmaster.

"We can't have this type of nonsense you know, Bishop."

"I'm terribly sorry, sir, a sudden wind tossed me over and before I could regain control…"

"Do you take me for a fool Bishop? I was there. You're on your way back to Upavon (air training school). You can come back when you've learned how to pilot an aeroplane."[9]

That afternoon a morose Bishop attempted to drown his sorrows in brandy. He was washed up as a fighter pilot and he knew it. He had no faith that another round of training flights in England would make him a better aviator.

Scott found him in the mess and tried to console him. The major had convinced Higgins to let Bishop stay until a replacement pilot could be called up. That meant Billy would be allowed to fly at least one more time over enemy lines. It would be his last chance to prove himself — and to stay on active duty.

CHAPTER FIVE

Jack Scott led four Nieuport fighters over the German lines in close diamond formation just before sunset. Low hanging clouds had afforded the patrol protection from Archie fire but, as the skies cleared, Scott had taken the flight up to 9,000 feet.

They droned along uneventfully for some time before Billy Bishop, who was bringing up the rear, spotted a trio of green and mauve Albatros D-3s coming in from the east at fantastic speed. Sunlight reflected off their swept-back wings, and large black Maltese crosses, outlined in white, could be seen distinctly on their torpedo-shaped fuselages. One of them sported a checkerboard insignia.

Bishop rocked his wings, signalling frantically to the others. They ignored his warnings and angrily motioned him to get back in formation. It was a trap! Scott was purposely luring the Germans in. He knew they would not accept combat unless they thought they had an advantage. So he let them approach from behind, planning all the while to turn and meet them at the last moment. But if his timing were off, even by a second, the enemy would draw first blood. And Bishop, as the rear man, would bear the full brunt.

Scott waited until the Albatroses were a scant 100 yards behind before wheeling the formation around to attack them head on.

Bishop, in his first dogfight, was a little slower than the others in spinning around and he turned just in time to see the German with the checkerboard insignia dive on the major's Nieuport. The enemy pilot had Scott cold and he bore in with both guns blazing.

Bishop reacted instantly. There was no wondering whether he could kill another human being, no hesitation of any kind. He dove straight for the Albatros and triggered his Lewis the moment the cross hairs in his Aldis telescopic gun sight met on the pilot's back. His combat report tells what happened next:

> Tracers went all around his machine. He dived for about
> 600 feet and flattened out. I followed him and opened fire
> from forty to fifty yards range, firing forty to fifty rounds. A
> group of tracers went into the fuselage and centre section,
> one being seen entering immediately behind the pilot's seat,
> and one seemed to hit himself. The machine then fell out of
> control in a spinning nose-dive. I dived after him firing.
> When I reached 1,500 feet or 2,000 feet, my engine had
> oiled up and I glided just over the line. The Albatros Scout
> when last seen by me was going vertically downwards at a
> height of 500 to 600 feet, evidently out of control and
> appeared to crash at —

If Bishop wasn't exactly sure where the enemy plane had gone down, he could be forgiven. Even as the German went into his death dive the Canadian's engine had conked out! The inexperienced lieutenant, who had dived too steeply and too quickly, worked the switches in front of him until he was literally shaking in his seat, but the motor stubbornly refused to respond.

Keeping cool, Bishop turned toward the Allied lines and began a shallow glide. He held out little hope of reaching the British side before his landing gear touched down. He wasn't even sure where he was. The skirmish had broken out somewhere over German territory between St. Leger and Arras but he couldn't be sure how far he was from home. He had visions of being hauled away unceremoniously by grey-clad soldiers. His worse nightmare was coming true.

Peering over the rubber rim of his cockpit he could see the shattered ruins of a village, farm buildings, coils of barbed wire and then an open shell-pocked field. He had no more altitude. It was time to come down and face the music. Selecting an area between the craters, Bishop executed a flawless, three-point landing. It was ironic, he mused, that his last landing should be textbook perfect.

The moment that the Nieuport rolled to a stop he scrambled out, grabbed his Very signal flare gun and dove into the nearest shell hole. Rather than surrender, he was prepared to fight it out with a flare gun! After crouching silently for several minutes, he finally risked a peek over the lip of the crater. Four hunched figures, rifles at the ready, were approaching. One of them pointed a finger in his direction. They were so caked in mud that it was impossible to determine their nationality. It wasn't until they were only a few yards away that Billy recognized them as British Tommies and let out a shout of joy.

The Nieuport had come down in No Man's Land, only 300 yards shy of the German front line positions. Enemy troops were directing rifle fire at them and an artillery barrage followed in seconds. But the cannon fire provided a smoke screen and Bishop and the Tommies quickly took advantage of it, dashing for the safety of their own trenches.

That evening, Bishop got a taste of conditions that the infantrymen faced every night. He slept, or rather tried to sleep, on the ground in the middle of a pouring rainstorm. Finally, he gave up and wrote a letter home by candlelight, starting off with: "I am writing this from a dugout 300 yards from our front line, after the most exciting adventure of my life."[2]

Next morning, Billy crawled out and attempted to start the motor of his plane. To his amazement, it caught at once and roared into life. Taking off proved less successful. A clump of mud flew up as he taxied between the shell holes and shattered the propeller. His plane had to be dragged to safety by rope, taken apart and shipped back to Filescamp Farm in a truck for reassembly.

It took Bishop himself two days to walk back to the aerodrome. When he got back, Major Scott greeted him with good news. A British anti-aircraft battery had seen his Albatros crash and he had his first officially credited victory. Better still, General Higgins had sent along his personal congratulations and word that Bishop could remain at the Front.

Billy was going to be allowed to continue his career as a fighter pilot and that was important to him because he had discovered something about himself during that first dogfight. Despite the danger, he realized that he had loved every moment of it. Soon he would be describing battle in letters home as "great sport," adding, "I never enjoyed myself so much in my life.'[3] Clearly, Bishop had discovered his calling.

Shooting down an enemy plane was a formidable task. Most fighter pilots took several weeks, or even months, to score their first kill. Indeed, the majority of 60 Squadron's veterans did not have a single victory to their credit. There were several reasons for that. Scoring hits on an enemy that was moving quickly out of your line of fire, while your own machine gun was vibrating with the roar of the Le Rhone engine, was not easy. And yet Bishop had destroyed one of the formidable Albatroses in his first dogfight — it really was quite a remarkable achievement.

Scott was so impressed that he named Billy a flight commander on March 30, 1917. It was a mistake because, victory or no victory, Bishop was too inexperienced to lead in battle. He proved that a few days later when he led his patrol into an ambush near Vitry.

Six Nieuports were flying over enemy lines when Bishop spotted a lone red Albatros 2,000 feet below. It was a trap, but he was too green to realize it. Without checking above for more of the enemy, he led the whole patrol down to the attack.

Watching all of this from cloud cover a few thousand feet further up, Manfred von Richthofen raised a gloved hand and motioned his Flying Circus to move in for the kill. Five ravenous Albatroses hurled out of the sun and straight onto the unsuspecting tails of the six Nieuports.

Bishop first became aware that he had walked into an ambush when he saw two lines of tracers passing directly between his wings. He launched the Nieuport into a lightning loop, zipping quickly out of the stream of lead.

Others were not so nimble. Lieutenant William Garnett was knocked out of the sky in the first seconds of the dogfight. His plane was hit in the fuel tanks and plunged to the ground in a mass of flames.

Young Frank Bower was also hit in the initial pounce. A hail of slugs tore open his stomach. Despite the mind-numbing pain, he gallantly battled his adversary for ten minutes before breaking off and, as Jack

Scott noted in the squadron history, gliding in for a perfect landing behind Allied lines "with his intestines hanging out."[4] Struggling out of his plane, the nineteen-year-old stumbled a few yards and collapsed. He died the next day. Scott was pleased that the youth had managed to bring his Nieuport home "completely undamaged except for enemy bullets."

The other four Nieuports only escaped the malevolent Albatroses by diving into a cloud bank after a lengthy fight. All four machines were damaged. None of the Germans had been shot down.

On the ground, Bishop was dazed and badly shaken. But he had no cause to fear for his position as flight leader. Despite the debacle, headquarters congratulated him for putting up a "splendid show."[6] The RFC was committed to taking the war to the enemy and was more than willing to accept terrible losses in order to maintain the offensive.

Bishop's luck as a flight leader didn't improve the next day (March 31) but he did score his second victory. With the surviving members of his flight he escorted a group of BE two-seaters over the lines near Arras. Richthofen was waiting for them again. A gaggle of murderous red Albatroses broke through the Nieuport screen and shot down one of the observation planes. In the whirling dogfight that followed, a German latched onto the tail of E.J. Townesend's Nieuport and blew it out of the sky. Bishop, arriving a split second too late to save his old RMC buddy, savagely poured a drum into the black-crossed biplane. "I opened fire twice, the last time at fifty yards range," he wrote in his combat report, adding, "My tracers were seen to hit his machine in the centre section. Albatros seemed to fall out of control, as he was in a spinning nose dive with his engine on. Albatros crashed at 7.30: Ref. 51B. 29-30."[7]

Jasta 11's records give no indication who the victim was, but there can be no doubt that Bishop's claim was legitimate. Attached to his report are confirmations from a British antiaircraft battery that saw the German plane crash, and another from Lieutenant L.H. Leckie of 60 Squadron, who wrote, "I was behind Lieutenant Bishop and saw the Albatros Scout go down in a spinning nose-dive."

Billy had his second confirmed victory but, in just two days as flight leader, he had lost four Allied planes and five men. Concerns about his leadership ability surfaced again a few weeks later when he was given charge of a newcomer named R.B. Clark.

Bishop and Clark were sent out together to attack German observation balloons. As they neared the German lines, Billy took off on his own, leaving the rookie to his own devices. Clark, who was virtually helpless on his own, was in for a ghastly fate. He was jumped by three Albatroses and shot down in flames. The Germans chased him all the way home, with Leutnant von Breiten-Landerberg delivering the coup de grace. Despite the flames, Clark was able to nurse his blazing machine down near an Allied field hospital.

Billy found him there the next day. The dying man, who had joined 60 Squadron just days earlier, was badly burned and had suffered several bullet wounds. Doctors had hacked off a leg but the operation had done nothing to improve his chances. Just before he died, he whispered to Bishop, "I came halfway around the world from Australia to fight the Hun. I served through the campaign at Gallipoli as a Tommy, and at last I got where I longed to be — in the Flying Corps. It seems hard to have to end like this, so soon."[8]

The scene had an unreal quality about it, almost as if it was out of a pulp novel — the hero watching helplessly as a comrade dies before his eyes, issuing a final tragic comment before succumbing to hideous wounds.

Bishop would not forget the scene and neither would some of his squadron mates. There was a suspicion that Bishop was nothing but a glory-seeker that cared little about the safety of fellow pilots. One 60 Squadron pilot, Sydney Pope, once recalled with annoyance how Bishop had left him in the lurch to go off on some private foray. Pope was taking photographs while Bishop provided overhead escort. They were operating deep behind enemy lines when Pope looked up for a moment and, to his astonishment, found himself absolutely alone and extremely vulnerable.

Bishop destroyed his third Albatros on April 6, but neither he nor anyone else ever found out about it. His combat report does not claim a victory. It reads like this: "I engaged an Albatros Scout at 15,000 feet, diving at him from above and behind. I fired a burst of fifteen to twenty rounds at 150 yards range. I dived again and opened fire at 100 yards range. He dived steeply but seemed to have his machine under control. I followed him down to 1,100 feet and he was still diving when I left him."[9]

Bishop did not see the Albatros crash and neither did British front-line observers on the ground. No claim was made and no confirmation granted. But German records show that a pilot named Eicholz was killed in action when his Albatros crashed that morning near Cherisy — the very time and place Bishop gave in his report.

The Allies were losing the war. Now well into its third year, the blood-bath on the Western Front was clearly going in favour of the Germans. The British had suffered a staggering setback at the Somme, where 420,000 Tommies had been killed, wounded or captured between July 1 and mid-November 1916. French casualties numbered more than 190,000 in the same battle. The French Army, utterly demoralized by the bloody carnage of Verdun and the Somme, was on the threshold of rebellion. On the Eastern Front it was no better. The Germans had scored spectacular victories. Russia, in fact, was on the verge of being knocked right out of the war. Romania had already given up.

On the sea, the Kaiser had finally agreed to unleash unrestricted submarine warfare. Allied shipping was beginning to suffer unaccept-ably high losses and it was feared that England might be starved into submission.

In the air the situation was even grimmer. The RFC had lost seventy-five planes and 103 airmen in the first five days of April. The Germans had established a new warning system that allowed Jasta leaders to know in advance of take-off where enemy formations were headed and what their strength was. Men equipped with binoculars and telephones had been posted all across the front lines to watch for incoming Allied planes. Once the enemy was spotted, the information was immediately forwarded to the nearest Jagdstaffel.

In the Arras sector, over which 60 Squadron flew every day, the Allies were hopelessly bogged down. As Scott so succinctly noted in his diary, the "skeletons of French soldiers still hung in the wire, where they had been since September 1915 at least."[10]

On the home front there was more bad news. Losses were becoming so severe that they could no longer be hidden from the general public. Statistics were not given out, of course, but on every street in every town in England and Canada, there was at least one home that had been visited by death. Everyone knew of a family that had lost a brother, father, son or husband in the war.

If those at home needed any further evidence that the situation was not what the newspapers claimed, they had only to visit London. German zeppelins and twin-engine Gotha bombers were now pounding the city almost at will. Although civilian casualties were not high, the raids often caused panic in the populace. Attendance at work the day after a bombing was shockingly low. And that was more serious, in the eyes of the High Command, than the deaths of a few thousand inconsequential civilians.

True, the Germans were on the defensive on the Western Front, but they were well dug in and appeared capable of turning back anything the Allies could throw at them. They had retreated in mid-March 1917 behind their famous Hindenburg line. As they fled, they employed a scorched earth policy, setting fires to countless communities in their wake.

No one had a better view of the devastation than the flyers. Bishop wrote: "The Germans had set fires to scores of villages behind their front. From where we flew we could see between fifty and sixty of them ablaze. The long smoke plumes blowing away to the northeast made one of the most beautiful ground pictures I have ever seen from an aeroplane, but at the same time I was enraged beyond words."[11]

In their new positions the Germans found themselves defending a shorter front. That meant any attack would face stronger resistance. Vimy Ridge, located not far from Filescamp Farm, was the key to the new setup. It was the point where the old line to the north met the new Hindenburg positions.

At first glance the ridge appeared to be impregnable. It was nearly 500 feet to its peak and was four miles long. From its top the enemy commanded the valley of the Scarpe River and the Plains of Douai. The

French had tried three times to capture it, and each time they had been smashed. Despite that, British Field Marshall Sir Douglas Haig decided that, in April, he would launch an all-out attack in the Arras sector. Vimy Ridge would have to be stormed again.

As the date for the attack neared, the RFC was ordered to throw every machine into the air. Every effort had to be made to prevent the Germans from observing the Allied build-up. That meant enemy two-seaters and observation balloons would have to be destroyed at all costs. The balloons were suspended at anywhere from 800 to 3,000 feet by wire cables, and their observers, dangling from wicker baskets just underneath the gas bags, had a bird's-eye view of Allied back lines.

Shooting down a balloon was, therefore, very important. The task also appeared to be rather simple, because the hulking gasbags often exploded in flames after only a few rounds of explosive bullets had been pumped into them. And they were so large that even a poor marksman couldn't miss from 100 yards range. All of that, plus the fact that a balloon counted as a victory in a pilot's personal score, led many to assume that the airmen relished a crack at one of the "drachens."

In fact, nothing could be further from the truth. Among flyers on both sides balloon bursting was the most feared of tasks. A handful of madmen actually specialized in destroying them, but they seldom lived long enough to enjoy their notoriety.

Balloons were heavily defended. A battery of Archie cannons and long range machine guns usually surrounded a single gasbag. Swarms of friendly fighters often patrolled nearby, offering further protection. And balloon crews could haul a sausage down with amazing speed if an enemy plane approached. The trick was to destroy it quickly, before it got too close to its lair, where ground fire became deadly accurate.

Balloon bursting was such dangerous work that Jack Scott was loath to send his veterans out on such assignments. A relatively inexperienced pilot could do the job, provided that he had the courage to descend through a hail of lead to get close enough to his prey. On April 7, he sent Bishop after a balloon. He didn't want to risk losing a man of such obvious potential, but he had no choice. All newcomers were expected to take their chances with the balloons.

On this mission, Bishop flew five miles behind the German lines before he found his target. It was a ghastly thing, floating in the evening sun like a bloated brown beetle. Its stabilizer was even thicker than the body. A huge black cross was stamped on its swollen side. In the basket, a lonely figure struggled with a parachute.

Bishop banked in a wide circle and started to make his run at the balloon. He was concentrating totally on his target when, without warning, bullet holes began appearing in his wings. Billy didn't waste an instant glancing back. If he had, he would have died. There was an Albatros perched just behind his tail and both of its spandaus were throwing out glowing red tracers.

The startled Canadian stood the Nieuport on its tail and held it there for several seconds. The German, obviously a rookie, simply roared underneath Bishop and continued on a parallel course. Billy quickly dropped his nose and found the tables had turned: he was on the German's tail. His combat report picks up the story: "I turned and fired fifteen to twenty rounds at 100 yards range. Tracers were seen going into his machine, he dived away steeply." Bishop didn't see the Albatros crash but he received credit for a victory in the "driven down" category nevertheless.

Without wasting a moment, Billy turned his attention on the balloon, which was descending at breakneck speed. He ignored Major Scott's orders not to go below 1,000 feet, pressing home his attack right to the treetops. Return fire was fierce. A bright green ball of fire suddenly came hurling up at him, aiming straight for his eyes. The projectile burned past the Nieuport, missing it by inches.

Flaming onions!

Bishop had heard of them but this was his first encounter with the batteries that fired cannonball-sized packages of flaming death. They were, it was believed, phosphorescent shells, but no one ever found out for sure, and that lack of knowledge only added to their fearsome reputation. But what was known for certain was that a single hit would send a plane down like a torch.

Machine gun fire and Archie bursts also laced his wings. The air over the balloon was filled with red-hot steel.

Breaking off the attack on the gasbag, Bishop dashed through the storm of lead and made straight for the anti-aircraft crews like an enraged bull. The Lewis gun scattered a group of grey clad soldiers. Several men fell and writhed in agony. Turning back to the balloon, he attacked with unrelenting fury. "I dived on the balloon, which was then on the ground," he explained in his combat report, "and opened fire at 800 feet, finishing my drum when approximately fifty feet above it. Nearly all the bullets entered the balloon and black smoke was visible coming out of it in two places."

But for Bishop there was no time to celebrate. At the moment of victory his engine died. And this time he was much too low to even attempt a glide for home. Worse still, he had killed some of the men below and it wasn't likely that the survivors would be in any mood to take prisoners. He'd always said he would rather die than go to a POW camp, but he had envisioned a clean death in the clouds, not a bayonet in the belly and a jackboot in the groin.

Bishop picked out a tree and aimed straight for it. Maybe they had him but they weren't about to get their hands on his Nieuport. If he played it right, he would be able to smash the wings off without seriously hurting himself. Then he would just have to hope that there was a good Prussian officer among his captors. Such men still believed in the gentlemanly rules of war and would never allow their troops to murder a helpless prisoner.

As he came down Bishop suddenly remembered something Walter Bourne had told him after his engine quit during his first dogfight. If his motor died he was to pump the throttle for all he was worth. He did just that and, as if by a miracle, one of the nine cylinders came back to life. A second kicked over and, a moment later, the whole engine had sputtered back into action. Bishop zoomed for altitude only yards from the ground. A dozen German soldiers vainly fired rifle shots after the retreating Nieuport. Bishop had his third and fourth victories and his second unbelievable escape from the clutches of the German infantry.

April 7 was not a day of celebration at 60 Squadron, despite Billy's success. Earlier that day, Richthofen's Circus had mauled a patrol led by Alan Binnie. Three Nieuports had gone down, carrying Knowles, Hall and Georgie Smart to their deaths. The Red Baron had killed Smart, pursuing him over Allied territory before setting his plane on fire. The Germans, who normally stayed on their own side of the trenches, were becoming bolder with each new success.

That night, Bishop couldn't bring himself to join in the drunken wake. Whether they were celebrating a victory or mourning a loss, the pilots had a party every night. He retired early to his barracks and cried his eyes out. Billy was an emotional man who expressed his grief with tears more readily than most males — a fact that he carefully hid from his mates. Before turning in he wrote Margaret "Three more pilots lost today. All good men. Oh how I hate the Huns. They have done in so many of my best friends. I'll make them pay, I swear."[12]

Next day, Smart was buried in a little country graveyard outside Izel-le-Hameau. A crumbling seventeenth century church was the only structure in view. A cold north wind added to the gloom as Smart was lowered into the mud. Three volleys were fired over the grave, someone played Last Post and 60 Squadron filed back to the war. An aeroplane propeller was left behind to serve as the tombstone.

CHAPTER SIX

The air war was becoming more savage with each passing hour. 60 Squadron's pilots were now flying three to four patrols per day; and each one of them was encountering fierce resistance. The offensive was taking its toll on flyers even after they had safely returned to Filescamp Farm.

Combat flying, contrary to popular belief, was even more physically demanding than ground fighting. The vibration from a Le Rhone engine was enough to make it impossible for a Nieuport pilot to relax for even a moment during the two-hour patrols. And the noise level was so loud that a quarter of all airmen who survived the war would be partially deaf.

Then there was the terrible cold and the lack of oxygen. Oxygen masks were simply not available, although the pilots needed them at two miles up. By the three-mile mark, breathing problems became acute. At 19,000 feet, where dogfights occasionally took place, lack of oxygen caused a stabbing pain behind the eyes, loss of concentration and high blood pressure.

The aerial duels themselves left many pilots exhausted. Loops, zooms, spins and tight turns caused temporary grey-outs and black-outs, and even moderate concussions. Blood drained quickly to and from the brain in such maneuvers, causing faces to redden noticeably. Mouths were forced open and cheeks were sucked into the mouth as pilots were bounced around inside their cockpits by frantic stunts. Just keeping a close eye on the rear necessitated constant craning of the head in all directions. Bishop noted that his neck was rubbed raw after each patrol. And he was often sick to his stomach from breathing nau-seating castor oil fumes.

Most of the airmen were too tired to do anything but sleep. But not

Billy: he had come to the conclusion that marksmanship was the key to success, and he kept busy at target practice during every spare moment. He spent hours diving on a ground target he called "Petit Bosche." Gunnery drill was not without its risks. He often dove within a few feet of the ground before breaking off. But the target was usually shot full of holes. "His invariable rule," Lieutenant Harold Lewis recalled, "was that unused ammunition in the drum on the gun should be fired into the ground targets before landing."[1] No one in his flight dared return from a patrol with a loaded machine gun.

Not content with that, he would gather up all the tin cans in the cookhouse, toss them overboard from three miles up and shoot them to ribbons as they tumbled to earth. The squadron cook was not amused by this, telling others "that the new Bishop lad is a bit batty." [2]

Next, he began shooting at pigeons with a rifle. One afternoon he fired 500 rounds, hitting only one bird in flight. But as anyone who has ever tried to shoot a bird in flight with a single shot rifle will tell you, the chances of obtaining a hit are one in thousands.

During evenings he could be found in the hangars, helping his mechanic, Walter Bourne, with his Nieuport. The lieutenant insisted on cleaning and loading the Lewis gun himself, even though the task of loading the three drums took half an hour.

All this target shooting very quickly paid off. On April 8, Bishop staged the most spectacular feat of the air war to that date.

At 9:30 A.M., over Arras, he teamed up with Jack Scott to shoot down a two-seater, giving him one of only two shared victories he would score throughout his career. A few minutes later, flying alone, he wrecked an observation balloon, peppering it with lead as it sagged to the ground. Then it happened. A lone Albatros that may have been flown by ace pilot Wilhelm Frankl came climbing up to greet him 4,000 feet above the tattered balloon.

A twenty-three-year-old native of Hamburg, Frankl had been one of the original Fokker Eindeckker aces and, after studying under the great Oswald Boelcke, had been given command of his own Jagdstaffel. One of only two Jews to win his country's highest decoration, the Ordre

Pour Le Merit, he was at his peak, having shot down three British two-seaters only two days earlier. That very morning at dawn he had registered his nineteenth kill, making him one of the top surviving German aces.

The German and Bishop came at one another head-on, closing the distance between them at a combined speed of 220 miles per hour. Both were unflinching, each waiting for the other to give ground. If either man broke off too soon he would expose his vulnerable tail to a murderous hail of fire. If neither gave way, the confrontation would end in a catastrophic mid-air collision. Both held like grim death to their course of flight.

The Albatros grew larger by the second until the instant when Bishop knew they must crash. He kept firing, to the last possible moment, before yanking savagely on his joystick. The wheels of the Nieuport skimmed only inches above the top wing of the Albatros.

The two went at one another again in another insane charge. Both planes seemed to be joined by smoking, burning tracers but, somehow, neither man was able to score a fatal hit. Then Bishop's gun jammed! He danced off to one side and anxiously struggled to clear the stoppage. The German, seeing his opening, bore in with both guns thumping. A hail of explosive slugs ripped into the fuselage just three feet behind Billy's head.

The Canadian somehow cleared the stoppage and turned hysterically on his tormentor. Two deadly accurate bursts of fire sent the Albatros spinning down out of control with a dead pilot's hand gripping the control column. Later that day, it was learned Frankl had been killed in the same sector where Bishop made his claim.

Ten minutes later, Bishop had an even more dramatic brush with death. Flying 10,000 feet over Vitry, he spotted a pair of single-seaters. They were, in fact, red Albatroses from Jasta 11.

Billy was about to attack the scarlet planes when he suddenly paused. The whole setup just wasn't right and he felt uneasy. He was beginning to learn the tricks of the trade. A quick glance around revealed three tiny dark specks hovering far above him. It was a trick: the three specks were German AEGs.

Billy decided to walk right into the lair — with both eyes open. He quickly calculated the distance between the AEGs, himself and the Albatroses, deciding that he could bag one of the Albatroses and have just enough time to turn and face the AEGs. It was a near suicidal gamble that would only be attempted by a madman — or by someone willing to take incredible risks to add to his victory score.

Bishop rocketed in behind the rear Albatros and opened fire. The German twisted to escape and, as Billy struggled to keep him in range, the second Albatros pilot, Sebastian Festner, slipped in behind the Nieuport and sent a shower of slugs right into its cockpit. One bullet actually creased the side of Billy's leather helmet, burrowing a three-inch scar in the material before shattering the windshield in front of his face. For the third time in his short career he had allowed an opponent to sneak up on him. And once again only a miracle had saved his life.

Badly shaken, but still in control of his senses, Bishop darted out of the gunfire and went after Festner. He gained the upper hand almost at once, sending the German down with a cracked wing after firing only one burst. Festner, one of Richthofen's more promising pupils, was forced down but escaped without injury.

Billy, who realized the high-level Germans must by now be almost breathing down his neck, swung around just in time to see all three dropping on him with guns flashing. He squeezed off a short burst of his own and watched as the lead AEG, a two-seater, fell over on its back and disappeared, its Benz engine having been reduced to separating wreckage by the Lewis bullets. Bishop, totally honest in his combat report, said the AEG "went down in a nose-dive but I think partly under control."[3] German records indicate no two-seaters were lost near Vitry that day, suggesting that the AEG was able to make an emergency landing in a cow pasture below. In any case, the victory, the fifth he'd claimed that morning, was not officially confirmed.

In one unforgettable patrol Billy was credited with four victories. It was a small wonder that his comrades now regarded him as "some sort of wild man, or fire-eater just escaped from the zoo."[4]

There was one humorous aspect to that bloodstained morning. As

Major Scott read Billy's report, he nodded and said, "Well, Bishop, after that lot I think you'd better have a rest."[5]

Visions of a week in London popped into Billy's head. A hot bath, the glitter of the capital, wine, women.

Scott looked up and added, "Take the afternoon off."[6]

Another consequence of the patrol was that Walter Bourne painted the nose of Billy's Nieuport a bright blue. It was, he said, the mark of an ace. When Albert Ball had been at Filescamp, Bourne had painted his nose scarlet.

Bishop was thrilled with the honour and flew to several neighbouring aerodromes to show off his new trademark.

Before long the silver Nieuport with the blue nose would be familiar to German pilots as well.

The officers' mess was reeling. Its walls rotated crazily and the floor vibrated unsteadily under Bishop's feet. Grabbing onto tables and chairs for support, he made his way toward the piano. Alan Binnie was seated at the musical instrument, pounding the worn yellow keys with great gusto. Everyone was in a riotous mood. Billy's four kills, which brought his official score up to eight, was the best news the squadron, or the entire RFC for that matter, had received in a month.

The man of the hour climbed atop the piano and launched into a sad Flying Corps ballad. The whole place erupted in boos. From the back of the room, General Trenchard advised Bishop against a singing career. There was loud laughter.

Trenchard was on hand to personally congratulate the man who was proving that the Albatros was not invincible. But once he had left, the party really heated up. Bishop crept up behind one pilot, grabbed him by the back of the collar and tore his uniform off his back. That precipitated a general uniform-tearing contest. The sport was becoming popular with the men, even though none of them could afford the bills of the London tailor who was getting rich from the practice.

Bishop, looking for new ways to break the boredom, and to relieve the tension, proceeded to smash gramophone records over the head of Grid Caldwell. Everyone quickly joined in, tossing records at one another in a giggling display of tomfoolery. No one protested the loss of the records. They had been played so often that everyone was sick of them.

Clearing the tables aside, the men engaged in a full-scale rugby match using a leather helmet as the ball. Part of English officer tradition calls for a man to pretend he is utterly disdainful of physical injury. Therefore, the pilots plunged at one another with bone-crushing abandon. Nobody was seriously hurt, although more than one ankle was sprained.

Major Scott, for his part, turned a blind eye to the whole affair. He realized full well that the partying, even though it had a certain forced-urgency to it, was essential to morale. Indeed, if not for his old injuries, he would have joined in. The lads needed an outlet to stop them from cracking under the terrible pressure.

All of this carousing did have its drawbacks, however. Pilots often had to fly the dawn patrol with a hangover. Bishop found the ailment could be at least partially relieved by climbing high into the cooler air.

But despite the obvious danger of fighting the Germans while suffering from a splitting headache, there were those who insisted that the drunken bashes were essential. They argued that casualties would have been even higher had pilots spent the evenings alone in their bunks, worrying about what the next day would bring.

There are vivid and delightful images of Bishop, 60 Squadron and life at Filescamp Farm available in the writings of the men who survived those desperate spring days of 1917.

Billy was the unit's clown prince and he kept everyone's morale up with a whole series of practical jokes. He had his detractors, but with the majority of his Squadron mates he was exceptionally popular.

Lieutenant William Fry, who joined 60 in mid-April, was initially very impressed with the ace. He wrote: "I was detailed to 'C' Flight, commanded by W.A. Bishop, commonly called "Bish," who had just been promoted to captain and flight commander and was rapidly making a name for himself and was highly thought of by the CO." Fry found the Canadian to be "good-looking, fair, strong, open and uninhibited, he was a success in the squadron and popular. He was friendly and I could not have had a better welcome." He remembered Bishop also as being an "extrovert to a degree," and as a man who "took the lead in every off-duty activity."

Lieutenant Harold Lewis, in a letter written in his eightieth year, told of how Bishop helped 60 shed the last remains of British military discipline. "I recall one day when the weather was dud with low cloud and rain. On call in the mess I was very expertly playing the piano to a lot of very rowdy singing of songs, probably from Chu Chin Chow and so forth. 'John Collins' had been flowing fairly freely for some hours, and Bill Bishop was sitting cavalry fashion astride the upright piano shouting to me to play a bit faster or slower or better, when the H-Ack Klaxon horn on the top of the mess drowned out our efforts. [The horn signalled the approach of enemy aircraft.] Bishop stiffened up and with his right foot came down with an almighty crash on about fifteen bass notes in an awful discord, shouting 'Come on chaps.' On reaching his machine he at least was S.C.S [Stone Cold Sober]."

Lewis continued: "Another Bishop memory is of a night when we had visitors from I think 70 Squadron. The party was fairly hectic and with one or two others I had gone to bed, and almost asleep, I realized that something unusual was afoot. Bishop, with a few other characters, was in the act of setting alight the net curtains on my Nissen hut windows, and those of others who had had enough of the party. A good supply of fire buckets avoided a major conflagration.

"Going back to the piano episode, Bishop called for a bottle of gin with which to lubricate the piano wires, which he declared much improved my efforts."[7]

Soon Billy moved his pranks outdoors, into the barnyard. Once he collared a huge pig and set the filthy brute loose in the mess. On another occasion he painted several animals in bright colours, decorating one sow with black crosses and inscribing on its flanks the name "Baron von Richthofen."

Tim Hervey remembered Bishop as being "the leading light in painting our long-suffering farmer's pigs red, white and blue." The Canadian was, he added, "very popular with his fellow pilots and mechanics and was always eager to fly and to take part in any off-duty fun."[8]

His example soon caught on. A favourite trick was to feed brandy-soaked breadcrumbs to ducks and drakes. The birds were soon wallowing about the yard in a comical fashion.

Once, one of the rookie flyers dashed into the mess, his face as white as a sheet.

"Seen a ghost?" asked Bishop.

"I gave too much drink to a prize drake and it keeled over, dead as a doornail," was the reply. "The farmer's enraged. He's going to report me to the CO. You've got to do something, Billy."[9]

Life at the aerodrome could indeed be pleasant during lulls in the fighting. Major Scott insisted that his pilots be given regular days off and the men used the time to relax or go horseback riding.

Lieutenant Yvone Kirkpatrick painted a pleasing picture in a letter home. He wrote: "This place is absolutely topping. Our quarters are in an orchard, and there's plenty of shade and green grass with an old horse on it. As I got here before the others I managed to bag a decent hut with wallpaper on the walls and linoleum on the floor, bookcases, cupboards, a table, electric light and a fair sprinkling of fair maidens on the wall who look, by their attire, as if 'La Vie Parisienne' was a pretty warm place."[10]

After the war, Major Scott admitted, "The contrast between our quarters and those occupied by the infantry and gunners in the line was striking. We had cream at every meal, a hot bath — made by digging an oblong hole in the turf and lining it with a waterproof sheet — whenever we felt so inclined."[11]

On especially hot days, wrote Captain "Moley" Molesworth, the pilots would loaf about the orchard in pyjamas, or lie naked in the makeshift pool with a book in one hand and a cool drink in the other. "These baths have been such a success," he wrote, "that we decided to dig a small bathing pool about twenty feet square by three feet deep. When we got this going the whole population of the nearest village had to come and watch us. This was rather disconcerting, as we used to bathe 'tout a fait' nude. Most of the chaps managed to rig up something in the way of a bathing dress by buying various articles of clothing in the neighbouring villages — I was forced to content myself with a type of female undergarment, which seemed to cause great amusement among the ack-emmas [air mechanics]. The village maidens were highly delighted, and thought it quite the thing, now that we were decently clad, to watch us at our aquatic sports."[12]

Molesworth, Bishop and Caldwell took over one of the Nissen half-circle shaped tin huts, kicked in a wall and hung a sign out front that read "Saloon Bar." Before long, said Molesworth, "most of the Squadron seemed to collect there, including Kate and Black Boy, the special pet dogs of the squadron, who made it their abode."[13]

Soon, Molesworth reported, pilots were often going aloft in "multi-coloured pyjamas."[14] Bishop occasionally scrambled into his Nieuport wearing only tennis shoes, a T-shirt and shorts. He started wearing his hair longer than regulations permitted, declaring, "A real gentleman always wears his hair a little long."[15]

All this relaxed behaviour created something of a crisis one morning when Bishop and Scott took off on dawn patrol wearing only bedroom slippers, pyjamas and snowboots — and without bothering to shave. They landed just in time to greet two generals who had arrived for a surprise inspection. The airmen were, Scott recalled afterward, given a stiff reprimand and saw the brass hats off with a "feeling of profound relief."[16]

Billy and his mates carried their pranks even into battle. When the squadron encountered a large white two-seater operated by a pair of woefully incompetent German airmen, they refused to shoot it down, amusing themselves instead by terrifying the crew. They launched attacks of grossly exaggerated ferocity, purposely firing wildly inaccurate bursts at the Germans. The enemy pilot was an oafish fellow who handled his machine with all the grace of a bear on ice skates. His observer was so fat that no one could imagine how he managed to squeeze into the rear cockpit. And his marksmanship was even more laughable than the pilot's flying ability.

The plane was dubbed the "Flying Pig" and formally adopted as a squadron mascot. Pilots were strictly forbidden to shoot it down. Once, when the burly gunner fired one of his aimless bursts, an entire flight of Nieuports turned and fled, feigning terror. That night, the Allied pilots sat around their mess trying to envision the scene on the German side of the lines as the Flying Pig observer boasted of how he had routed single-handedly six opponents with one burst. The thought was enough to make Bishop laugh until tears welled in his eyes.

The Germans, in fairness, weren't the only ones capable of glaring stupidity. 60 Squadron demonstrated that one afternoon when a flight of Nieuports forced down an Albatros two-seater behind the British lines. The six Allied pilots, in their eagerness to prevent the enemy from destroying the plane, attempted to land in a crater-pocked field adjacent to the damaged two-seater. The first Englishman to set down, a Lieutenant Grenfell, crashed on impact, breaking his leg and demolishing his plane. Three of the other five also wrecked their planes, so that, as Scott noted, the German was "flanked by a crashed Nieuport in every adjoining enclosure."[17] Meanwhile, as the men of 60 were busy smashing up their own planes, the German pilot was able to set fire to his Albatros. The plane, in fact, quickly exploded, with the resulting blast seriously wounding a swarm of British Tommies, who had come to capture the enemy airmen. The Germans, quite by accident, had knocked out four Nieuports and several infantrymen after having lost the dogfight! It is doubtful that they could have inflicted that much damage had they remained on operations for the rest of the war.

Bishop's pranks and carefree attitude showed only one side of the man; the other side was less attractive — he was becoming a hardened killer. The war was changing the young extrovert in more ways than even he realized.

At first the spine-tingling excitement of aerial combat had aroused something within him. But now it was more than that He was beginning to enjoy sending his adversaries to horrible deaths. This dark side of his personality surfaced graphically one afternoon when a lull in the fighting gave the squadron some unexpected time off. Major Scott, along with Bishop and another pilot, decided to spend the afternoon looking for a German plane that had crashed on the Allied side of the trenches. It wasn't often that an enemy plane fell inside British territory and the airmen were anxious to collect a few souvenirs from the wreckage. They made their way by automobile through the shattered streets of Arras, weaving in and out of long columns of tired British Tommies. At one point they passed by a cemetery that had been violated by an artillery bombardment. Headstones had been smashed to pieces and the bodies of men, women and children had been ripped from their graves and hurled about, Bishop said, "like rag dolls."[1]

Eventually, the three airmen made their way to the ruins of Monchy. The town had been the scene of intense house-to-house fighting during the Battle of Arras and it had been reduced to little more than a pathetic pile of rubble. Allied infantrymen were still checking cellars when the 60 Squadron contingent arrived.

This was the full horror of warfare at close range and Major Scott, at least, was shocked and sickened by what he saw. Pilots faced undeniable danger in the air, but at least fighting above the clouds was clean. A vanquished opponent or a slain comrade simply tumbled out of the clear blue sky and left behind no trace. There was something very tidy about it all.

On the ground it was much different. Dead men were strewn about all over the place. Twisted corpses littered the streets, alleys and door-ways. Lifeless figures hung out of windows. Broken bodies were draped across piles of rubble. Many had been dead for days and the stench of rotting flesh filled the air. One dead German soldier was propped in a sitting position, his back resting against the wheel of an abandoned peasant's cart. His face was stiff and waxen and the front of his grey coat was smeared with a reddish-brown. A bolt-action rifle was clutched firmly in his hand and he was still wearing a coal-scuttle hel-met and full battle gear.

Scott grimaced at the sight but Bishop, according to one writer, exclaimed "What a trophy! If we take him back it will prove to the mess that we were really at the Front."[2]

Other accounts of this ghoulish incident explain that Jack Scott refused to go along with the idea. Indeed, he did. But the episode does not appear to have ended there. There is evidence that Bishop laid his hands on the corpse, intending to bring it back with the aid of the other pilot.

When Billy was on home leave in October 1917, he granted an inter-view to a reporter from the *Owen Sound Sun*. The journalist wrote: "His stories of the Front have a grim humour that is amusing even while they are sometimes most tragic. In company with another officer he was walking over a part of ground that had recently been a battlefield and hundreds of Germans, yet unburied, dotted the ground. The two of them decided to take one of the dead Germans into the mess as a surprise to the others and picked on one that was apparently sitting up. They went over to him and were surprised to find that he had been buried to the waist and when touched he fell apart. Needless to say they did not bring a German to the mess that day."

Billy himself admitted in a letter to Margaret that "a bloodthirsty streak" had appeared in him. "You have no idea how bloodthirsty I've become and how much pleasure I get in killing Huns," he told her.

In another letter, he said matter-of-factly: "Margaret, my machine, my new one, is a wonder. It fairly tears through the air. Tonight, just to celebrate it, I shot down a Pfalz in flames from 17,500 feet. There were four of them and I was so pleased to see a Hun again ... that I just had to try my gun on them. Sure enough, down they went and one in flames. 'Twas a merry sight withal. I'm so glad you're taking painting lessons."[3]

His letters to her are filled with detailed descriptions of his kills. In one, he relates how he shot two German airmen down in flames and added, "That made my heart feel good sweetheart, because that's so much less misery that they will bring to the world." After returning to the Front from an extended leave he told her, "It's somehow good to get back closer to the war."[4]

Just how deep-seated Bishop's bloodthirsty streak had become was made clear on April 20, when he shot down a big, square-winged Aviatik two-seater for his ninth official victory. He closed within just five feet of the black-crossed plane before veering off. He was so close that he could look right into the eyes of his adversaries. The observer had stopped firing and slumped wounded in his chair. The pilot, staring stonefaced over his shoulder at Bishop, was unhurt.

Suddenly, as the ace gazed back, the Aviatik erupted in flames. Fire shot from the engine and ripped through both cockpits, enveloping the aircraft in flames from nose to tail. The ship staggered to one side, wallowing across the sky like a pregnant water buffalo. Yellow tongues of flame licked at the crewmen. Expressions of raw terror were stamped on their faces as the Aviatik tumbled away, engulfed in fire. Fanned by the wind, the flames transformed the huge craft into a blazing inferno. It would be several minutes before the plane reached the earth, where a shattering explosion would signal a merciful end to the suffering of the two men.

Recalling this terrible scene later, Bishop wrote: "I must say that to see an enemy going down in flames is a source of great satisfaction. The moment you see the fire break out you know that nothing in the world can save the man, or men, in the doomed machine."[5]

He admitted reflecting for a moment on the fate of the crew, "into whose faces I had just been looking." But he quickly added, "it was fair hunting and I flew away with great satisfaction in my heart."[6]

Days later, he forced a two-seater down and then strafed the helpless crew on the ground. It was not a violation of the rules of war because the Germans had landed behind their own lines and would not have been captured. However, pilots on both sides usually refrained from firing on downed airmen.

In combat he showed no mercy whatever. He gained his twenty-third victory by mowing down a Rumpler crew after the rear gunner's Parbellum gun jammed. As the observer struggled to clear the stoppage, Bishop closed in point-blank and raked the two men with fifteen rounds.

It was said that he would go to just about any length to obtain a victory. In one incident, it was said that Bishop destroyed an Albatros by brushing up against it with his Nieuport! According to the story, the German's top wing had been weakened by Billy's fire. But just at the moment when victory seemed assured, his Lewis jammed. Rather than allow his opponent to escape, the Canadian knocked the top wing off the German plane with his own wing-tip serving as a battering ram. Perhaps. But the story has a fantastic ring to it. The Nieuport was rather fragile to begin with and it seems highly doubtful that any pilot would risk bumping into another machine while flying one of the little French fighters. The structural limitations of the Nieuport were well known to Bishop because no less than five 60 Squadron pilots had crashed when their planes broke up in mid-air for no apparent reason. (Major Scott blamed the manufacturers, claiming they used unseasoned wood and inserted screws in main spars, thus seriously weakening them.) Besides that, Bishop does not mention the episode in any combat report, in his book or even in private letters home. Still, there are those who insist the story is true. What is known for certain is that Bishop's fifty-seventh victim, a Pfalz pilot, died after Billy literally drove the poor man into the ground. The German had become so distraught at being unable to shake Bishop off his tail that he plunged his machine into a reckless nose-dive. The Pfalz — like the Nieuport — couldn't stand up to that type of strain and its airframe crumbled. None of the ace's bullets had found their mark, but Bishop's single-minded attack had resulted in the death of his foe nevertheless.

It is also beyond dispute that Bishop used ghastly Buckingham incendiary bullets on at least one occasion. Such ammunition, if used accurately, virtually guaranteed the other man a fiery death. He admits using these hideous blunt-nosed bullets in an April 27, 1917, combat report, stating flatly: "I attacked it and fired about sixty rounds of Buckingham into it."[7] The words fairly jump off the page because General Trenchard had issued orders strictly prohibiting the use of such pellets.

Even the moody Irish ace, Mick Mannock, whose hatred for everything German was notorious, spurned the use of Buckinghams. He explained his feelings in a tearful speech to a fellow pilot, declaring, "That's the way they're going to get me in the end — flames and finish! I'm never going to have it said that my own right hand ever used the same dirty weapons."[8] As it turned out, Mannock's prophecy of doom was correct. He died in a burning SE5 after a German gunner set his fuel tank alight with incendiaries.

But perhaps Bishop did not know the rules because he did, after all, openly mention use of Buckinghams in a combat report, which he knew full well was an official document that would be scanned by superiors. The penalty for using the ammo varied, depending on who found out about it. On the Allied side of the lines it could mean anything from a reprimand to a court martial. If the Germans caught you with Buckinghams they forsook the niceties of a courtroom. You faced a firing squad.

That Bishop might not have known the rule is quite possible, considering the fact that he had a history of not paying a lot of attention to regulations. What is more surprising is that Major Scott apparently did not know about it either. Or at least there is no record that he said anything to Bishop about it.

A possible explanation for Bishop's blood lust is this: the Germans had killed so many of his close friends that he hated them with a burning passion. During one weekend in April alone, Jack Scott noted in the squadron history, no less than ten of the eighteen pilots were shot down. On April 14, Bishop was shattered when four of the men in his flight were gunned down in a shoot-out with the Richthofen Circus. The Red Baron destroyed one of the Nieuports and his men got the other three. Bishop was not with them that fateful afternoon, but Alan Binnie was, and the gregarious Australian was listed among those who did not return.

Scott told what happened: "Binnie was leading, and was hit in the shoulder when trying to extricate two of his patrol from a cloud of enemies. The blood from his wound spurted all over the nacelle, obscuring the instruments, and in addition to this his machine caught fire. He extinguished the flames and then fainted when gliding homeward. The machine must have turned west after this, for he woke up in a small park in Lens, having hit the ground while still unconscious, without further serious injuries. He lost his arm at the shoulder, and was a prisoner till the spring of 1918, when he was repatriated and immediately commenced flying again. He was a very great loss to the squadron, as he was a first-class flight commander who had already destroyed several Huns and would have got a lot more."[9]

At first, the squadron knew only that Binnie's plane had been seen on fire in the air and it was assumed that he had been killed. For Bishop it was a severe jolt. He and the Australian had become almost as close as brothers. He wept and wrote Margaret a letter that gives a clear insight into his frame of mind during that period of his life.

He confided: "My heart is full these days. We are having the most awful time. Yesterday, Binnie, a friend of mine and three others were shot down and today, four of my flight went under in a scrap. Oh, those damned Huns. I'll pay a few of them for this, I swear I will. They were such good people and one was at RMC with me."

Billy won the Military Cross for his double victory over a balloon and an Albatros on April 7. He was also promoted to captain simply because he was one of the few men left with any front line experience.

His phenomenal personal success continued throughout Bloody April. On the 22nd he employed new tactics to sucker a pair of Albatros D-3s to their fate. Using Major Scott as a decoy (without the major's permission) he ambushed a flight of Germans, driving two down with near surgical precision.

Bishop had changed his technique. He realized he could not survive much longer if he continued his no-holds-barred style of fighting. Already he'd had too many close calls. Once, mechanic Walter Bourne had counted 210 bullet holes in his Nieuport after a patrol. From now on he would use the sneak attack. And in future he would show no hesitation to run for the hills if the fight became too hot to handle.

The surprise-attack method quickly reaped impressive results. Bishop forced a two-seater to land on the afternoon of April 23, and destroyed an Albatros on the same patrol. That gave him four victories in just two days. There was a brief lull in his scoring but he made up for it on the 27th when he sent a balloon down smoking.

On the 29th, while escorting a flight of 11 Squadron FE2Bs near Baralle, he broke away and pounced on a lone Halberstadt D-3, sending it down in flames with three bursts. There can be no doubt about the honesty of Billy's report because the kill was registered in full view of several FEE crewmen, one of whom called 60 Squadron to confirm the kill, although Major Scott did not bother to record that fact in writing.

In any case, as the bloodiest month of aerial fighting that the world had yet seen drew to a close, Bishop intentionally began seeking out two-seaters. He went after them with a vengeance — crashing two, driving a third down out of control and forcing a fourth to land — all in the space of three days. His bag included one Aviatik C-5 and three Albatros C-3s. The carnage opened on April 30, when he shot down the Aviatik.

Moments later he forced an Albatros C-3 to land. Two days after that, on May 2, he attacked a pair of big Albatros two-seaters, destroying one and driving a second down out of control.

Bishop said in his autobiography that he went after the slower reconnaissance planes because he was looking for some easy targets after several weeks of tough sloughing against German fighters. But Hanns-Gerd Rabe, a gunner/observer who had more than one brush with the Canadian ace, had a different theory as to why Bishop began preying on two-seaters. He wrote: "The basis of his strange behaviour lay in the fact that a German observer crewman had shot down a friend of Bishop's."

Whatever the reason, it was more than obvious that Billy was becoming an extremely polished air fighter. Just how well polished is best outlined in a letter written home by Moley Molesworth.

Led by Bishop, Molesworth and one other British pilot had boldly attacked seven German fighters. Molesworth tells what happened next: "Our numbers were not overwhelming this time, but we knew the Huns had got pukka wind-up by the way that they disappeared when we arrived on the line, so we felt quite confident in taking on twice as many as ourselves. Of course we were all out for trouble, as we wanted to show what the new machines could do. As soon as our leader spotted a formation of Huns, he was after them like a flash. I think there were seven of them but we were all much too excited to count. Suddenly they saw us coming and tried desperately to escape, but our leader got into his favourite position, and the rear Hun hadn't a ghost of a chance. The next instance he was a flaming mass." [10]

Bishop discussed tactics with anyone who would listen and, as a result, there were numerous surviving descriptions of his tactics. One of the better ones came from squadron mechanic A.A. Nicod. He wrote: "Captain Bishop was now making history. Enjoying a roving commission, he went off any time and always fired a Very light [flare gun] on his return to the aerodrome if he had destroyed a German machine. Sometimes he would fire two. Everyone would surge round his machine on landing to hear his account of how he had put paid to a Hun. Captain Bishop developed a style entirely his own. Taking advantage of the sun, he would stalk his victim and send a stream of lead just in front of the enemy machine, using Buckingham tracer ammunition. The German machine would invariably fly straight into this burst of fire, and in the majority of cases, would dive to the earth in flames." [11]

As April 1917 came to a close, Billy was the only man in the squadron who could claim success. He had scored fifteen kills during the month and raised his overall total to twenty by May 4, when, with the help of Willie Fry, he shot down an AEG two-seater. It was the second and last Bishop victory listed in Royal Flying Corps records as a "shared" triumph. Fry recalled the incident in his book: "During luncheon that day, a message came in that there was a German two-seater doing artillery cooperation on our front. The CO asked Bishop and me to go up and we did so at once. We soon picked up the machine from AA shell bursts at about 5,000 feet and attacked it."[12]

The intruder was quickly shot down and, said Fry, "what I recall about the occasion is that we were only an hour in the air and returned to finish our luncheon which had been kept for us."[13]

In his autobiography, Fry would write a passage about this particular fight that Bishop's critics would latch onto in later years in a bid to discredit the ace. Fry wrote:

> *Strangely, although I must have flown with him constantly as his deputy leader in the flight this is the only mention in my logbook of being involved with Bishop in a fight.*

Fry added it was the only time he could ever remember being in a fight with the Canadian. Some of Billy's detractors would claim Fry was implying that Bishop was not a very aggressive pilot, at least when flying as a member of a patrol. But it's more likely just an example of how pilots did not always record every detail about their missions in their logbooks. For there's evidence that Fry was in at least *seven* dogfights with Bishop. Because Fry's comments have been used to damn Bishop so frequently, it's important to prove this point. The first fight the two men took part in together came on April 6, 1917, when Bishop wrote in his combat report:

> *While leading the Offenseive Patrol I saw six HA and followed them up and down in front of Vitry for three-quarters of an hour trying to engage them. Lt. Fry dived twice at them, but both times they managed to escape. I dived once, but was unable to get near them. They seemed determined not to fight.*

In a combat report on May 4, 1917, Bishop wrote:

The OP (offensive patrol) was attacked by five HA (hostile aircraft) from above and out of the sun. One HA attacked me and then zoomed up. He dived again vertically and by pulling down my gun I fired a short burst at him. He flew away. The other three machines in the patrol were attacked at the same time. Lt. Fry fired a burst at one without effect. The whole five then escaped us.

On June 1, 1917, at the bottom of Bishop's combat report we find the following note from Fry:

I dived after Captain Bishop and fired one half of a drum at fairly long range.

Two weeks later, on June 15, Bishop and the rest of his flight attacked a two-seater. In his combat report, Billy wrote:

I fired one drum, Lt. Fry 70 rounds, Lt. Rutherford one-half drum, Lt. Lloyd 30 rounds.

We also know from 60 Squadron records that Fry was present on April 22, 1917, when Bishop downed two planes. On top of that, Arthur Bishop notes in his book that Fry was involved with Bishop in fights on April 30 and May 2. Throw in the shared victory on May 4, and that's seven battles they participated in together.

Apart from Bishop, the pilots of Squadron 60 were having a dreadful time. By the end of the month, Major Scott had to report the loss of twenty men in just thirty days. It was a casualty rate in excess of 100 per cent. Only five veterans, including Bishop, Caldwell, Scott and Molesworth, had survived the ordeal. The other thirteen pilots, and seven of the men who came up to replace them, had been shot down.

Some of the newcomers had been killed before Bishop had even been introduced to them. One young pilot named Stedman was lost on the very day that he arrived. Others quickly followed him into the rolls of those killed or missing in action: Russell, Henderson, Chapman, Townesend, Clark, Cook, Bower, Williams, Robertson, Garnett, Elliott, Languill, Smart, Milot, Kimball, Binnie, Tim Hervey (who was a prisoner) and others, whose names Bishop had forgotten or had not had time to learn. Scott had even been forced to call a halt to operations for a few days. The most famous fighter unit in the RFC had been decimated in a single month.

The strain of such staggering losses took a heavy toll on the survivors. Lieutenant Fry, recalling the havoc, wrote: "Casualties were heavy and there were always new faces in the mess. From my recollection it seems to me that the pressure and pace were so great that the nerves of a number of the pilots were a little stretched and nearly everyone was liable to flare up at the slightest provocation."[14] There was an odour of fear in the barracks and the mess that not even the drunken parties could eradicate. Pilot Jack Rutherford insisted: "You could smell fear when there was a run of several days with casualties."[15]

In such a pressure-cooker atmosphere there was a great risk of suffering a nervous breakdown or lapsing into complete insanity. The French ace, Jean Navara, was already hidden away in a mental institution. Mick Mannock, the British marksman, suffered from bouts of near-hysteria until the day he was shot down in flames.

Every dogfight was justification for going a little crazy. Bishop sometimes found himself laughing in the midst of extreme danger and speculated that the reaction was his body's way of dealing with the tension. Pilots went temporarily "bonkers" and no one paid the slightest attention. Few noticed if a man didn't snap out of it several hours after the battle was over.

Lieutenant Sholto Douglas explained the tension this way:

"Ours was a strain of a new and peculiar temper that even now is hard to analyze. In some cases the abrupt change from the quiet of our way of life on the ground to the heat of being in a scrap in the air over the lines, often in a matter of only a few minutes, led to tension or strain that, I must admit, had severe effects on the nerves. Stomach ulcers became one of the hallmarks of our trade."[16] Some, he noted, went to pieces and never recovered. They were sent home but were never formally recognized as war casualties.

Scott himself came close to going over the edge. He became so distraught after posting the initials D.N.R. (did not return) on the blackboard beside the name of an overdue pilot that he suddenly took off alone for the Front. An apprehensive Bishop followed a few minutes later. Over the German trenches, Billy spotted his commander flying upside down above the heads of enemy troops. German gunners were blazing away furiously. The major, who appears to have gone temporarily berserk, later claimed he had pulled the stunt to show his contempt for the enemy.

Some men reacted much differently — they simply quit before cracking up. Cowardice was a very real problem. It was not uncommon for pilots to return home early from patrols, faking gun jams or engine trouble. The situation was so serious, 60 Squadron pilot Spencer Horn suggested in a letter, that Major Scott made a habit of personally inspecting the plane of any airman who returned ahead of schedule. This may explain why Lieutenant Penny felt compelled to explain his decision to return to base after his Nieuport began breaking up in mid-air: "My lower plane [wing] came off, so I thought I had better land," he told Scott. "Sorry I left the patrol." [17]

And at least one squadron member smuggled flasks of rum along on patrol in order to screw up enough courage to fight.

In neighbouring squadrons the situation was worse. One RFC officer refused to fly a mission, was confined to quarters and promptly blew his own brains out rather than face a court martial. And an entire squadron once defied an order, flatly refusing to embark on a dangerous mission. In fact, Flying Corps doctors estimated that half of all airmen fell victim to serious neurosis problems before completing a tour.

Such statistics make Bishop's exploits during this period, the darkest in RFC history, seem even more remarkable. But it would be a mistake to believe the often-repeated tale that he was a "man without fear." Bishop was under as much strain as anyone. He once admitted that his hands shook and his throat went dry at the sight of enemy planes.

When his own machine was hit, he added, he always felt the muscles in his anus retract involuntarily. But he was better able to cope with his fears than many of the others.

That he was still able to maintain his fighting edge despite six weeks of daily adversity was amply demonstrated on May 7, when he drove two Albatros pilots down, gaining his twenty-first and twenty-second victories.

His first victim of the day went down trailing thick black smoke without ever knowing what hit him. Bishop used a new trick, diving under the German and then climbing directly toward him from below. Just yards away, the ace grabbed his Lewis and pulled it down on its mount so that it was facing skyward. Pointing to the spot where he knew the pilot was sitting, he squeezed off twenty rounds. All twenty tore through the underbelly and both Bishop and 60 Squadron's Lieutenant G.L. Lloyd saw the machine fall completely out of control.

CHAPTER EIGHT

Our crack flight commander has had a spinner made up and painted blue, which he says puts the wind up the Huns. I should think they must be getting to know him by now, as he has crashed twenty-five of them, two of which he got in flames yesterday. He always lets us know when he has got one by firing a red Very light over the aerodrome before landing.[1]

So wrote Moley Molesworth in a letter home. And Molesworth was right. The aircrews of the Imperial German Air Service were noticing Bishop's distinctive blue-nosed Nieuport. In Jagdstaffels immediately opposite Filescamp Farm, pilots were referring to the Canadian as "Hell's Handmaiden."[2] German pilot Ernst Udet described him as "the greatest English scouting ace,"[3] and at one Jasta a bounty had actually been placed on his head!

What the Germans noticed about Bishop, remembered gunner/observer Hanns-Gerd Rabe fifty years later, was the personal trademark on his plane — and the single-minded determination with which he drove home his attacks.

"I had aerial combat with Bishop twice," Rabe wrote in a 1968 letter. "Once he succeeded in surprising me during artillery adjustment far behind the English lines. I was flying with the two-way radio-telegraph in a Hannover CL3A, a two-seater fighter that was equivalent to the Sopwith. My pilot put the Hannover on its wing-tip in the tightest curve, scarcely losing altitude since the fuselage provided a good amount of lift. Bishop attacked us two more times, but at a distance of 150 metres he flew into a burst of my swivel-mounted machine gun. He turned immediately into a dive.

"The second time he attacked me was during a long-range reconnaissance mission in a Rumpler C-7 at an altitude of about 5,000 metres. I had him in view for a long time, however, so I was able to catch him and hold him down with a well-placed machine gun burst as he tried to squeeze under the tail. My pilot effortlessly pulled up the 260 horsepower Maybach-powered Rumpler to over 5,500 metres, where Bishop could not climb."[4]

But Bishop, Rabe remembered, was not about to give up, despite the limitations of his own plane. The Canadian's aircraft "floated at that altitude and drifted down like a leaf. I waved to him ironically from above as he, with threatening fist, accompanied my flight for some time," substantially deeper into German territory.[5]

Although Rabe's letter provides vivid testimony to Bishop's tenacity in combat, it is hardly surprising to discover that Billy's machine was well-known on the other side of the trenches. Pilots of the First World War decorated their planes with distinctive markings, and the opposing flyers often knew whom they were up against. Richthofen, for instance, was the only man on the German side fighting in an all-red Albatros. One of his comrades, Hermann Goring, would make his mark in a white Fokker.

The Royal Flying Corps frowned upon such actions and most of its pilots did not sport any kind of individual markings. But a few exceptions were made for the leading aces. Albert Ball flew an SE5 with a red nose and Ray Collishaw was running up his fantastic score in an all-black Sopwith triplane. In the Arras sector, Bishop was the only man hunting in a blue-nosed machine.

What all this meant was that the war was now extremely personal. Leading aces on both sides were on the lookout for one another. When they found each other, the results were often spectacular.

The Red Baron, for one, was trying to bag Bishop. One of his pilots, Carl August von Schoenebeck, confirmed as much in an interview long after the war. He recalled that his famous commander was searching for a certain Allied plane believed to have been flown by a well-known ace. Although Schoenebeck could no longer recall the name of the pilot involved, the type of plane and the date he gave indicate that the man was almost certainly Billy Bishop.

Bishop, for his part, was anxious to get a crack at the Baron. Richthofen had shot twenty-one British planes out of the sky during April alone. The carnage brought his victory total to a world record of fifty-two. He was the enemy's best and Billy wanted to pit himself against him. A showdown seemed inevitable.

Bishop was certain he encountered Richthofen on April 30, 1917, just a day after the Red Baron had destroyed four English aeroplanes.

It happened just after lunch, when the Canadian and Major Scott collided with four red-painted Albatros D-3s over Drocourt. Before the smoke had cleared, Billy would be engaged in one of the toughest dogfights of his life.

In his autobiography, he wrote:

> The Major reached them first and opened fire on the rear machine from behind. Immediately the leader of the scouts did a lightning turn and came back at the Major, firing at him and passing within two or three feet of his machine. In my turn I opened fire on the Baron, and in another half-moment found myself in the midst of what seemed to be a stampede of bloodthirsty animals. Everywhere I turned smoking bullets were jumping at me, and although I got in two or three good bursts at the Baron's 'red devil,' I was rather bewildered for two or three minutes, as I could not see what was happening to the major and was not at all certain as to what was going to happen to me .... Around and around we went in cyclonic circles for several minutes, here a flash of the Hun machines, then a flash of silver as my squadron commander would whizz by. It was a lightning fight, and I have never been in anything just like it.

The battle only ended when a flight of British Sopwith Triplanes showed up and the Germans retreated.

For the next eight decades historians assumed Bishop had clashed with Richthofen and three of his best men. But Canadian author David Bashow proved that wasn't the case in the year 2000, uncovering evidence that Richthofen did not fly that day.

Some have since criticized Bishop, claiming he made up a story of a fight with the Red Baron to enliven his autobiography. But that doesn't seem likely. Major Scott's combat report proves he and Bishop did indeed take part in a tough fight with four Albatroses that afternoon. In fact, Scott admits his plane was damaged and that he had a difficult time escaping from a skillfully flown Albatros. And in a letter written to Margaret just a few hours after the fight, Bishop wrote:

> The CO and I went out and got mixed up with four really good Huns. We chased them away, but oh heavens, did they shoot well. Seven bullets went through my machine within six inches of me, and one within an inch.

Bishop knew that Richthofen's Jasta 11 was operating directly across the lines from 60 Squadron. He knew also that a deadly marksman was leading the Germans he encountered that day. It was only natural for him to assume he'd collided with Richthofen. But based on what we now know, it seems likely that the two Nieuport pilots had run into the Richthofen Circus, minus the Red Baron.

Whoever it was that Bishop fought on April 30, it was obvious he was becoming an outstanding pilot. Long gone were the days when he would smash up planes on landings. In fact, he was a much better pilot than has commonly been thought.

Folklore has it that he was a ham-fisted aviator who wrecked literally dozens of Allied aircraft with his heavy landings. Billy, perhaps mischievously, added to the myth by once claiming he had destroyed more British planes than Richthofen — a good story, but it just wasn't true.

60 Squadron historian Joe Wanc, in a letter to author, stated:

"Please discount any long-held statement that Bishop was a 'crasher.' He flew Nieuport B1566 continually for many months — few aircraft lasted that long on a scout squadron." Bishop's log book, now on display in Ottawa with the historical branch of the Department of National Defence, proves Warne correct. Bishop put some 400 hours on B1566. And he had equally good luck with other machines. In all, he flew only six different aircraft to score seventy-five victories — an astonishing accomplishment for the time. Flight instructor Harold Balfour, the man who taught Bishop how to fly, also dismissed the legend that Billy was a poor pilot. First World War aircraft were difficult to fly and, said the old flyer, Bishop would have had to have been "adequate just to handle his Nieuport or his SE5."

But perhaps the purest tribute to Billy's flying skills is the story of how he bested a French ace in a mock aerial duel. Foul weather had socked in 60 Squadron for the afternoon one spring day in 1917 when the airmen, who had been passing the time in the mess playing cards and drinking, detected the sound of an airplane engine. Rushing outside, they were just in time to see a Spad fighter from the French airforce pop through the soup and make an emergency landing. It was a sturdy-looking plane — not as wonderfully sleek as the Nieuport, but certainly more reliable under stress. It had pale yellow wings and fuselage to go with its brown engine hood. Just behind the cockpit was the red stork insignia of the most famous outfit in the French Air Service — "Les Cicognes."

Bishop was the first to greet the pilot. The Frenchman's flying coat was unbuttoned, revealing a blue tunic, scarlet trousers, the red propeller emblem of a *sous-officier aviateur* and, on his breast, the ribbon of the Croix de Guerre.

The visitor explained in halting English that he had become lost while testing a new machine in the overcast. He had flown aimlessly for some time before, low on fuel, he was forced to descend through the haze in search of a cow pasture to land in. To his great relief he found himself directly over an RFC aerodrome. The British treated him like a conquering hero just back from the crusades, carrying him into the mess to join in the festivities. When everyone was roaring drunk, Bishop decided to introduce the guest to the squadron's uniform-tearing tradition, ripping the man's tunic from his back in one quick motion.

The Frenchman, feigning anger, demanded satisfaction, declaring that the honour of his nation was at stake. Someone suggested they settle the matter with a flying duel — a contest to determine who was the best pilot.

With that, twenty intoxicated airmen stumbled out to the flight line, several taking bets as the two contestants strapped themselves into their fighters.

They took off together, climbing to 200 feet before levelling off. The Frenchman went first, throwing the Spad through a series of tight loops and barrel-rolls. Then, he danced to one side and signalled to Bishop to show his stuff. The giddy Canadian put his more agile machine through its paces, staging a series of daredevil maneuvers that gave him an undeniable edge in the contest.

Doubtlessly fuming at the turn of events, the French pilot decided to rely on the Spad's strength — its diving power.

He dropped the nose and the square-winged fighter fell like a dead weight. With a split second to spare, the cowling came up and the plane's wing-tips brushed through the tall grass at the end of the runway. There was a collective gasp from the onlookers.

Then the blue-nosed plane was diving at breakneck speed. Bishop came in with his engine wide open, aiming straight for the mess. He raised his nose only a fraction, rolling his wheels over the roof before coming in for a bumpy landing. He was the clear winner.

The next important development in Bishop's life came in late April, 1917, when a green, moth-shaped SE5 biplane came in low with its motor wheezing in short bursts. Levelling out, the pilot made a picture-perfect landing, the wheels and tail-skid touching down almost simultaneously. The machine settled in smoothly, without the slightest hint of a bounce, causing onlookers to shake their heads in admiration.

Two mechanics appeared out of nowhere, grabbed the red-nosed fighter by the wing-tips and guided it toward the tarmac. The four-bladed propeller had not even stopped spinning before a crowd materialized around the curved-winged machine.

A dark-haired young man swung his short legs over the side, gingerly avoiding the red-hot exhaust pipes as he jumped down. Fawning ground crews and aviators surrounded Albert Ball, snapping out salutes and slapping him on the back and shoulders.

Ball had come to see Bishop.

The boy-ace was a different person than the one Billy had met in a London waiting room a year earlier. He had a faraway gaze in his eyes and he looked exhausted.

Pilots at 56 Squadron said that Albert no longer mixed socially with them. He had moved out to a shack behind one of the hangars to be by himself. At night, he could be seen prancing around a roaring bonfire, playing mournfully on his violin. Some feared that he was cracking up.

Bishop poured himself a brandy and offered the Englishman a drink.

Albert had come with a proposal. He wanted to attack Richthofen's Circus — catch it on the ground at dawn, just as the pilots were preparing for the first patrol of the day. Such a scheme had never been tried before and Ball believed the element of surprise would allow them to carry it off. Bishop drained his glass and thought for a moment. The men were deathly quiet, the silence overlapped only by the churning of minds. Jagdstaffel 11 would be no piece of cake, but with the great Ball along, Bishop thought they might succeed. Maybe they would even bag one of Germany's better-known flyers — perhaps even old Richthofen himself.

Billy agreed to the plan, but added he could not go on the raid right away because he was due for leave. Fine, the Englishman said, he would be back near the end of May and they would draw up specific plans.

Bishop saw Ball out to the tarmac, shook hands with him and waved goodbye as his friend climbed into a pink sunset, wings rocking gently up and down in a teeter-totter motion.

On May 9, Bishop arrived in London on leave and went directly to Lady St. Helier's mansion. The next day, word came through that he had been awarded the Distinguished Service Order, the empire's second-highest award for valour. He had won it by taking part in nine combats in one day, scoring two victories.

But there was chilling news as well, news that left Bishop with an

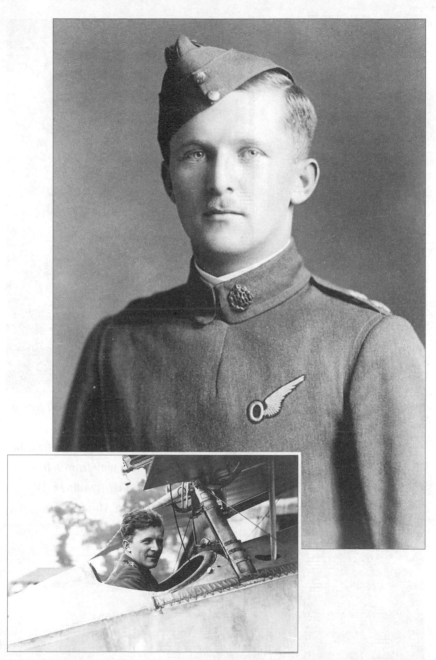

Top: Billy Bishop as a gunner/observer with 21 Squadron in 1916.
Bottom: Bishop about to take off on a mission. He sometimes flew with-
out helmet and goggles, claiming that he enjoyed the wind in his hair.

Above: An Albatros that crashed without bursting into flames. In cases in which the pilot survived — as may well have happened here — German records would not mention the loss of the plane.

Above: Bishop in full flying gear in front of 60 Squadron headquarters. In the doorway from left to right, Lieutenant H. W. Guy and Major Scott.

Bishop (left) with Major Jack Scott.

An informal photo taken at the height of Bishop's career.

Above: Bishop, standing, clowns around with three fellow pilots. Seated from left to right are: Captain William 'Moley' Molesworth, Lieutenant Graham Young and Captain Keith Caldwell.

Right: Bishop, centre, with friends William Molesworth, left, and Keith Caldwell.

Playing with a pig at Filescamp Farm Aerodrome. Bishop later painted German black crosses on the animal.

Below: In front of his famed Nieuport B1566 fighter. Bishop claimed nearly forty victories with this machine before switching to the faster SE5.

An official photo of Bishop widely distributed during the war for propaganda purposes.

A row of 60 Squadron aircraft hangars.

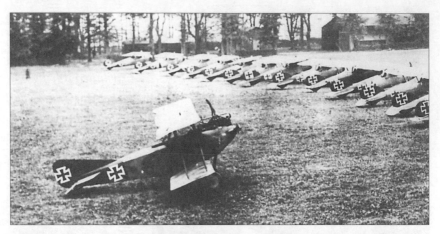

A German two-seater is shown in the foreground, with Albatros fighters in the background.

Above: 60 Squadron pilots locked arm-in-arm, August 4, 1917. From left: Jenkins, Soden, Steele, Bishop, Caldwell and Molesworth.

Above: Bishop (left) with William Molesworth and Graham Young outside 60 Squadron's "Saloon Bar."

Above: A badly damaged Albatros from which the pilot probably walked away unhurt. In such cases there would be no record indicating the German pilot had lost a dogfight.

Right: A downed German plane.

An Albatros with a splintered propeller, once again showing the type of battle damage that would not normally show up in German records.

Above: Paul Billik, the high-scoring German ace who was lightly wounded by Bishop, stands beside his swastika-decorated Albatros.

Left: Bishop relaxes between missions.

Bishop, left, and Lieutenant-Colonel William Barker pose with a captured German Fokker.

empty feeling in the pit of his stomach. Albert Ball was missing in action. The words leapt off the page of the *London Times* and stabbed him between the eyes. Newspaper reports were sketchy, but Bishop was able to gather further details from other pilots over drinks at London's RFC Club on Bruton Street, where the latest rumours from the Front were always available. Number 56 Squadron had been sent out on Offensive Patrol near Douai with instructions to draw the Richthofen Circus into a shoot-out.

In fact, the squadron had been formed for the specific purpose of killing the Red Baron and decimating his troublesome Jasta 11. To do that, Trenchard had brought together handpicked British pilots, including Ball and McCudden, to form a special unit. He had equipped them with the new SE5, which was much superior to the old Nieuport. The theory was that Richthofen had made his reputation mostly by picking off helpless observation planes. The RFC brass was confident that its best pilots, in brand-new fighters, would make mincemeat out of the red Albatroses.

Unknown to the British, the Red Baron was on the leave at the time. But his Flying Circus was still very much in evidence, with the red and yellow Albatros of Lothar von Richthofen, the Baron's younger brother, at the helm. Lothar was a high-scoring ace in his own right, and would eventually claim forty enemies in individual duels.

It was an overcast evening on May 7, when Albert Ball led 56 Squadron into a head-to-head showdown with Jasta 11. What followed was one of the bitterest aerial battles in history. The gruesome clash opened at 15,000 feet and continued all the way to the treetops before nightfall set in, forcing the weary belligerents to withdraw. Fighting was so intense, reported 56 Squadron Captain C.M. Crowe, that his goggles were shot from his face.

During the action, Lothar found himself tangling with a skillful Sopwith triplane pilot who had stumbled onto the scene and joined in. After a lengthy fight in which neither man was able to gain much of an edge, the British naval flyer decided to call it a day and broke off. But Lothar's evening was far from over.

Somewhere in all of this madness, Albert Ball was fighting with his usual savage intensity when he spotted a lone Albatros on the fringe of the fight. He quickly fired a red signal flare to alert his mates that he was attacking, and then dove down after the German. The two opponents were last seen being swallowed up by a huge cloud bank.

Lothar saw Ball coming for him but, in the confusion and fading light, he mistook the charging SE5 for the triplane and assumed that the naval pilot had decided to have another go at him.

In the ensuing fight both Ball and Richthofen crashed. Lothar was hit in the hip and, bleeding profusely, came down just inside German lines. He was out of the action for several months, although he would eventually recover. Ball was not so fortunate. Observers on the ground saw his machine come out of the cloud bank with a dead engine. Albert himself had not been hit by gunfire but was mortally injured in the crash. He died in the arms of a young French girl.

Stories conflict as to what happened to the two aces. Lothar claimed to have shot down a triplane and the British latched on to that fact in a bid to discredit the theory that he had killed Ball. The British had various versions as to how their star pilot met his end. Some had him falling to a machine gunner in a church tower. Others insisted he simply spun into the mud in poor visibility. As for Lothar, some believed he, too, was hit by ground fire, while others preferred to think that Ball had shot him down.

There can be little doubt that the two men were at each other's throats. German pilot Wilhelm Allmenroder, for one, clearly remembered seeing Lothar in fierce combat with an SE5 biplane, not a Sopwith triplane. Although it is now impossible to say anything for certain about such a confusing dogfight — which was being waged in misty near-darkness — it is entirely possible that Ball and Richthofen shot each other down. Whatever the truth, the fact remained that one third of 56 Squadron was missing — along with the first great British air hero. The RFC had learned the hard way that the Richthofen Circus could handle anything thrown at it.

Bishop wept at Ball's fate. That night he wrote Margaret: "They have killed my dear friend, Richthofen and his scarlet gangsters. They are going to pay for this, Margaret!"

The war was wearing on Bishop psychologically. His emotions were on a continuous roller-coaster ride featuring fear of violent death, joy over his triumphs, hatred for his enemies and grief for lost friends.

In just six weeks the clumsy newcomer had become the leading living ace of the Royal Flying Corps. He had risen to the rank of captain and had won the DSO and MC. But the success had not been won without paying a fearful price. Bishop was tired. Photos of him taken at this time showed bags under his eyes, and he looked at least a decade older than his twenty-three years. By now he had survived countless narrow escapes and the corrosive strain of it all was building to the breaking point. In London, free for the moment from the fear of sudden death, he planned to live life to the fullest.

CHAPTER NINE

Wartime London was a sinful city. The capital of the mighty British Empire was filled with weary soldiers on leave and each one was determined to cram as much living as possible into a few short weeks.

Nightclubs, dance halls and theatres were never livelier, jammed as they were each evening with lonely young men, some many thousands of miles from home. Canadians, Australians, New Zealanders, Rhodesians, South Africans, Indians and even the odd American mixed with the Brits, looking for pleasure wherever they could find it.

Liquor flowed freely as servicemen sought to escape from the horrors of the front lines. The results were predictable. There was much laughing and singing, considerable lovemaking and the occasional barroom brawl. Many a soldier awoke with a severe hangover only to find a strange woman in bed beside him. Others came to in jail, or alone in hotel rooms to find their wallets missing.

The Victorian era was long forgotten. By 1917, permissiveness had reached the point where authorities were compelled to establish the London and Home Counties Venereal Diseases Scheme. Letters to the editors warned fathers to keep a close eye on their daughters. Men from the colonies were especially dangerous to a young lady's honour, a reader informed a leading newspaper. Records showed a startling thirty percent jump in illegitimate births, compared to prewar days.

Everyone on leave seemed anxious to forget the war. Sellout crowds jammed into the Old Bailey and the Scala to watch live entertainment. Light comedy was devoured by servicemen. The biggest and most lavish extravaganza of them all was "Chu Chin Chow," an oriental musical hit featuring thinly clad belly dancers in an erotic production. One critic noted that it had "more flesh than dress." Another production, "Maid of the Mountains," was a close second in popularity, enthralling the troops with exuberant acts performed by beautiful women. Civilians, on the other hand, flocked in droves to see such plays as "The Kaiser — Beast of Berlin."

There were occasional blackouts imposed because of German night raids, but the fearsome Gothas and zeppelins did not stop the parties. Soldiers and their girls could still be seen strolling along the narrow streets or under the stone bridges that crisscrossed the River Thames. Public displays of affection between men and women, frowned upon in peacetime, were now commonplace. There was simply no time for the prewar rituals.

The relaxed moral standards did not harm the business of London's prostitutes. With the streets literally teeming with Tommies, the prostitutes had all the work they could handle. The chief of police reported that nearly 20,000 young women were charged with soliciting, in three years of war.

London had changed in other ways too. For one thing, women could now be seen working at jobs that had traditionally been reserved for men; they appeared at the wheels of buses, operated subway cars and laboured in munitions factories. They did their jobs well.

At the same time, city life was not as colourful as it had been before the hostilities began. Lovely parks and gardens had been transformed into refugee camps for desperate souls who had fled France and Belgium in order to escape the advancing Germans in 1914. Even Alexandra Palace was soiled by the ramshackle structures that had been thrown up almost overnight by foreigners who had deserted the mainland.

Annual sporting events, including boat races and the ever-popular cricket matches, were cancelled until the end of the conflict. Museums and art galleries were ordered closed. Some of London's finest hotels, clubs and private mansions had been seized in order to provide working quarters for a new army of bureaucrats.

There were shortages to cope with, too. Clothing, coal and fuel for private motor cars were in short supply. Food, fortunately, was readily available.

Bishop, as the Royal Flying Corps' newly crowned ace of aces, unexpectedly found himself something of a celebrity when he arrived in London. Air heroes were very much in vogue at this time, partly because aerial combat was new and exciting, but also because trench warfare produced no glamorous figures of its own. A foot-soldier might perform one spectacular deed of valour that would win him a decoration and a mention in army dispatches, but after that he disappeared back into the anonymity of the trenches. Nobody was keeping track of the number of men he killed. A "poor bloody infantryman" could display great courage on a daily basis and go completely unnoticed by the press and the general public.

With the air aces it was different. Conquests were easy to verify and could be quickly tabulated to feed a population thirsting for some good news from the Front. A whole nation had rejoiced in the exploits of Albert Ball. When he died, there was a far greater outpouring of genuine public sorrow than when 60,000 Englishmen had been slaughtered in half an hour at the Somme.

Flying was still new enough that civilians looked upon aviators with a certain degree of awe. It was assumed that you had to be something of a swashbuckler just to take one of those flimsy crates off the ground. To joust to the death in man-to-man duels above the clouds was something that staggered the imaginations of millions.

To the propagandists, the swaggering aces were a godsend. They could do nothing to break the stalemate in France, but tales of their deeds were instrumental in the recruitment drive.

As might be expected, Bishop took full advantage of the opportunities available to a dashing young air hero. He was wined and dined by the upper crust of English society and by members of the royal family. He was often seen visiting the plush mansions of the West End, showing up in places such as Park Lane and Mayfair.

He spent an evening with the lovely Princess Marie Louise and, "under the influence of champagne," delighted her with his charm. She was so enthralled with the youthful knight of the air that she insisted he simply must meet her father, King George V.

A prominent British Member of Parliament, Bonar Law, wanted some of his time, but Bishop had none to give. He made an appointment to see the politician but broke it when he stumbled on an opportunity to dine with a pretty young stage actress instead. Deciding he would rather be in the company of the glamorous star, he picked up the nearest telephone and contacted the MP's office. He claimed he was Captain Bishop's secretary and announced that the ace had suddenly been ordered back to France.

Throughout the city Bishop was frankly amazed at the raw hatred of the Germans. He had learned to despise them only because they had killed so many of his friends and because he had to fight for his own life against them on a daily basis. But the civilians loathed the enemy far more than the soldiers. Their abhorrence for everything German even outmatched the bitterness in France, where the Kaiser's legions were wrestling for control of the French soil.

Newspapers were partly responsible for this — the *Daily Mail* and the *Globe* whipped the populace into angry hysteria with fabricated tales of German brutality. One of the most absurd stories was headlined: "Hun Airmen Drop Poisoned Candy."[1] It went on to explain that the incident had caused "the death of many children who ate it." Bishop and other fighting men laughed at the story, but the general public believed it was gospel.

Anti-German feelings were so pronounced that ladies with dachshunds were spat upon. German musicians, who had become practically fixtures on the streets of London, had been arrested and locked away. Music by Wagner and Beethoven was instantly unpopular. There was even talk of banning all German music, until someone remembered that that would include Handel's *Messiah*.

Perhaps most absurd of all, the royal family was forced to change its name. It was decided that the House of Saxe-Coburg and Gotha had too much of a "Hun" connotation to it. The name was switched to Windsor.

Bishop found he had little in common with the civilians. He was annoyed with their outspokenness about the war, a subject that they knew nothing about. And he was angered when a man in a pub declared, "With those bloody zepps it's more dangerous right here than in the trenches! Why don't you RFC blokes do something about them?"[2] Bishop knocked the fellow down and stormed out. He was quickly discovering that the only people whose company he enjoyed were other fighting men. There was a bond, a powerful comradeship that was difficult to put into words. Once he had been well rested, Bishop was anxious to get back to Filescamp Farm.

He returned to France in late May. Several new faces greeted Bishop when he arrived at the aerodrome. The Grim Reaper had claimed five more pilots during the two weeks that he had been absent. The losses brought to thirty-five the number of airmen 60 Squadron had lost since Bishop had joined in mid-March. Their replacements were raw rookies — overzealous fledglings who couldn't wait to get into combat. They were certain that they knew everything there was to learn about the game and there was nothing the veterans could to say or do to persuade them otherwise. The captain was careful to avoid getting to know them too well, realizing they were probably doomed men. In his letters home during this period he talked mainly about the few old hands still alive, such as Molesworth, Caldwell and Scott.

The Billy Bishop who returned to Filescamp Farm aerodrome that spring was a different man from the one who had departed for England only a fortnight earlier.

Bishop had tasted fame and he liked it. The small-town Ontario boy had been feted by royalty and had rubbed shoulders with the key political, military and social figures of his generation. For a lad practically out of the Canadian backwoods, the filet mignon, aged brandy, sparkling champagne and lavish balls in his honour were things he had not dreamed of just three months earlier.

He knew now that if he played his cards right, this could be just the beginning. The pilot who finished this war as the ace of aces would be set for life. He would have financial opportunities and contacts in high places that were otherwise unattainable. With Albert Ball dead he had a clear opportunity to become the top Allied scorer.

Billy made no bones about his goals. He wrote: "By this time I had become very ambitious, and was hoping to get a large number of machines officially credited to me before I left France."[3]

But more than just victories, he wanted decorations to prove his prowess to the whole world. He especially coveted the Victoria Cross. It was the ultimate military award; the most prestigious medal on the planet. Holders of the VC were assured of lasting fame.

There was only one obstacle standing in his way as he made plans to expand his reputation as an air fighter. The Germans were nowhere to be seen. Most of the Jagdstaffels in the Arras sector, including the Richthofen Circus, had packed up and moved further north to participate in the upcoming Ypres offensive.

As a result, one 60 Squadron flight after another was now returning home in frustration. They scoured the skies but could not even see a black-crossed plane, let alone do battle with one.

Curiously, Bishop continued to return home from lone wolf patrols claiming victories. He said he drove one of six Albatroses down out of control on May 26, and claimed to have crashed a Rumpler two-seater on the 27th and yet another Albatros on the 31st. He had no witnesses, either on the ground or in the air, for any of these conquests. Nevertheless, Major Scott granted Billy confirmation for all three.

Scott's actions caused a great deal of discontent in the squadron mess. But the major had his reasons. He knew that Bishop, with a roving commission, was free to fly forty or more miles behind enemy lines. He often covered four times as much territory as the other pilots, who flew together on escort duty or offensive patrol near the front lines. Billy's chances of finding — and surprising — a German were much better than those of his comrades.

But several pilots had doubts nevertheless. It was not uncommon in aerial combat for a man to submit accurate reports until he built up an impressive score and then, with an inflated opinion of his own ability, to begin over-claiming. Because his earlier, well-documented successes had made a favourable impression on the commander, such a man would have his exaggerated claims taken as gospel. This, some 60 Squadron flyers were now convinced, was exactly what Bishop was doing.

Whether they were legitimate conquests or simply flights of an overly active imagination, the three victories had been officially accepted and Bishop's score was, therefore, still climbing. However, he was far from satisfied. He still ached for a Victoria Cross. But how to get one? In his gloomier moments, he must have thought he would have to commit suicide to obtain the VC. The British were very stingy with Queen Victoria's bronze medal. Of the many thousands of men who served in the English flying services between 1914 and 1918, only nineteen won the VC. Of those, only ten would live to see the armistice, and two of those would die of war-related injuries less than a year after a weary peace settled over Europe.

If Bishop had known that Jack Scott had already recommended him for the VC a few weeks earlier and that the War Office had turned down the proposal, he would have been even more depressed.

But Billy had an idea that he thought just might get him his medal. He hinted at it in a letter home on May 31, writing: "I have a great plan in mind. A real hair-raising stunt which I am going to try one of these days."[4]

To his comrades he was more specific. At a mess party on the evening of June 1, he told his mates that he was going to attempt Albert Ball's aerodrome plan by himself. He proposed to go in at dawn and strafe a German field, picking off the pilots one by one as they tried to get airborne.

The others argued fiercely against the scheme, insisting it was too risky. Even Ball, who always threw caution to the wind, had thought the job was too big for one person to handle. Grid Caldwell pointed out that, at dawn, there would be no wind. That would mean German pilots could take off in every conceivable direction. Several of them could take off at the same time, making it impossible for Bishop to get them all. And if even one German got into the sky, he could keep a lone Nieuport busy long enough for the whole Jasta to get airborne. Even if Bishop did manage to escape, other German aerodromes would be alerted by phone and more black-crossed planes would be on the lookout for him on his return journey. Dromes were protected by long-range machine guns and any attacking pilot would have to come in at treetop level, presenting the German gunners with an inviting target.

But Major Scott, who by now regarded Bishop as almost invincible, did not forbid the Canadian from going ahead with the raid.

Billy made one last-minute pitch to talk his deputy flight leader, Willie Fry, into coming along on the mission. Unable to get a commitment out of the Englishman, he left the mess party early and asked his batman to wake him up at 3 A.M.

When he was summoned, Bishop's ears detected the gentle patter of a light drizzle on the corrugated tin roof of his Nissen hut. The sound must have brought a frown to his features. No one would have blamed him if he had crawled back under the covers. He would be aloft in an open cockpit in less than an hour, and rain would not help matters. Bishop could have cancelled the mission and no one would have thought less of him. The idea had to have crossed his mind. But obviously, he dismissed it rather quickly. He was determined to carry out his plan, no matter what.

He decided against peeling off his yellow silk pyjamas, contenting himself with pulling on a tattered old football sweater, a leather coat and fur-lined flying boots that extended up to his knees.

It was not the first time he had done that; RFC men often flew the dawn patrol wearing only pyjamas under flying gear, despite the fact that if they were forced down behind enemy lines they would have no proof of rank. That could mean sitting out the rest of the conflict in a prisoner-of-war camp without the considerable benefits bestowed on an officer. One thing you could say for the Germans, they treated captured officers with respect. As for an enlisted man, that was a different matter.

In any case, Bishop had long since vowed there was no way that they would ever take him alive. It was all he could do to stomach British regulations, never mind a German jail. He would rather die.

Fitting individual fingers into a pair of gauntlet gloves, he grabbed an oil-stained leather helmet and stomped out of his quarters.

It was grey and soppy outside. A thick pre-dawn mist hung heavily over the aerodrome, streaking the hangars and barracks with a glistening coat of dew. The early morning darkness was chilly and the imminent threat of more rain only added to the gloominess of the dank surroundings. Bishop could not see more than a few yards ahead, but the cool night air felt good. He was wide awake as he went next door, marching into the hut of Willie Fry. Bishop came right to the point, asking him if he was coming along on the raid.

Fry's head was throbbing from the evening's drunken bash and he was so tired he could barely keep his eyes open. Recalling the scene sixty years later, he wrote: "The night before, we were enjoying one of our noisy parties in the mess — probably celebrating a decoration awarded to someone. Bishop approached me during the evening and said something about shooting up an enemy aerodrome early the next morning and would I care to go with him. I did not take much notice, was non-committal and soon afterwards went to bed. Early the next morning, before light, he came to my room and asked if I were going with him. I had a headache from the night's party and answered that I was not for it, turned over and went to sleep again. It should be explained that it was an entirely voluntary effort and that there was no question of him having been detailed for the job."[5]

Bishop trudged off in the direction of the sergeants' mess, where he could see a yellow light burning. He was a disappointed man as he crossed the clearing; there is courage in numbers and he had hoped that Fry would come with him.

The burly sergeant looked up in astonishment as Bishop walked in, admitting a gust of wet night air as he entered. Without bothering to salute, the NCO blurted out, "You don't expect to find any Huns out there at this time of day, do you sir? It's still dark."[6]

Bishop grinned and poured himself a cup of scalding hot tea. There was a whimpering cry at the door, followed by scratching sounds. As the captain opened it, a great black hound bounded in and proceeded to smear him with drooling affection. Bishop patted the dog lovingly.

The mess sergeant was not touched by the scene. Not only did the animal harbour an army of fleas; it also reeked with the foul stench of an unwashed runaway. One of the pilots had once tried sprinkling face powder over the mongrel, which was called "Nigger," but the ugly mutt had smelled worse than ever.

"I don't understand that dog," he muttered. "The horrible cur has never taken to anyone. He just scrounges his meals here. If anyone but you tried to stroke him he'd probably take an arm off. What is it he likes about you?"[7]

"We're kindred spirits. Come on Nig, let's go and rouse Jerry out"[8]

As Bishop and his dog left, the mess sergeant must have been impressed with the air of self-confidence surrounding the captain. He wasn't like the rest of the airmen. Oh, they did their duty alright, but they cherished their sleep and what little time they had to themselves. For many of them, it was all they could do to stop from going to pieces after months of hellish combat on a daily basis. But not Bishop. He was somehow different. He loved the war — loved to fight — even at 3 A.M. on what was supposed to be his day off.

Before sauntering over to the decaying hangars, he visited briefly with Grid Caldwell, who was quartered in a hut near his own.

Caldwell tried, as he had the previous evening, to talk him out of going. What Bishop was proposing, he repeated, was "sheer suicide."

But the swarthy New Zealander could see he was not getting anywhere. Bishop noted, in his lispy voice, that he would have the element of surprise. Such a stunt had never been tried before and he was counting on that fact to pull him through.

Caldwell had no answer to that. If Bishop was determined to kill himself, there was nothing that anyone could say or do to stop him. There was never any hope of reasoning with him once he put his mind to something. He wished the Canadian good luck and went back to sleep.

Bishop wandered over to the line of hangars where his nose caught the whiff of castor oil mixed with stale sweat. It was a sickly sweet smell that tingled the nostrils. Two grimy mechanics in bulky brown overalls were rolling his Nieuport out of one of the tents.

Walter Bourne had a look of deep concern etched on his face. He signalled to the sky, which was still a dark, greyish hue. It continued to rain gently.

"How's everything, corporal?"[9]

"The machine's alright sir. Your gun is serviced and loaded but I don't like any of this sir."[10]

"Don't worry. Keep an eye on Nig. I'll be back in just over an hour and I'll want the bus for a gunnery test after breakfast."[11]

"Good luck sir," Bourne said.[12]

Bishop climbed easily into the small cockpit and strapped himself into his leather-and-wicker seat. He made a quick check to make sure all three 99-round drums were on board, glanced briefly at the fuel gauge and altimeter and squeezed the pump handle until there was enough pressure to start the engine.

Bourne was at the front of the Nieuport now, seizing the propeller in his hands. He swung it mightily as Bishop worked the switches in front of his face. The engine barked, emitted a white puff of smoke and roared deafeningly to life.

Bishop repeated a silent prayer, whispering to himself: "God give me strength. God be with me now."[13]

The ace signalled his grease monkey to remove the wooden wheel chocks (there were no brakes on a Nieuport) and opened the throttle before taxiing toward the runway. The machine picked up speed quickly, lifting gracefully off the rain-soaked turf before disappearing into the overcast. It was 3:57 A.M.

Billy Bishop was off on what was to become the most controversial mission in the history of aerial warfare.

CHAPTER TEN

The Nieuport circled slowly overhead. The sun, although still cold and white, was now well above the horizon. Daylight sparkled against the propeller. Bishop fired off a red signal flare, alerting those below that he was returning in triumph.

Corporal Walter Bourne ran excitedly alongside the fighter plane as it rolled to a halt. Bishop climbed out and reported he had destroyed three Albatroses over a German aerodrome seventeen miles behind the line — picking two off while they attempted to get airborne and bagging a third in a dogfight over the enemy camp. Others were soon gathering around the blue-nose, inspecting her for battle damage. Almost immediately, some of them noted something curious about the combat scars.

Willie Fry was one of the first on the scene. "At breakfast," he wrote later, "there was a buzz of talk in the mess. On going over to the flight hangar I saw that Bishop's machine was the centre of attraction. I remember clearly seeing a group of about five bullet holes in the rear half of his tailplane, within a circle of not more than six inches diameter at the most."[1] Another man saw twelve holes grouped close together behind the cockpit.

Most of the men thought nothing about it. Bishop, after all, was flying at treetop level and executing slow stall turns just over the heads of German ground gunners. Under such conditions it should have been expected that the holes would be close together. But others were not so sure. To them, the punctures were just too close. They thought the Nieuport might not have been moving at all when it was hit.

Someone noticed that the plane's Lewis gun was missing. A completely false rumour started, innocently enough, to go around. Somebody assumed that Bishop had tossed the gun overboard to reduce weight and thus make good his escape.

Bishop himself never made such a claim but the story spread quickly and it raised a few eyebrows among the more experienced pilots. To remove a weapon from its Foster mounting and to disconnect the trigger cable from the control column while at the same time flying the plane would have been an extremely difficult task. Just changing the ammo drums in flight was a tricky task. And, of course, the absence of the Lewis would not go unnoticed by any sharp-eyed Albatros pilots. An opponent who saw an unarmed aircraft would be encouraged to press home his attack with vigour. Bishop said there were four Germans chasing him on his way home. An aviator being pursued by that many enemy planes, some would later argue, could hardly be expected to spend precious seconds struggling to discard his gun. A man in such a hot spot would be running at top speed for the security of the Allied lines — over which the Germans almost never ventured.

While 60 Squadron pilots pondered those points, Bishop stalked into Jack Scott's office and filled out his report. He typed it out and handed the document to the major. Scott devoured it eagerly, realizing at once that it was a report of historic significance. It read: "I fired on seven machines on the aerodrome, some of which had their engines running. One of them took off and I fired fifteen rounds at him from close range sixty feet up and he crashed. A second one taking off, I opened fire and fired thirty rounds at 150 yards range, he crashed into a tree. Two more were taking off together. I climbed and engaged one at 1,000 feet, finishing my drum and he crashed 300 yards from the aerodrome. I changed drums and climbed east. A fourth HA 9[hostile aircraft] came after me and I fired one whole drum into him. He flew away and I then flew 1,000 feet under four scouts at 5,000 feet for one mile and turned west, climbing. The aerodrome was armed with one or more machine guns. Machines on the ground were six scouts [Albatros type 1 or 2 and one two-seater]."[2]

Scott was ecstatic. He ordered Bishop to get into a dress uniform. He was taking the Canadian over to 3rd Army Advance Headquarters for a face-to-face meeting with General Allenby. Scott was going to recommend Bishop for the Victoria Cross for the second time that spring and he wanted the general to meet Billy personally.

What the major apparently did not notice was an unusual entry at the top of Bishop's report. The ace had taken off at 3:57 AM and had returned at 5:40AM after a high-speed chase at low levels. Under such conditions, a Nieuport would have exhausted its fuel in about an hour and twenty minutes (the plane normally had a much longer endurance but much fuel was used up in combat situations) and Bishop had been gone for an hour and forty-three minutes. In other words, he had set his machine down at Filescamp Farm at least twenty-three minutes after he should have run out of petrol.

Billy had an explanation. He told Willie Fry that he had become lost and had landed behind Allied lines in the French army sector to ask fieldhands for directions. Neither in his combat report nor in his auto-biography did he mention that he had been on the ground before returning to base or that he had returned without his gun.

Jack Scott believed Bishop's story, as did most other members of the squadron. But some thought he had made the whole thing up. To them, the close grouping of the bullet holes in his plane, the missing machine gun and the fact that he admitted landing behind Allied lines before returning to base meant only one thing — Bishop had landed in safe territory before riddling his own plane with bullets from his own gun, and then flying home to tell a completely false tale about an attack on an enemy aerodrome.

Soon, doubts about Billy were being spread outside the squadron. The three kills credited to him on June 2 gave him six in a row without any Allied witnesses.

One of those with suspicions was Sir Archibald Henry James, a pilot in a neighbouring RFC unit. James told what he thought of Bishop in a tape-recorded interview in his eightieth year. The tape is on file with the British Imperial War Museum. On it, James makes the claim that "everybody" in the Royal Flying Corps knew that Bishop was padding his score with false claims.[3]

James said Bishop "began very well. He was genuine." But, said the old pilot, as Billy's ambition to become the leading ace grew, he began claiming victories that were "completely mythical." He offered no proof in the interview to back up the charges, saying only "Everybody knew it. It became common knowledge ... but it couldn't be proclaimed at the time because the Canadians were so proud of him that it would have been damaging to Allied unity."[4]

In June 1977, on the sixtieth anniversary of Bishop's famed solo raid on a German aerodrome, England's Royal Air Force Museum issued a commemorative stamp/envelope to mark the occasion. It asked surviving 60 Squadron pilots from the era to sign the envelope, called a "flown cover." Of four men contacted, only one agreed to do so. The others flatly refused.

One of the men who would not sign was Grid Caldwell. He explained his reasons in a letter to Willie Fry dated June 17, 1977: "I cannot do what they wish, sign and endorse the picture of Bishop doing his VC act, when I have to doubt its authenticity .... I do not expect you to do anything about it, as it would put you in a similar difficult spot, as I think we hold alike views on the VC incident."

In a letter to another 60 Squadron man, A.V.M. Pidock, Caldwell was just as blunt:

"All references to poor Billy Bishop do raise a problem because some of us know upon cross-checking with German archives that many of B's claims were unreal, including his VC job when no German aircraft were reported lost — it's all very sad, but he is dead."[6]

Caldwell was not alone with his doubts. Air historians rummaging through German First World War casualty records found startling information for June 2, 1917. Three German airmen died on that day but they all perished deep inside Germany on training flights. The records made no mention of fatal casualties on the Western Front. Weather conditions were poor that day and very little operational flying took place.

By 1984, when doubts about Bishop's feat had gone public, one Canadian newspaper reported that 60 Squadron's Spencer Horn had once claimed to have flown over the German airfield later in the afternoon of June 2, and had seen the damage that Bishop had wrought.

Unfortunately, the tale cannot be backed up with facts. Squadron records indicate Horn never crossed the lines that day. Weather reports for the Arras sector show it was raining in the early morning hours, clear just after dawn, clouding over by afternoon with storms by early evening. Pilots flew only four patrols — and none of them crossed the lines. Each flight lasted only about one hour.

Beside that is the fact that Horn was one of those who had doubts about Bishop's record. There is a letter on file at 60 Squadron in England, signed by Horn, that strongly suggests that incidents described in Bishop's autobiography was exaggerated. Indeed, Horn warns a historian not to rely too heavily on the book because it contains "too much 'line shooting.'" Line shooting was RFC slang for telling tall tales.

The mutterings of the doubters were unknown to the public in 1917. But even if they had been common knowledge, it is doubtful whether many would have believed them. That spring, the Royal Flying Corps had been bled white. In May it had lost Albert Ball and by early June, as the losses mounted, morale was at an all-time low. In these circumstances, the RFC and the public as a whole were aching for an air hero. Jack Scott believed in Bishop and that was enough. He had connections in high places. As Fry noted in his autobiography, Scott "had access to General Allenby" and was a friend of Lord Dalmeny. With the major pulling strings, Bishop would get his Victoria Cross whether there was the slightest shred of evidence to back up his story or not.

In the days following the raid on the aerodrome, Bishop's popularity with some of his peers continued to falter as more and more pilots began to doubt the accuracy of his combat reports.

Billy said he destroyed an Albatros north of Lille on June 8, and in the last five days of the month he made claims for five German planes.

Not all of these kills were scored on lone wolf patrols without witnesses. When he picked an Albatros pilot off the tail of an antiquated FE2B on June 24, the gunner aboard the British plane saw the German go down and verified the victory. And Billy was operating with

Lieutenants Soden and Young of 60 Squadron when he drove down out of control one of ten enemy planes that he attacked a day later. But there were no witnesses for any of the others.

Still, Jack Scott signed his name to Bishop's reports, giving Billy a victory total of thirty-four by month's end.

Tension mounted in the mess as Scott continued this practice. Bishop sensed the hostility of the others and withdrew into himself. One of the pilots who knew the ace at this stage of his career was Sholto Douglas. He described Billy this way: "There was something about him that left one feeling that he preferred to live as he fought, in a brittle, hard world of his own. He has been described as a lone wolf, but I do not think that any of us came to know or understand his motives well enough to be sure about that. He was not a lone wolf in the sense that we applied that term to Albert Ball."[8]

Canadian pilot Roy Brown painted a picture of Bishop as a hard-nosed loner. "Aces like Barker and Collishaw were idols," Brown said. "Their fellows felt kinship. But Bishop was austere, aloof, godlike." He was also, Brown added, a man who "kept his feelings corked."[9]

And Willie Fry, who had found a charming, happy-go-lucky comrade when he reported to 60 Squadron in mid-April, had an entirely different impression of Bishop by the end of June. He wrote: "Although I had lived and flown with Bishop as my flight commander during the previous two months, I had never really got to know him or to make friends with him — but then I found it difficult to make friends. He was very popular in the squadron, yet I do not remember him having any particular friends."[10] All three of these descriptions are in marked contrast to the picture painted of Bishop before his London leave.

Fry's relations with Bishop soured noticeably. They reached the breaking point one night when the Englishman made a scurrilous remark to Bishop's face. Jack Scott demanded that Fry apologize. When the lieutenant refused to do so, Scott had him declared mentally unfit to fly and posted him back to England.

Fry, in his memoirs, admits that Scott had him shipped home because of a remark he made to Bishop. However, he does not reveal what it was he said to the ace. Paul Cowan of Canada's National Film Board spoke with Fry in 1981 and claims that Fry told him he was dismissed for making "the mistake of openly criticizing Bishop's many unconfirmed kills to Scott."[11]

Fry, when contacted by the author, was reticent about the whole affair. He waited six months before replying to a letter and then would only say, "I much regret being unable to help you."[12]

Whatever it was that Fry had said, he must have felt it very deeply because he could have avoided being sent home simply by apologizing to Bishop — a step he refused to undertake.

Billy, ostracized by several of his peers, sought out the company of animals. His autobiography is filled with pleasant tales of playing with rabbits, pigs and dogs. Soon, he had four dogs of his own, although his favourite was "Nigger," the big black hound he had taken into his hut one rainy night. The animal followed him everywhere after that.

The new Bishop was also an unforgiving flight commander. Harold Lewis, who flew only four patrols with "C" Flight, recorded two instances in which he had run-ins with the ace.

Once, after performing some fancy flying, he got a frosty reception from the Canadian. "After landing," he remembered, "Bishop sent for me and dressed me down in no uncertain manner and said, 'Don't show off like that, next time you go in for that sort of thing you will not get away with it,' or words to that effect, but in stronger language."

"I got into trouble with Bishop on returning from another patrol," he said, recalling that he had emptied his gun into a ground target just before landing. "Very pleased with my gunnery efforts, I got a roasting from Bishop for firing into his target. I still know that the mistake was his."[13]

July 10, 1917, 8 A.M.: the four pilots were split into pairs as they scampered to and fro, locked in a vigorous tennis match. They were dressed in shorts and t-shirts. If not for the grass growing in the cracks of the court and the advanced rot in the netting, they could have been mistaken for a group of young aristocrats at some private club. This idyllic scene was almost enough to make onlookers forget that there was a war on.

Almost, but not quite. Suddenly the Klaxon horn sounded its shrill alarm. Jack Scott hobbled out of his headquarters and waved a cane in the direction of the tennis players. A dozen Germans were strafing British troops near Monchy.

Bishop and the others dropped their racquets and dashed to the tarmac where five Nieuports were lined up. Minutes later, with Scott leading the way, the five RFC pilots swooped into the middle of twelve Albatroses caught in the act of strafing English soldiers.

There was no time for fancy acrobatics. Airmen twisted and turned in close quarters. Risk of a mid-air collision, or even an accidental nose-dive into the mud, was very real.

Bishop was about to nail an opponent when a second Albatros got behind him and stitched his Nieuport's fuselage with a stream of lead. Before the German could deliver the deathblow, Jack Scott streaked out of nowhere, sending the plane down in flames.

Another Albatros dove on Billy, but the Canadian got out of this jam on his own, looping around and raking the D-3 with a prolonged burst. The Albatros tumbled away out of control. Scott saw the German go down and confirmed the victory.

That was enough for the enemy. The Germans broke off the dogfight and fled. But before they left, one of them took a parting shot at Scott, shattering the major's arm with a well-directed burst. Bleeding profusely, Scott had to thrust his wounded limb into the cool slip-stream to check the loss of blood. Back at the aerodrome the major gave no hint to the mechanics that he had been hit, going to his office to make out a combat report before summoning help.

Billy was distraught at the turn of events and blamed himself for Scott's misfortune. The commander tried to cheer him up, dismissing the wound as a "blighty." A blighty was the RFC's term for a minor injury that would land the injured man back in England for a short rest. However, the truth was evident to everyone. Jack Scott's flying days were over. The arm was too badly damaged to allow him ever to return to action.

On July 12, Bishop shot down and killed a German during a short skirmish near Vitry. Billy was directly behind, watching the enemy pilot's leather-helmeted head twist and pivot in the cockpit as he stole glances back over his shoulders. The Canadian was so close to him that he saw one of the bullets slam into the man's face, smashing his features into a bloody pulp and smearing his brains over the instrument panel and windshield. Sopwith triplane pilot Robert Little was trailing just a few yards behind this action and confirmed Bishop's kill.

Little wrote:

> While on special mission I observed a Nieuport east of Roeux. We met and went east together when I observed a formation of Nieuports fighting with some Albatros scouts. I joined the fight.
>
> During the fight I saw Captain Bishop shoot down an EA which crashed near Vitry en Artois. Captain Bishop and myself then attacked another EA together. The German pilot waved a white handkerchief during the fight so I stopped firing at him, but seeing he was going east, I opened fire again. I think he was wounded.

Another Allied pilot in this fight, Lt. A.W.M. Mowle, wrote at the bottom of his combat report:

> I saw this machine spin into the ground a few seconds after Captain Bishop attacked it.

If we are to believe the German records, Bishop did not shoot down the plane that day. But as the eyewitness testimony of Little and Mowle proves, those documents are clearly not reliable.

Billy's thirty-seventh conquest was also solidly verified. He got in two bursts from point-blank range at an Albatros that was harassing a pair of Bristol two-seaters from Number 11 Squadron. Lieutenant Barnett, a gunner aboard one of the Bristols, saw the German go into a hideous spin minus part of his tail. As Barnett's eyes continued to follow the red and yellow plane downward, it suddenly burst into flames and crashed. Twelve minutes, later Billy blew apart yet another luckless Albatros.

And the hot streak did not end there. Bishop sent his thirty-ninth victim down out of control on July 20. Yet, despite his mounting score, 60 Squadron was by no means having everything its own way. A particular thorn in the unit's side at this time was Oberleutnant Adolf Ritter von Tutschek, the infamous leader of Jagdstaffel [12].

Although von Tutschek is not well known among First World War aviation history buffs, he was one of Germany's deadliest aces. In photographs he is often shown preening and strutting arrogantly, posing with Allied aircraft that had fallen under his guns. In the air he flew a black Albatros with blue and purple wings. And he came to 60 Squadron's attention on July 15, when he shot down Lieutenant G.A.H. Parkes. A few weeks later he had a brush with Bishop.

Bishop had been patrolling with Grid Caldwell and a raw rookie named Bill Gunner when von Tutschek led four Albatroses into the attack. A bitter struggle followed, with neither side able to gain the upper hand until, without warning, Gunner's engine failed and he dropped out of the battle and began the long, slow glide for home. He never made it. Von Tutschek was all over the lame duck in a flash, with both of his guns blasting. Bishop tried to intervene, firing ineffective bursts at long range. The German ace ignored the salvos and continued his own attack until the helpless Gunner crashed in flames.

The squadron's new SE5s had arrived. Bishop was not impressed with their outward appearance. They were rugged, boxlike planes, two feet longer than the Nieuports and 700 pounds heavier. Moreover, they totally lacked the graceful lines of the little French fighters.

The exhaust pipes, Billy noticed at once, were its most distinctive feature, running almost the full length of the fuselage. He had to admit, however, that he liked the feel of the cockpit. It was more comfortable than the old Nieuport and visibility was simply outstanding.

What really surprised him was the sound of the 200 horsepower Hispano-Suiza engine. Those long exhaust pipes had reduced the familiar ear-splitting roar of a Le Rhone engine to a gentle purr. Better yet, it wasn't a rotary engine, which meant there were none of the sickening castor oil fumes that had so often turned his stomach.

Walter Bourne was quick to get his hands on the plane, painting Billy's SE5 red and white with a blue coat of paint on the square-shaped radiator. It was easily the gaudiest plane in the Royal Flying Corps.

On his first flight in the SE5, Bishop was astonished at the swiftness with which it picked up speed. It literally jumped into the sky, pinning him forcefully into the back of his seat. He completed the circle in seconds, making a Nieuport's loop seem by comparison to be a slow-motion maneuver.

Bishop was exhilarated with the performance. He headed for German territory, along with two other 60 Squadron pilots, anxious to try out the added firepower of the two machine guns on an enemy. For in addition to the top wing Lewis, the SE5 had a Vickers gun mounted on the engine hood that fired through the propeller.

Crossing the lines, he quickly encountered an Albatros, swung onto its tail and opened fire. Twin lines of tracer sliced the machine to shreds. The captain had discovered another of the SE5's secrets. It was an incredibly stable gun platform. In the hands of a marksman such as Bishop, it would be an extremely potent weapon indeed.

A day later, as if to prove the point, Bishop gained his forty-first victory when he drove down another Albatros.

Bishop was reverting back to the reckless form that had marked his first days at Filescamp Farm. He was so obsessed with increasing his score that he was beginning to take foolhardy risks.

On the flight in which he scored his forty-first kill, for instance, he found himself alone in the midst of seven enemy pilots. He only lived to tell the tale because Grid Caldwell happened on the scene and saved his life. Caldwell, with both of his guns jammed, nevertheless dove into the fray and scattered the Germans in every direction.

On August 12, Billy found himself in an even tighter corner. He had chased an Albatros a full ten miles behind German lines at dusk before giving up. The SE5 was faster, but the German had a head start and dove steeply to increase his speed. Bishop had followed him very low to the ground before finally admitting he had to abandon the hunt and return home. As he wheeled around he took in a sight that must have made him tremble in his seat. Twenty German fighters were coming straight for him. They had hidden above the clouds while the lone Albatros had intentionally led him far behind the lines. Now, with a sixty mile per hour gale in his face and an entire circus of enemy planes between him and home, Bishop found himself hopelessly hemmed in.

There was only one way out and he seized it. The ace turned the SE5 around and roared off like a bat out of hell, deeper into German territory. After a time the Germans, in their slower machines, had completely disappeared. But Bishop was now thirty miles behind the lines and night was coming.

He climbed for altitude because at dusk there was still some light in the upper sky. Soon the sun had gone down and the high wind was working against him.

Relying on his compass, Bishop headed for Allied lines. More by luck than skill, he found his way to Filescamp and fired off flares. Shortly after that, the runway was flooded with lights and he was able to land without incident. In fact, he was just in time to drink a toast to his departed soul! The squadron had been certain that "poor old Bish" had finally gone west and they were surprised when the familiar tri-coloured SE5 came down out of the darkness.

A possibly even more hair-raising episode occurred around the same time. Again, Bishop's desire for kills got him into hot water. And again, fantastic cunning saved his hide.

Bishop, flying alone, spotted a flight of three Fokkers on the same level as his plane. Normally, when going after three single-seaters by himself, he would zoom for altitude and strike from above.

When he was 300 yards behind, he received a shock: the Fokkers executed a hairpin turn and came at him with guns winking atop their horseshoe-shaped cowlings. Bishop involuntarily ducked and bullets riddled the fuselage behind his cockpit. The Germans were so excited about catching the troublesome blue-nosed ace off guard that they failed to score a fatal hit on that first pass. Banking smartly around, they came at him again, guns firing.

Suddenly Bishop had a brainstorm. The Fokker pilots knew who he was — they were aware of his reputation. They would expect such a dauntless opponent as Billy Bishop to fight it out, regardless of the odds. But he would fool them.

The SE5 lurched over on one wing and tumbled down, totally out of control. For the first time in his life Bishop had gone purposefully into a spin. The Fokker pilots would likely have followed any other Allied airman down to make sure he was not faking. But they simply watched in astonishment as the SE5 fell away, disappearing from their view as it was swallowed up by a cloud bank 1,000 feet below.

Bishop was not out of danger yet. A damp grey mist enveloped him; one moment he had been catching alternate glimpses of sky, sun and brown earth and the next instant the whole world disappeared. He could not pull out of a spin inside a cloud. He had to wait until he was clear of it and then hope there was room enough left to recover. If the vapour reached too close to the ground it would be too late.

"Well," he told himself, "Better to die voluntarily crashing than to have the enemy send you down in flames." [14] Seconds later he popped into the blue. Lady luck was still with him. There were 3,000 feet to spare.

Bishop's boldness continued to pay off. On August 5, he led Moley Molesworth and one other pilot into an attack on seven Albatroses, shooting down Leutnant Burkhard Lehmann and sending a second German down out of control. Molesworth, who destroyed a third German, confirmed both of Bishop's kills. The carnage brought his score up to forty-three — just one behind Albert Ball's RFC record. Bishop said nothing about the mark to his fellow pilots but they knew full well that he desperately wanted to achieve at least two more victories.

He tied the mark on August 6, when he shot down an Albatros D-3. The victory was confirmed by the Bristol fighter crew of Captain Clement and Lieutenant Carter from Number 11 Squadron. One more to go. The hunter found what he was looking for three days later, destroying an Aviatik two-seater 6,000 feet over Drocourt. There now wasn't an airman in the British Empire — alive or dead — who was officially credited with killing as many Germans as Billy Bishop. At long last he was known across the Front as the RFC "ace of aces." It was a title he did not intend to relinquish.

Bishop added to his record four days later. The truculent SE5 tore through a flight of three Albatroses, firing two quick bursts. Both salvos hit home. Two of the black-crossed planes crashed in flames in a field below, coming to rest almost on top of one another. Billy was especially thrilled with the second kill because the man he had shot was flying a silver D-3 that had been a thorn in his side for weeks.

General Trenchard phoned with the news — and to offer his personal congratulations: Bishop had won the Victoria Cross.

Billy had been expecting the award because the newspapers had been predicting it for days. And he bad even written home telling Margaret that he thought he deserved the medal. Still, when word came through it was an emotional high for him. The bad boy from Royal Military College was now the toast of the empire. He was officially a hero. Billy went straight to the NCO's mess to share the news with the men with whom he was most comfortable — the grease monkeys. The ace moved in and sat down beside Walter Bourne.

"Anything wrong sir?"

"Not particularly."

"I replaced that interrupter-gear piston, sir," Bourne said, a bit defensively.

"It's not that. I just wanted to tell you that we've won the Victoria Cross."[15]

Bourne, who had heard rumours that the honour was on the way, showed no change of expression.

"Thank you, sir. That means of course ...."

"Nothing of the kind! They'll not send me back!"

The captain pointed out that Albert Ball had been left at the Front when his score was in the forties. And he added, "Jimmy McCudden over at Number 56 is going like a house on fire."

Bourne groaned and then pointed out: "We've lost practically every VC airman so far, sir. There was Rhodes-Moorehouse, Warneford, Hawker, Liddell, Ball and Sergeant Mottershead. Leefe-Robinson is a prisoner of war. They won't risk you any longer."

"I'll have something to say about that!"[16]

60 Squadron, which never needed much of an excuse to stage a wild party, celebrated Bishop's VC with a drunken bash that outstripped anything yet seen at Filescamp Farm.

After drinking the mess dry, the flyers poured out the door and formed a torch procession over to 40 Squadron. The boisterous celebrants tossed everything — including a few 40 Squadron pilots — out the windows and doors. Flare guns were fired through broken windows and only through the grace of God was a major fire averted.

Soon Bishop began to fear that Bourne was right. Rumours about his imminent departure were rampant among the squadron pilots. They huddled in groups, whispering, when suddenly he would walk in and the talk would abruptly come to a halt. The silence was deafening.

Finally, one of them told him, "You're to be sent to London for your investiture. And they say you won't be posted back to the Front."[17] Bishop was stunned. He was in danger of losing his job simply because headquarters did not want to risk losing another hero. Such a setback would not be good for public morale.

Still, orders for his posting would have to be processed before they became official. There was still time to bag a few more planes.

CHAPTER ELEVEN

It had been two months since Bishop had returned to the Front and his nerves were once again stretched to the breaking point. In a letter home he confided that his nerves were "shaky," adding, "I find myself shuddering at chances I didn't think of taking six weeks ago."[1] Clearly, he was suffering from combat fatigue. If he didn't find a diversion soon, he'd likely be killed in action.

Billy found a much-needed tonic from the war in the city of Amiens, where he met a beautiful young French girl named Ninette. While on a weekend pass, he spotted her outside a drugstore and followed her in, boldly introducing himself despite the fact that her mother accompanied her. Ninette confessed that she had seen Billy several times and had longed to meet him. But she refused to frequent Charlie's Bar, the local establishment that attracted servicemen on leave from across the region.

Billy started to see Ninette often. Amiens was a three-hour drive from Filescamp Farm, but the pilots thought nothing of making the trip by lorry in the early evening, often returning just in time for the dawn patrol. In her company he found a gentle woman who seemed to understand his needs. She placed no demands on him and never seemed the slightest bit concerned for his safety. That, in turn, made it easier for him to relax and forget the war for a few hours at a time. During the bitter days that lay ahead, Ninette would help Billy through some very traumatic times. And although he had by no means forgotten about Margaret, without Ninette as his mistress during this stressful period, he probably would not have survived.

Amiens itself was a pleasant diversion. Located seventy miles north of Paris on the banks of the Somme, in the middle of gently rolling hills, the former capital of Picardy province was a beautiful sight to behold. Its red brick homes with slate roofs, and the Gothic church spires are still visible for miles around.

For the flyers, however, the main attraction of Amiens was Charlie's Bar and Le Hotel du Rhin. Charlie's was especially popular because its proprietor somehow managed to keep it stocked with fine wines and delicious French food. The food was a pleasant relief for the RFC men, who normally had to put up with meals boiled to excess in steam and coated with a sticky sauce that tasted like dried glue.

At Charlie's, where greasy-haired waiters scurried between the marble tables, they were served salad, fish, mutton and herb-flavoured soup. After meals, the pilots headed for the cellar, where a bar was continuously open, and where young women could be picked up for a few francs. Servicemen were more popular in Amiens than elsewhere in France, partly because the city had been captured by the "Boche" early in the war and was then liberated.

Before he met Ninette, Billy often went to Charlie's. On one occasion he was seen there with two vivacious women. He instituted a game in which each pilot who managed to charm a garter from a girl in Amiens would hang it as a trophy in the squadron mess. Included in it would be the lady's name and address. The airman who brought in the most garters had almost as much prestige as the man who had shot down the most enemy planes. Before long, Billy led the squadron in both departments.

Why was he able to attract female company with such ease? The *Owen Sound Sun* noted the attraction Billy had for the opposite sex in a story written while he was on leave in the autumn of 1917. It reported that, upon his return, he was greeted by a group of ladies "in a manner that made the young hero blush. It looked for awhile that this method of salutation might become general, until a young lady said that she was tempted to kiss him but was afraid."[2]

George Stirrett explained his success this way: "Bill had that fun-loving bounce of a schoolboy about him. He was a real charmer. I saw him woo them in the Grand Hotel in Folkestone. They were falling all over him, and this was long before he became famous. Oh, he was a real womanizer back then, although I think his future wife was the only woman he ever really loved.'[3]

If anyone needed to find solace in the company of women, it was Bishop. For by August 1917, the bloodthirsty streak that he had displayed in the spring was beginning to leave him. Indeed, feelings of remorse and guilt had set in.

Such emotions were dangerous for a fighter pilot: it was his killer instinct that had helped keep him alive. But now Bishop was sick to death of the bloodshed. In this, he was not unusual; it was not uncommon for men who had been at the Front for an extended period to grow tired of it all. Just before his death, Albert Ball had written home telling his father that he felt like a murderer. Jimmy McCudden was expressing similar feelings in his writings. On the German side of the lines, Manfred von Richthofen was in the same boat. After a year of constant killing he wrote:

> I am in wretched spirits after every aerial battle. When I set foot on the ground again at my airfield after a fight, I go to my quarters and do not want to see anyone or hear anything. I think of this war as it really is, not as the people at home imagine, with a Hoorah! and a roar. It is very serious, very grim.[4]

At first they had all found it very exciting. But as such men piled up more and more kills, the glamour began to wear off and their consciences began to bother them. Bishop was no different. He knew that the Albatroses and Fokkers were piloted by flesh-and-blood human beings. He had flown within five feet of some men before snuffing out their lives.

This feeling of remorse surfaced for the first time the day after one of his few remaining friends was killed. The squadron had not lost anyone in some time and Bishop took the setback hard. He wrote to Margaret, telling her, "I am thoroughly downcast tonight. The Huns got Lloyd today, such a fine fellow too, and one of our best pilots. Sometimes all of this awful fighting in the air makes you wonder if you have a right to call yourself human. My honey, I am so sick of it all, the killing, the war. All I want is home and you."[5]

Here was a new Billy Bishop. The letter contains none of the bitter vows of vengeance that usually marked his correspondence after a friend had been killed. In his autobiography, Bishop admitted that he was now having trouble sleeping at night because the fact that he was killing people kept bothering him. It was an astonishing public admission that somehow got through the wartime censors.

In one recurring nightmare, he relived the moment that he had killed a German pilot over Vitry. He told his friend George Stirrett that he would never forget the look of terror in the enemy pilot's eyes just before he opened fire. "My bullets," he said, "shattered his face and skull. I can't get that picture out of my mind."

Allied propaganda had helped make the killing easy in the beginning. After all, the newspapers had spread countless lies about German brutality. The world was told that the Germans had slaughtered large numbers of helpless women and children when they trampled over Belgium. Bishop and thousands of others had no way of knowing it was all a lie.

He knew for certain that the Germans were bombing defenceless civilians in London because he had seen that with his own eyes. And they had done other despicable things too, such as sinking passenger liners with U-boats. Or using poison gas at Ypres. Or shooting a French woman who they accused of spying.

The Allies had also committed acts that, by the fighting standards of the nineteenth century, would have been considered immoral. But the German propaganda machine had not been skillful enough to take advantage of the various incidents. The French had shot female spies as well. And the British were killing more civilians — starving them with their naval blockade — than the Germans were butchering with their Gothas and zeppelins.

But whether or not the war was bothering Bishop did not matter at this stage. The senseless killing had to continue because both sides had lost too much to settle for anything less than total victory. Neither side was fighting for an altruistic cause. Revenge was the only motive left to spur on the belligerents.

On August 15, Bishop shot and killed a man in an Albatros, gaining his forty-eighth victory. The next day, his last at the Front before returning to England, he slew three more men, shooting down an Albatros and an Aviatik two-seater.

The Aviatik disintegrated in mid-air and its two crewmen, both still alive, were hurled into space. They tumbled past Bishop, screaming madly and clutching wildly at the thin air. With arms and legs flailing in all directions, the two men plunged 13,000 feet. It would take several minutes for them to reach the ground northeast of Lens. They knew, as they fell, that their bodies would explode upon impact in a shower of blood and bones. It would be like an egg hitting a kitchen floor after rolling off a table.

Bishop, who might have smiled at such a sight a few months earlier, was horrified. He even considered trying to shoot them as they fell, thus granting them a more merciful end. But he decided against it, realizing the chances of scoring hits were not good.

A pair of Albatroses came on the scene, saw it was too late to help the two-seater, and turned for home.

Bishop followed them for a time but eventually decided they had too much of a headstart to be overtaken. They were 300 yards ahead of him. On an impulse, he decided to take one final parting shot. The range was almost impossible but, what the heck! He was going home and might never get another opportunity. His guns hammered a brief burst. The rear Albatros spun down out of control. Its pilot had been killed by a thousand-to-one shot. Bishop looked on in bewilderment as his fiftieth officially confirmed victim dropped more than two miles and crashed.

As he flew home, the bright orange ball that was the sun was setting in the west. The whole sky — the entire world — was orange. It was high summer and as the SE5 glided over the Allied lines, not more than a few hundred feet up, Billy's nostrils caught a revolting stench from the trenches. It was a smell that he had not often noticed because in the winter it had been suppressed by the cold. But in late summer there was

no hiding it. Millions of men were living below in their own excrement
— and amid the bodies of thousands of decaying corpses of friend and
foe. The rotting flesh, combined with the tons of human body waste,
was enough to make a person gag.

Billy Bishop was *late* for his investiture! He hurried down the vast cor-
ridors of Buckingham Palace, rushing past white marble columns with
no idea of where he was supposed to go.

A general flagged him down and asked if Billy was to receive the
Military Cross. When the Canadian said he was, the man quickly
rushed him into a massive ante-room where a large group of MC winners were seated in red velvet chairs, anxiously awaiting the start of the
proceedings. Billy was more nervous at the prospect of meeting the
king face to face than he had ever been when facing a German aviator
in a duel to the death.

The general burst into the room, looking terribly flustered. He was,
he said, missing a DSO man. Was anyone in the room to receive the
Distinguished Service Order? Billy volunteered that he was to be
awarded a DSO and was ushered into another room.

Moments later, the general reappeared, demanding to know if anyone
in the room was to receive a VC. One of the Victoria Cross winners was
missing. Billy, red-faced, admitted that he was again the culprit who had
been holding up the proceedings. The King of England, Ruler of Ireland
and Emperor of India and the Dominions beyond the Seas, had been
kept waiting while the boy from Owen Sound sorted himself out.

The general was almost beside himself. Billy would have to go out
and meet the king without a rehearsal.

Fortunately, Bishop had memorized the awards drill. Marching ten
feet into the centre of a vast hall, he turned to his left and bowed stiffly
before a delegation of generals, admirals and other high-ranking officers in braided uniforms. His polished boots squeaked audibly during
those ten paces and the ace was deeply embarrassed as he came to rigid
attention.

The hall was massive, with a high domed ceiling, gigantic silver chandeliers, wall-sized mirrors trimmed in gold, priceless seventeenth century furniture, red carpeting, historic paintings and marble pillars cut from blocks of veined carrera marble. Along the sides were impressive sculptures of winged figures.

The room went silent. A staff officer began reading from a scroll.

"His Majesty the King has been graciously pleased to confer the Military Cross on Lieutenant William Avery Bishop, Canadian Cavalry and Royal Flying Corps.

"For conspicuous gallantry and devotion to duty. He attacked a hostile balloon on the ground, dispersed the crew and destroyed the balloon, and also drove down a hostile machine which attacked him. He has on several occasions brought down hostile machines."

Bishop flushed, feeling terribly self-conscious with the knowledge that all eyes were on him. The staff officer was droning again, reading his Distinguished Service Order citation.

"For conspicuous gallantry and devotion to duty. While in a single-seater he attacked three hostile machines, two of which he brought down, although he himself was attacked by other hostile machines. His courage and determination have set a fine example to others."

Bishop twitched nervously. Papers were shuffled. The staff officer announced that Bishop was also to receive the Victoria Cross.

"For most conspicuous bravery, determination and skill. Captain Bishop, who had set out to work independently, flew first of all to an enemy aerodrome; finding no machines about, he flew on to another aerodrome about three miles southeast, which was at least twelve miles the other side of the line. Seven machines, some with engines running, were on the ground. He attacked these from about fifty feet, and a mechanic, who was starting one of the engines, was seen to fall. One of the machines got off the ground, but at a height of sixty feet Captain Bishop fired fifteen rounds into it at a very close range, and it crashed to the ground.

"A second machine got off the ground, into which he fired thirty rounds at 150 yards range, and it fell into a tree.

"Two more machines then rose from the aerodrome. One of these he then engaged at a height of 1,000 feet, emptying the rest of his drum of ammunition. This machine crashed 300 yards from the aerodrome, after which Captain Bishop emptied a whole drum into the fourth hostile machine and then flew back to his station.

"Four hostile scouts were about 1,000 feet above him for about a mile of his return journey, but they did not attack.

"His machine was very badly shot about by machine gun fire from the ground."

Another staff officer was walking about the room, displaying Bishop's three medals on a satin pillow.

Suddenly, the king was before him. He was an impressive figure, with a dignified air about him, a well-trimmed, reddish-brown beard, a high forehead and deep-set eyes. Then, sternly and unexpectedly, he spoke.

"This," he announced gravely, "is the first occasion on which I have bestowed all three of these honours on any one subject.'[6] With that, he pinned the decorations on Bishop's tunic. Bishop found himself thinking that the VC was a rather unimpressive-looking medal; a simple bronze cross with the words "For Valour" inscribed on it.

He tried to speak but only a garbled sound came from his lips. He was almost disabled by fear. His brain seemed completely paralyzed and his body was quaking. King George flashed a fatherly smile and said, "You have been making a nuisance of yourself out there, haven't you?"

The king then talked to the young flyer for fifteen minutes before dismissing him. Bishop took his leave, with his boots squeaking again at what seemed to be an almost deafening level.

The next time he saw the Canadian, to pin the Distinguished Flying Cross on his breast, the king, who was not usually noted for his humour, quipped: "You now have the VC, DSO, MC and DFC after your name. If you distinguish yourself again we shall have to give you something to put in front of your name. Perhaps we could call you Archbishop!"[7]

The "Old Boy," as Bishop called him in a letter home, also informed him that he was glad not to have been the one with the squeaky boots at their first meeting.

Billy did not yet realize it, but he was now considered more important as a propaganda tool than he was as a pilot.

King George had been anxious to present the empire's three highest awards to one man, at one ceremony. Two British soldiers had won the trio of decorations, but both had been killed in action before they could get to Buckingham Palace.

Bishop had another thing going for him, in the eyes of the British. He was a colonial officer, and that was important. The colonies were making enormous sacrifices and the king had decided the best way to maintain colonial enthusiasm for this European war would be to make an elaborate production out of Bishop's investiture.

The British tended to overlook men from the colonies when it came time to hand out decorations. While Britishers Albert Ball and Jimmy McCudden, for instance, were both awarded the VC, Canadians Ray Collishaw and Donald MacLaren were overlooked, despite the fact that they had comparable combat records. English pilots were almost automatically given a VC for shooting down a zeppelin, but no Canadian ever received the medal for such a feat, even though half of the zepps that were bagged during the war were, in fact, destroyed by Canadians. Indeed, Canada's Robert Leckie was ignored even after becoming the only airman to send two of the giant dirigibles down in flames. Now, Billy Bishop was to serve as Canada's token VC fighter pilot.

The British were not the only ones who saw him as an important symbol. The Canadian government was now demanding that he be returned to the Dominion to help stem the tide of growing anti-war sentiment. The RFC complied.

By the time Billy sailed out of Liverpool on his way home in September, he had every reason to be proud of himself. He had fame. The newspapers had spread his name around the globe, referring to him as the "Lone Hawk." He had decorations. Six of them, in fact. Before he left for home he was informed that he had been granted a second DSO. And the French government had bestowed on him the Croix de Guerre with palm and the Legion of Honour. That made him the most decorated individual among the millions of servicemen in the ranks of the Allied powers.

Rank? He was now a major, having received the promotion in mid-August. Five months earlier he had been a mere lieutenant, and it had only been three years since he had been on the verge of being expelled from cadet school.

Money was also on the horizon. He had been persuaded to write a book about his exploits and there was the promise that it would bring in thousands of dollars. He finished it before his leave was up and it became a bestseller.

But there was a stiff price to be paid. Reporters, dignitaries and ordinary people hounded him wherever he went. Public appearances in places such as restaurants, theatres or even boxing rings, were strictly off limits. He found that out when he walked into a boxing match and the whole audience rose and gave him a standing ovation. Both fighters stopped punching one another long enough to join in the applause. Bishop, who had only wanted to relax and watch the event, turned around and stomped out.

He did not realize that when he got back to Canada the adulation would be almost suffocating.

CHAPTER TWELVE

Bishop's life took a new turn when he arrived in Montreal in October 1917. Margaret was there to meet him, and after an ecstatic reunion the couple decided to get married, setting October 17 as the wedding date. Given Billy's antics with women in France and England, his decision to get married may seem surprising. But it wasn't really. Margaret was the woman he loved, and there was never any doubt between them that one day they would be husband and wife.

There was little time to plan the wedding. After the decision had been made and the date set, Billy set off on a triumphant procession that ended in Owen Sound. Along the way, he was greeted with wildly enthusiastic, flag-waving crowds. Major William Avery Bishop, VC, DSO and bar, MC, had come home — and Canadians were desperate for a glimpse of him.

The tour had a clear political purpose: Billy was on display, much like a prize steer at a country fair, in the expectation that his appearance would rekindle public enthusiasm for a war that had lost its glamour.

By 1917 the war was tearing Canada apart. Casualties were now reaching catastrophic proportions. The Canadian Corps, which had won spectacular victories in 1916 and 1917, was now badly depleted and there were not enough volunteers coming forward to fill the holes created by German machine guns. The situation was so serious that the House of Commons passed a conscription act in April of 1917. Unfortunately, conscription created bitter divisions in the country, splitting the population along racial lines. In Quebec, French Canadians viewed the war as simply another of Europe's endless conflicts and bitterly opposed the draft. English Canada had a different opinion: it was willing to see the war through to the end, no matter how many Canadian boys had to be slaughtered in the process. Yet even in English Canada, enthusiasm for conscription was not universal. Many farmers, who needed help in the fields, were opposed to the drafting of their sons, and there were angry demonstrations against conscription in Toronto and Calgary.

It was an ugly time. Churchmen and politicians railed against able-bodied lads who were "not doing their duty to king and country." Scandals rocked the nation. Industrialists, bankers and financiers were making huge profits from the war. The minister of defence, Sam Hughes, was forced to resign from the federal government after it was revealed that the army was being supplied with massive amounts of useless equipment. The public was also upset over passage of a new bill implementing an income tax. Politicians explained that the tax was needed to pay for the war and that it would disappear once the conflict was over.

It was in this atmosphere of suspicion and resentment that Billy Bishop made his way to Owen Sound. When he reached his home town, the *Owen Sound Sun* reported his return in a fascinating story that, inadvertently, also captured the insanity of the war and the tensions it was creating in Canada. It reads in part as follows: "The welcome home to Major Billy Bishop on Friday last was enthusiastic and wholehearted to a degree. There were thousands of cheering people along the route of the procession and at the market square, and in every breast was the knowledge that Major Bishop had done wonderful things for the empire in this great war, and a respect for him and his prowess was unbounded. He had been received by the king at Buckingham Palace, he had been feted in England and ever since his return to Canada, but he is still the same modest Billy Bishop that the English papers call him.

"There were probably five or six thousand people around the station, standing in autos, on the roofs of buildings, when factory whistles along the east shore of the bay denoted the fact that the train, bearing the youthful aviator, was approaching the station. Other vehicles throughout the town took up the welcome and at the station the cheering was added to the noise of the auto horns and engine whistles. A special car was attached to the CRR for the use of Major Bishop and his family and friends, and from the rear of this, the crowd received its first view of the gallant airman since he left here over a year ago and since winning honours unequalled in the British Empire."

The story went on to relate that numerous high school bands, with youngsters in brilliant red coats, were performing, and that "all along the route were cheering crowds." Children were "wearing wreaths of maple leaves and carrying flags. They cheered lustily as the VC warrior and other returned men passed." The streets were, the *Sun* reporter continued, "a mass of moving humanity," and were "profusely decorated for the occasion."

Eventually, the motorcade made its way through the throng to the town market, where an elevated platform had been set up, along with chairs for fifty VIPs. The crisp autumn air was filled with the pungent smell of burning leaves.

The mayor kicked off the proceedings, introducing Billy in gushy terms. He described him as "the greatest hero of Great Britain or the empire."

"We are here," he blustered, "to do honour to some of the brave boys who have been adding to the name and fame of Canada. The heroic acts of Major Bishop will live on as long as time itself!"

The crowd spontaneously broke into a verse of "The Maple Leaf Forever," led by a Salvation Army band. Local high school students, including some boys eager to reach enlistment age, broke into their football rallying cry.

A whole parade of politicians then took to the microphone and, unintentionally, drove home the fact that enlisting was just about the most dangerous thing a young man could do. One, an MP, declared that Billy "is the only living man who has won the three decorations, the VC, DSO and MC. Owen Sound is proud of him. Two others have been given these awards but they have gone to the great beyond."

The mayor added, "The first VC to come to Canada was won by a Grey County boy, Captain Frederick Campbell. He served in the South African War and lost his life in the present struggle."

Strong pitches were made to young men in the audience still not yet in uniform. It was a blatant effort to embarrass and shame them into enlisting. Dr. Jamieson, a local MLA, strutted up to the podium and, with jowls flapping, thundered: "One thousand men such as Major Bishop would settle the war!" He expressed the preposterous opinion that the war would be won in the air.

MP J.R. Bell wondered aloud "whether or not some people realize their great duty during the present crisis?" The war, he continued, "will cement the different parts of Canada as nothing else could have done." The most ludicrous remark of all came from the lips of a local judge, who told the gathering: "I am sure that I speak for everyone here today in saying to Major Bishop how glad I am to welcome him home. It is impossible to say how important his work has been to Canada, the empire and to Christianity itself!"

Billy, having killed a good many German airmen and an un-determined number of ground troops in strafing attacks, must surely have cringed. Even someone with a limited knowledge of the teachings of Christ is aware that the machine-gunning of people does not pro-mote Christianity. Interestingly enough, German airmen had the words "God is with us" inscribed on their belt buckles. They, too, claimed to be killing for Christ.

Billy, nevertheless, played his role as war hero very well. After being presented with a ring from the town, he addressed the worshipping crowd. "Mr. Chairman and citizens of Owen Sound ...."

Thumping applause interrupted him.

"I have little experience in speech-making but I am absolutely over-whelmed by this reception and the presentation of the ring and civic address. I cannot fittingly express my feelings but I take it as a sign of the great interest taken by the people of Owen Sound in the war.

"I have flown over Vimy Ridge and around Lens this past spring and have seen much of what Canadians have accomplished. Everywhere there are reports of the wonderful work of the Canadians and, particu-larly, their success in making trench raids has become a byword of the whole army. At present they are in such demand that every squadron commander eagerly grabs one every chance he gets.

"I'm sorry that my work has kept me from seeing many of the Owen Sound boys while in France, so that I could tell their relatives about them. I have had many proud days during the past three months, including a trip to Buckingham Palace, but never anything to equal this. It is a dream come true. I thank you from the bottom of my heart."

The *Sun* concluded the story by appealing to its female readers to continue knitting and baking for soldiers overseas. They now had, the writer said, "a newer realization of the worth of the recipients, for that worth is emphasized by a young soldier who is all on fire with the enthusiasm of one who has seen for himself how splendid Canada's men have fought and are fighting."

After the festivities in Owen Sound, Bishop was sent around the country giving speeches. In Toronto, crowds broke through barriers to get at him and he rode down Bay Street in a parade. And in Massey Hall a wildly enthusiastic standing-room-only audience greeted him.

He was all over the place. One day he was in London visiting sick children in hospital. The next would find him in Dayton, Ohio, meeting with Orville Wright, one of the inventors of the aeroplane. Indeed, he was in just about every community from Montreal to Dayton. There was a brief stop in Ottawa and, although he did not get to see Prime Minister Robert Borden, he was pleased when Parliament recognized his exploits with a congratulatory motion.

From there it was on to Kingston for a visit to Royal Military College. Here he was wined and dined by the very men who had treated him like a contemptible dog only three years earlier. The instructors who had branded him a liar and a cheat, and who had run a school in which he was forced to eat spiders and kiss the seniors, sat around a table with the new national hero and lavished praise on him. They were, of course, attempting to take credit for helping to make him such an outstanding military success.

After another round of spectacular public appearances, it was off to Toronto for his wedding at Timothy Eaton Memorial Church. Billy, in typical fashion, was late for the service. Along with his best man, he had stopped off at a bar to build up his courage with several drinks. At the church, they were refused entry by the honour guard, which announced gruffly that there were no empty pews left for guests!

After it finally got underway, the wedding was a fairytale affair, of a kind not seen before in Canada. The handsome young war hero marrying his beautiful childhood sweetheart — it was a made-to-order romance that took the public's mind off more pressing matters. As Billy and Margaret left the historic old church, they passed under an arch of ceremonial swords that were drawn by Canadian cavalry officers. Throngs of spectators followed the newlyweds to the Burden home and, later, to the train station as they left for their honeymoon in New York's Catskill Mountains.

Following his honeymoon, Bishop was sent on a tour of the United States. Officially, his mission was to help organize American aircraft production, but his main task was actually to stimulate enlistment.

He made speeches wherever he went. And although he was rather shy at first, he had overcome his stage fright by the time he addressed a crowd of 800 that had assembled at the Biltmore hotel in New York City. A reporter was on hand to record the event. He described Bishop as "a mere slip of a boy, looking not at all his twenty-three years and weighing not much more than 100 pounds." He added: "Looking like a college freshman, he told of his exploits in a manner as cool as if he were reciting a lesson in a classroom."

It was a bloodthirsty crowd and Billy told them what they wanted to hear.

The journalist wrote: "He said the greatest thing about air fighting was to get bullets into the heads of the Hun flyers — not just one bullet, but 'hunks of 'em.' If one brought them down in flames, he said, one was lucky because the job was complete."

The speech brought wild cheers from the audience.

Warming up to the occasion, Billy then told them he had occasionally flown as high as 22,000 feet, and added, "There is always the danger of being attacked from above." There were gasps from the gathering.

"Bombing is an interesting part of our work," he added. "At first, all the bombing was done from a height of about 12,000 feet. In the Battle of the Somme, some great airman missed a bridge with two of his three bombs at a height of 12,000 feet.

Then he flew down to about 200 feet and blew up the bridge with his last bomb. Now we all do it."

Low level flying was "awful," he told them, because of the danger of ground fire from both friend and foe.

Then, being overly melodramatic, he told them that his squadron had once gone through fifty planes in "two or three days." The audience loved it and accorded him a thunderous standing ovation.

From New York it was on to Washington, to advise the American government on aircraft production.

Pompous American politicians were strutting around the countryside beating their breasts and promising that US machines would darken the skies over Europe. When Billy got an inside look at the situation, he was shocked to discover that the Americans were woefully unprepared to produce military aircraft. Back in Canada, he outlined his concerns in a speech to the Canadian Club in Montreal.

This was no recruitment drive pep rally. He frankly told a hushed audience that American aircraft production was far behind schedule. He predicted that, because neither the French nor the British were able to churn out planes at the same rate as Germany, the Allies would face a terrible ordeal in the spring of 1918.

Finally, in January 1918, the touring ended. On the twelfth of that month, with orders in his pocket assigning him the task of organizing his own fighter squadron in England, Billy and Margaret boarded a ship in Montreal. No sooner had they settled when a knock came at the cabin door. Bishop opened it to be greeted by a military policeman. He was placed under arrest!

Billy, although now facing a possible court-martial, did not seem particularly disturbed by the turn of events. He was a national hero and realized it was most unlikely that a VC man would be drummed out of the service in disgrace. Nevertheless, he was in hot water. His remarks to the Canadian Club had been carried in major newspapers in England and France, and had also been reprinted in Germany.

The major was called up on the carpet and given a severe reprimand. What he had said, Billy was told, was true — the admiral delivering the tongue-lashing conceded that much. But the point was that it should not have been said publicly. He had offended a valuable ally and had handed the enemy a morale boost.

Billy, a lifelong rebel, always seemed to know instinctively when to draw back. He did not push matters too far, pretending he was remorseful. As he had expected, he was let off with nothing more than a stern lecture.

Then, he was off to England.

CHAPTER THIRTEEN

The motor car pulled up in front of a fashionable four-storey mansion in Berkeley Square. A pretty young chauffeur — she didn't look a day over eighteen — stepped from the vehicle and opened the rear door. Major Billy Bishop emerged from the back seat, fitted his cap on a rakish angle atop his head and instructed the girl to park the car.

Bishop had arrived for a 6 P.M. party being staged by some of the pilots whom he had chosen for his new fighter squadron, Number 85. Several of them had chipped in to rent the house, which was owned by an elderly English lord, for the not inconsiderable sum of ten pounds per week. The old gentleman had retreated to the countryside and his elegant home had become 85 Squadron's unofficial headquarters.

The major was welcomed at the door by a butler who took his coat and cap. The servant, as well as a cook, was included with the rent.

Bishop strode purposefully across a bright red carpet into a large, comfortable study. The room was immense. A huge oak desk, situated in front of a massive stained glass window, was barely noticeable. Quaint oil paintings of Sussex farm scenes were positioned prominently. The lord had a superb collection of antique weapons: ancient swords, flintlock duelling pistols, battle axes, sabres, daggers, maces, war clubs, British army bayonets and machetes hung from the walls. There were, as well, hunting trophies, including stuffed heads of animals from Africa and Europe, above doorways and the fireplace mantel.

Bishop proceeded to the dining room, where his men greeted him.

He had handpicked them and, because of that, they worshipped Bishop. It was a great honour to be chosen by the most decorated man in the empire. Little did they realize that Bishop had selected them simply because they were the only pilots available. Front line squadrons were clamouring for reinforcements in a desperate effort to beat back a major German offensive and, consequently, most of the best flyers had been sent to France to bolster existing units.

The major had put together a curious collection of greenhorns and old pros. The group included three Americans, six Canadians, one South African, two New Zealanders, an Irishman, two Scots, a pair of Australians and six Englishmen.

One of the young Americans, John Grider, had heard rumours that 85 Squadron was going to be sent out after Richthofen's Flying Circus. Old Richthofen was still playing havoc with Allied units. Since returning to the Front after an extended leave, the Red Baron had bagged another fifteen British pilots, bringing his score up to seventy-eight victories.

But Grider, like the rest of the "Flying Foxes," as Number 85 had been dubbed, was confident that the group could give Richthofen a run for his money. With "The Great Bishop" as their leader, Grider was certain the outfit would distinguish itself.

Bishop had done nothing to harm morale when he announced that every pilot who scored two or more kills would be allowed to attach a fox tail to the struts of his plane. Clearly, he anticipated success and that confidence was rubbing off on the others.

In the dining room, Bishop found his men in a joyous mood. Elliott White Springs, one of the Yanks, stood at the head of the table, acting as master of ceremonies. He was serving dinner, grabbing fish by the tail and tossing them around the table. His aim was remarkable, with most of the seafood landing on or near the plates it was targeted for. The English cook watched the proceedings with an incredulous look on his face.

Springs was a Princeton graduate who had left his wealthy family to seek adventure in the skies over France. He was a fun-loving, hard-drinking womanizer whom Bishop was counting on to keep spirits high.

Off to the side was a tub that was filled to the brim with eggnog. At each table setting was a bottle of champagne and one of port.

At about 8 P.M., when all the fish, soup and drinks had been consumed, everyone except Grider got up and began chasing one another around the mansion. The harried butler tried for a few minutes to restore order and then, defeated, slumped into a chair. Finally, the roughhousing culminated in a wild wrestling match in the study. When they were all too tired to continue, the flyers lay on the carpet and laughed until they cried.

Someone suggested that they top off the evening by going to a nearby theatre.

It would never do to go unarmed! one man cried.

With that, they proceeded to pull the antique weapons out of their racks and spilled out into the street. Grider could not believe that they weren't arrested before they reached the theatre. It was an incredible scene: nineteen of the king's officers, including a Victoria Cross winner, wallowing drunkenly in the streets of London brandishing axes, spears and war clubs.

Somehow, the group found its way to the theatre and into one of the boxes overlooking the stage. The inevitable happened. In the middle of the first act one of the Americans, a lanky Kentuckian named Larry Callahan, stood up and, in an egregious pantomime of awkwardness, stumbled against the railing, dropping his war club. It fell like a rock, crashing with unexpected suddenness into a drum on stage. An actor nearly jumped out of his skin and a collective gasp went through a stunned audience.

Another pilot, Lobo Benbow, leapt to his feet to steady Callahan and lost his own balance, tumbling headfirst out of the box. Benbow, an Englishman who wore a monocle in his eye, had a rather dignified air about him when he was sober. But now he was dangling helplessly out of a theatre box while Bishop and the others struggled to pull him back in by his polished boots. Those looking on from below were flabbergasted.

Eventually, London Bobbies escorted the Flying Foxes out of the theatre. Only some quick talking by Bishop, who reminded the police that his lads were about to leave for the Front, saved them all from a night in jail.

Bishop was having a good time in England. He had been allowed to pick his own chauffeur and, in true form, had selected an attractive girl. But Billy could hardly take advantage of the situation because Margaret was now close at hand. The couple had rented a house near the aerodrome where the Foxes were training. Margaret, in fact, was kept busy entertaining the pilots in her home. They often stayed late into the night, shocking her with their wild parties and heavy drinking.

Still, she was so happy to be in England with her husband that she hardly complained at all. And when there weren't any pilots around to entertain, she occupied herself with painting lessons, trying to keep her mind off the fact that Billy would soon be going back into combat.

For his squadron, Billy had used every trick in the book to ferret out the best men available. He had snagged his three Americans by devious means, virtually snatching them away from other squadrons.

Springs, for instance, had been on his way to a squadron in France when Bishop submitted a false report to the War Office recommending that the Yank be kept in England for further training. Springs was fuming until he discovered that Bishop had held him back so that he could get the American for 85 Squadron.

Grider and Callahan had been destined to join one of the new American aero squadrons when the Canadian again intervened. Grider described how the coup was accomplished, writing in his diary: "They are letting Bishop pick his own pilots and he went with us to the US headquarters to try to arrange it. Colonel Morrow said it couldn't be done. The whole staff nearly lost their eyes staring at us when we strolled out, arm and arm with the great Bishop."[1]

After the squadron was formed, the Flying Foxes moved to the country for a rest, taking up residence in a little community by the sea called Eastbourne. Before long, several pilots got drunk and drove up to a cliff overlooking the town. There, Springs lost his balance and tumbled over the side of the ridge. He hung on for dear life while the others attempted to lower a rope to him. Looking down, he could see that he was about 100 feet above a pile of jagged stones. His intoxicated companions barely managed to pull him to safety.

Springs indeed seemed determined to kill himself. Once, he dove head first into an empty swimming pool and ripped a layer of skin off the side of his face.

But Bishop came closest to losing the American when Springs

became involved in an altercation with a group of Tommies. He was seated in a bar next to about half a dozen British soldiers when a tall guard officer announced loudly: "I've been reading in the papers until I'm bloody well sick of it, about the number of American troops that have come over. But what I can't understand is why none of them will fight. Paris is full of them, London is full of them, but they all jolly well stay away from the Front. None of them will fight. He directed the venomous words at Springs, along with a menacing glance.

Springs froze for a moment, looking down at his drink. Before Bishop or anyone else could intervene, he took matters into his own hands.

"Well," Springs declared, "Here is one of them that will."[3] Without another word he spun around like an uncoiling cobra and lashed out with an overhand right. The fist smacked into the Englishman's jaw with resounding force. The Tommy's head snapped back and he collapsed in a heap.

A second guardsman came forward and took a wild swing. Springs ducked it and raced out the door with a swarm of men running after him. He scrambled down to a dock, dove into a rowboat and made good his escape. But he was not out of trouble yet; the boat had no oars and he drifted helplessly down river in the dark. He only avoided going over a raging waterfall by swimming to shore after he detected the sound of rushing water just ahead.

The War Office, in a rare display of common sense, insisted in early May that Bishop and his men undergo a brief refresher course before flying to France. It had been nine months since Bishop's last dogfight and since that time both the Allies and the Germans had introduced new, more powerful aeroplanes.

However, before long, their training flights over the green English countryside degenerated into a series of wild barnstorming displays, with the pilots often terrorizing the civilian population.

On one sunny afternoon the Flying Foxes steeple-chased down a meandering river, skimming their wheels just above the surface. Spencer Horn actually dipped his landing gear briefly into the water. Callahan roared over a bridge, clearing the structure by no more than an inch or two. Springs came back trailing 200 feet of telephone wire from his wheels.

Bishop contented himself with bouncing his undercarriage off a raft.

Along one stretch of the waterway they found a well-to-do couple out for a boat ride. The gentleman was outfitted in a red blazer and was standing by the stern. His lady friend was seated in the bow, twirling a rather large pink parasol when the flight of SE5As came screaming down on top of them. Grider recalled: "As we dove on them, the man fell overboard and the girl lost her parasol. I looked back to see it floating down the river and the man in the blazer floundering about in a regular whirlpool."[4]

When the airmen landed, an RAF colonel was waiting for them, flanked on either side by hulking military policemen. "Bishop was told the man he'd buzzed on the river was a cabinet minister and a personal friend of Prime Minister Lloyd George," said pilot Tommy Williams. "The poor fellow had nearly drowned ... had to be rescued by the lady with the pink parasol, which was rather embarrassing. All hell had broken loose and he was demanding somebody's head. When the colonel asked for an explanation, Bish said, 'We were chasing a hedge-hopping Hun raider down the river.' The colonel replied, 'You'd better come up with something better, Bishop, or you'll be spending the rest of this war in the stockade.'"

The politician was insisting that someone be disciplined and was threatening to call for a full-scale inquiry. When the colonel suggested Billy blame the incident on one of his young Americans, he flatly refused. "We were all guilty and I won't throw one man to the wolves," he retorted. Just when it appeared that he was headed for a major showdown that he could not win, Bishop heard that the woman with the parasol was not the cabinet minister's wife. He let it be known that he was in possession of that fact and that he would welcome an inquiry: "I'll just get on the stand and say Springs had engine trouble and was looking for a spot to ditch, if that became necessary. We were following to mark the spot where he went down, when we flew too low over the minister and his mistress ... I mean his lady friend."

When informed of Bishop's plan, the cornered politician agreed to drop the whole affair.

Needless to say, Billy's popularity with his men, especially the three Yanks, was growing in leaps and bounds.

He cemented the friendship even further one afternoon when he was having drinks with the trio, who had by now been dubbed the "Three Musketeers." An American Air Service colonel showed up asking for an audience with Bishop.

"Well," Billy asked his three lieutenants, "Should we invite him in to tea?"[5]

"Certainly not!" Grider snorted. "No colonel would ever invite us to anything but a court martial."[6]

"Tell him to wait," Bishop instructed an orderly.

Twenty minutes later, the colonel was astonished to see three junior officers emerge from Bishop's office. He had been kept waiting by a group of subalterns in slacks and shirts.

Amid all this, the Foxes did find some time for military flying. On May 17, with RAF generals looking on, Bishop led the squadron through an impressive performance of tight formation flying and followed it up with a dazzling display of aerial acrobatics. The nineteen pilots performed flawlessly, until Springs crash-landed, completely burying his head in mud. The Flying Foxes were almost ready for the Front.

The situation on the Western Front had been grim for weeks as the Flying Foxes prepared to move out for France. Germany's defeat of Russia had allowed it to transfer a million men from the east. Realizing that they had to win the war before the United States could reinforce the Allies in significant numbers, the Germans had launched an all-out offensive in late March.

The attack had fallen with devastating force, hurling British and French armies back forty miles. Paris was threatened for the first time since 1914 and, in London, there was a state of near panic. The Allies were in almost total disarray.

In the air, the Richthofen Circus, equipped with the deadly new Fokker triplane, was winning one spectacular victory after another. The

Red Baron himself shot down two Sopwith Camels on April 20, killing another British squadron commander in the process. The double victory gave him the unprecedented total of eighty officially confirmed conquests. If Bishop was to become the war's leading ace he would have to get back into action soon.

He had already lost the title of RAF ace of aces. While he had been in Canada, Jimmy McCudden had surpassed the fifty mark, bringing his score up to fifty-seven. But the Englishman was now home on leave himself, and Bishop hoped to regain the lead in the coming weeks.

On April 21 came news from the Front that struck like a bombshell. Richthofen had been killed. The mighty ace had gone down behind Allied lines after a fierce dogfight with two Canadian Camel pilots. One of them, Roy Brown, was credited with the victory.

Richthofen had been pursuing a novice from Edmonton named Wilfred May at treetop level when Brown approached from above and behind and got in a burst from his twin Vickers guns.

There is no doubt that Brown's fire struck the German Fokker tri-plane. Captain Oliver LeBoutillier, another Camel pilot who was in the middle of the famous scrap, confirmed as much in a 1959 interview. He said: "Brown's speed was terrific — at least half again of the two hedge-hopping planes over the Somme. In fact, his speed was so great that when he pulled out above and behind the German plane, he had only a very few seconds for firing. I clearly saw his tracers strike the red triplane, and I would judge he had only time to fire about forty rounds from both guns. The red triplane immediately pulled up and to the right."[7]

At one point in his dive, LeBoutillier recalled, he was only two plane lengths away from Richthofen. About forty-five seconds later, he esti-mated, the Fokker crashed. During that time, he added, he did not see the German's guns fire or any further movement in the cockpit.

Although it appeared to be a clear-cut case of a victory for Brown, complications quickly arose. The Red Baron crashed smack in the midst of Australian machine gun positions near Corbie Hill in the Somme Valley and several Aussies immediately claimed to have laid him low.

Most of the witnesses to Richthofen's death were Australians and, perhaps not surprisingly, they backed up the various stories of their countrymen. Many aviation historians and writers have taken their accounts as gospel — to the extent that it has now become standard to accept the story that the Red Baron was killed by ground fire.

But the truth is that the Australians could not even agree among themselves as to what really happened. At least three different machine gunners claimed the honour of downing the ace, along with one soldier who fired a single shot at the triplane with a rifle! They all insisted that the Fokker crashed just after they had fired on it. Some of the Aussies who examined the body of the dead German reported it was riddled with bullets while others said Richthofen had been shot through the heart by a single slug. Most of the Aussies even went so far as to claim that there were only two aircraft involved in the action — Richthofen's Tripe and May's Camel. But here again there were contradictions. A few Australians did admit that a second Sopwith was on the scene — at least for a few moments. In fact, there were no fewer than four Camels in the immediate vicinity. Three of those pilots — May, LeBoutillier and Francis Mellersh — all submitted combat reports backing up Brown, and each of them had a much better view of the fight than anyone on the ground.

Much has been made of medical evidence, with many insisting it proved that the fatal shot came from below. But again there is conflicting documentation, as some medics reported that the killing burst came from the sky. In reality, the medical examinations were nothing more than surface probes of the wound, with no attempt being made to open up the body.

Many denied Brown the victory because the Fokker continued to fly for forty-five to sixty seconds after the Canadian stopped firing and before it struck the earth. But it is possible that the machine could have continued that long on a level course — even with a dead pilot at the controls — before gliding in to crash. Indeed, Mellersh reported that the triplane was in a glide when it crash-landed.

In fairness to the Australians, they were not the only ones to rush forward with claims from the ground after a famous pilot met his fate.

After the death of each of the war's greatest aces there was, almost inevitably, a claim from below. Mick Mannock died while engaging the crew of Leutnant Schoepf and Vizefeldwebel Hein, and although it is entirely possible that the air gunner Schoepf delivered the fatal blow, most histories automatically give the credit to a man in the trenches. Schoepf never did submit a claim because he and Hein were killed in that same fight.

And when Albert Ball died in a pitched battle with pilots from Jasta 11, an unnamed gunner in a church tower was presented to the world as his victor. Because thousands of people preferred to believe that such legendary figures as Richthofen, Ball and Mannock could not possibly be bested by other airmen, the claims of the various ground gunners have probably been given more credence than they deserved.

All of this does not rule out the Australian claims completely. Ground fire was always a possibility when any aircraft was shot down, so there is at least a chance that an Aussie snared Richthofen. But it is also known for certain that Brown, an experienced ace with a dozen kills to his credit, got within a scant two plane lengths of Richthofen's Fokker (an incredibly close distance in aerial combat) before pouring tracers directly into it. And shortly after that, Manfred von Richthofen was dead on the ground.

Thus, although the Australian claims should not be dismissed out of hand, the fact remains that the odds are every bit as good that it was the Canadian Roy Brown who shot down the war's greatest fighter pilot.

The RAF was more than satisfied and granted Brown a second Distinguished Service Cross.

Bishop, for his part, did not greet the news with the joy that one might expect. He felt a strange sense of regret, even sorrow, now that his old nemesis was gone. Later, he was quoted as saying he wished Richthofen had been captured alive.

Billy had indeed mellowed since the days when he had had a burning ambition to take the Red Baron's life. If Richthofen's violent end disturbed Bishop, it may well have been because it drove home to him his own mortality. He would soon be going back into combat and, although he was an old hand at the game, there was no guarantee he would survive. If a fabulous ace such as Richthofen could be killed, no one was safe in the dangerous skies over France.

Before leaving for the Front, the Flying Foxes took London by storm one last time. The nineteen airmen, Grider told his diary, downed 200 bottles of champagne in a single drunken binge. Obviously, the figure is an exaggeration. Each man would have had to consume more than ten bottles to dispose of that much alcohol. But there is no doubt that they all dipped a little too heavily into the stuff. One pilot had to be physically restrained when he attempted to "fly" to France right then and there by jumping out a third storey window.

When Number 85 finally left for the coast in mid-May 1918, a leading British actress was overheard to mutter, "Thank God, Bishop and his crowd have finally gone to France."[8]

The next morning the pilots, all of whom were nursing painful hangovers, assembled at Hounslow Aerodrome for an 11 A.M. departure.

The sendoff of an RAF squadron had become something of a social event. A huge crowd of well-wishers, including families and friends of the airmen, members of the royal family, a few representatives of the top brass and several local dignitaries, was on hand.

Margaret was clearly nervous. She took some of the pilots aside when Billy wasn't looking and asked them to take care of her husband. "Promise me that you'll stick to the major and not let a Hun get on his tail?" she pleaded.[9] They all agreed, although none of them believed there was a German pilot alive who could outfight their leader.

Despite the audience, Margaret passionately kissed Billy good-bye. When they parted he could see she was on the verge of tears.

On the tarmac, nineteen ochre-winged SE5As sat with their 200 horsepower Wolseley Viper engines idling. Bishop's bluenose was out in front with the other aeroplanes arranged behind it in three V-shaped flights of six each.

Bishop called his men to attention while a Royal Air Force general delivered a brief speech. When he had concluded, Bishop huddled his pilots together for his final instructions before take-off. They were to fly to a drome at Petit Synthe near Dunkirk.

Then, forgetting that he was within earshot of a huge civilian audience, he pointed to the windsock and yelled out: "Be sure to look at the condom when you're coming in to land. Land squarely into the wind."[10]

Bishop suddenly turned as red as a beet. Margaret hid her face and several of the other ladies, their mouths open in horror, lowered their parasols. The major turned quickly away, jumped into his machine and took off. The others followed just behind him.

The flight across was not uneventful. One pilot suffered engine trouble and made a crash-landing near Croydon. The squadron stopped at Folkestone for lunch and a second pilot smashed his SE5A there. A third man crash-landed on the beach just as the Foxes headed out over the English Channel. Grider's motor skipped badly and he kept picking out ships below so that he could ditch beside one of them, if the need arose. Two more pilots wrecked their planes landing in France.

No one was hurt, but it was not a noteworthy beginning for the squadron. It seems likely that excessive drinking was to be blamed for much of the misfortune. Springs, for one, was seen drinking out of a flask as he flew over the channel.

Nevertheless, the Flying Foxes were now in France. Billy Bishop's second, and most sensational, tour of duty as a fighter pilot was about to get underway.

Bishop took in a magnificent view as he flew over Dunkirk in search of Petit Synthe aerodrome. Below him, tiny boats fishing for cod and herring cut through the Atlantic waters just offshore. Dunkirk, a little fishing village on the northeast coast, was a vital manufacturing centre and seaport. It was one of the few harbours in all of France capable of accommodating ocean ships, and he could see three canals jutting out from the town to the sea.

The communities around Dunkirk were lovely, surrounded by ancient walls and moats. One of them, a place called Gravelines, was noteworthy for its star-shaped walls. As the Flying Foxes flew overhead, sunlight reflected off the moat, giving it the appearance of a giant, glittering jewel.

Bishop found the Petit Synthe aerodrome two miles south of Dunkirk. It was the home of two DH9 bomber units as well as 85 Squadron. The major could see that a network of trenches and sandbag dugouts surrounded the airfield. In a clearing beyond the drome, thousands of Chinese coolies, dressed in padded blue uniforms, were busy with shovels, filling sandbags. They had been brought halfway across the globe to build defensive positions behind the front lines.

The Foxes had arrived with nothing more than their planes and the few personal belongings they could fit into their cockpits. But the DH9 crews welcomed them with open arms, gladly sharing their provisions with the men who would be providing them with fighter escorts on their raids on German submarine pens farther up the coast.

Bishop talked at length with the bomber pilots in an effort to find out as much as he could about the opposition facing them in the district. The Dunkirk area was relatively quiet, with the competition being provided mainly by lesser-known Jagdstaffels. The enemy airmen were among the greenest in the Imperial Air Service and they were equipped with old Albatros and Pfalz fighters. They were good planes — by 1917 standards — but not a match for the new, high-powered SE5A.

There was even an Austrian anti-aircraft battery in the vicinity that fired pink-coloured flak! Although it was every bit as dangerous as the traditional black-coloured Archie, nobody could take an exploding pink puff-ball very seriously.

There were some skilled German flyers in the area, notably Theodore Osterkamp and Paul Billik. Billik was perhaps the most brilliant, having scored more than thirty victories, including the downing of Canadian ace Nick Carter.

But the real action was farther south, where the aces of the Richthofen Circus were hunting in the new Fokker D-7 fighter. It was easily the best German single-seater of the war.

Bishop was told his outfit would be stationed at Petit Synthe for about a month before heading south.

Billy spent his first night sleeping on a beat-up old mattress with a moth-eaten blanket. Before turning in, he wrote Margaret a letter, concluding with: "Goodnight my darling, you were a real brick and it made my heart ache to see tears so near to your eyes."

Bishop and a handful of his men went into Dunkirk the next morning to seek out supplies for the mess. While two pilots loaded up a truck, he strolled down to the wharves. The smell of fish and salt water filled the air. Tubs full of iced cod and cabbage lay in neat rows on the docks. White building façades and boathouses crowded the shoreline. The whole town seemed crowded up against the sea.

Suddenly, Bishop noticed that people were closing up their shops and carting goods indoors. The streets were quickly emptying. Walking up to a shoe salesman, he asked why the whole town was closing down so early in the day.

The Frenchman urged him to take immediate cover. The Boche fired exactly four shells at Dunkirk every morning at this time, he said. They were unimaginative people, the Boche, he added. You could set your watch by them. Four rounds every day at the same time. Minutes later, as if on cue, four shells from long-range cannons at Ostend ripped into Dunkirk.

Bishop, who had taken shelter in an alley, emerged to see the front of the shoestore had been torn away, scattering merchandise all over the street. People had come out of their houses and were going about their business as if nothing had happened. The shoe salesman was even selling damaged boots at discount prices right in the middle of the road!

A few moments later, down on the dock, Bishop spotted a young boy fall into the water. The lad, who was no more than five, thrashed about helplessly while his panic-stricken schoolmates cried for help. Without hesitation, Billy dove into the bay and pulled the toddler to safety.

"The boy was fishing when he fell in," pilot Tommy Williams recalled nearly seventy years later. "Bishop saved him, no question. And it was never reported. You won't find it in any of the books or articles about him. He wasn't the type to toot his own horn about that sort of thing. But another 85 Squadron man saw it and told me about it after the war. I've always felt that a man known for killing didn't get any credit for saving a little boy's life."

While Bishop was plucking the child from the water, his men were buying provisions, including a piano, a phonograph, an ice cream maker and several boxes of champagne.

Soon there was a vacation atmosphere around the aerodrome. The Americans taught the cook how to make Eggs Benedict, which made breakfast an event each morning, and the Foxes were the only squadron in France that enjoyed ice cream after every dinner. As Grider noted in his diary: "In the midst of life we are in death. And in the midst of death we manage to have a hell of a lot of fun. Bronx, cocktails, chicken livers en brochette, champagne, strawberry ice-cream and Napoleon brandy. That's the way we live. I don't think Bish is sorry he brought us along."

There were the obligatory drunken parties too. The Foxes invited the DH9 crews over and a wild scene ensued. Table dancing followed a bottoms-up competition. The commander of the two-seater outfit, a full colonel, collapsed a table he was standing on and had to be carried out, stone drunk, and tossed boots first into his staff car. Bishop was right in the midst of the action, playing quarterback in a football game right in the mess. To liven things up, someone turned out the lights. Bishop and Callahan slammed together in the dark and were both knocked cold, although no one noticed for several minutes.

But it was not all fun and games — there was a war on. Bishop was slow to commit his men to battle. He had decided to make them all familiar with the region before allowing any of them to go hunting over the lines. And he demanded that each pilot sit in his aircraft on the tarmac for hours at a time, checking dials, gun sights and maps. He insisted that they practise continuously the loading of the Lewis gun on the top wing, realizing a quick change could make the difference between life and death in a dogfight. He wanted them to feel totally at home in their new machines. As one airman noted, "Bishop was determined not to make the same mistakes that had cost men their lives when he was a rookie flight leader in the spring of 1917."

But that did not mean he couldn't go looking for Germans on his own. On May 27, he decided it was time to give the Foxes a demonstration of what he expected from them.

In mid-afternoon he took off alone for the Front. It was his first combat mission in nine months and he later admitted he found himself savouring the anticipation of impending danger as he climbed into the cockpit. Even the hum of the engine on the flight line before a patrol was always enough to get his adrenaline flowing. The excitement of aerial combat gripped him firmly once again.

It was 4:30 P.M. when, flying 14,000 feet above Passchendaele, he spotted a German two-seater. His heart began beating a little faster as he prepared for his first combat since August 1917. Would his marksmanship still be with him? How about his nerves?

He found out soon enough.

Out of the clouds above him came ten Albatros D-5s. He stood his SE5A on its nose and roared through the enemy formation, firing as he went. The Germans scattered and Bishop dodged quickly into a cloud. They had almost nailed him and the experience did nothing to reassure him that he had not lost his touch.

But as the ace emerged from the fluff he was just in time to spot another black-crossed observation machine. The escorting fighters had vanished. The two-seater pilot, Kark Andrieson, spotted Bishop at the same instant and sideslipped to give his gunner, Leutnant Keil, a clear shot. Too late. Twenty rounds from the blue-nosed fighter ripped into the fuselage of the big biplane. Keil threw up his arms, jerked violently backward, and disappeared into his cockpit. Andrieson, too, had been hit and the two-seater lunged over like a wounded duck. It was obvious from its erratic movements that a living foot no longer guided the rudder. Bishop followed the plane down to make sure, showering fifty more slugs into it. The doomed aeroplane shed both wings and the tail fell away. That night an excited John Grider scrawled in his diary: "The major got a Hun two-seater today the other side of Ypres. First blood!"[1]

The next day, flying at 13,000 feet east of Ypres, Bishop climbed above nine Albatros D-5s from Jasta 7 before launching a bold single-handed thrust. The inability of the enemy pilots to maintain a proper formation immediately gave away their inexperience. The major swooped down mercilessly. Unerring fire from both guns tore into an oafishly flown Albatros, hacking up canvas and chewing the gas tank to tattered junk. Corporal Siche's machine exploded in flames and tumbled to earth. Bishop raced straight through the debris, continuing his power dive for another 600 feet before swerving to line up Corporal Peisker in his sights. He whipped out a short burst and watched as glowing red tracers sent a second D-5 down. Peisker, despite a bullet wound, managed to crash land in a field below. In two days Billy had shot down three planes and four men. He was back in the groove.

The thrill of the hunt — the urge to kill and kill again — seized him. His letters home indicate that his earlier compunction over the taking of human life had been overpowered by the incredible excitement of aerial combat. And there was his ego. He had taken great pride in his status as the top RFC ace. During his long layoff Jimmy McCudden had dethroned him and that irked him. It was time to restake his claim as the empire's ace of aces. He would worry about the remorse later.

In three days, from May 30 to June 1, he did just that. Flying and fighting like a madman, he shot down six Germans, bringing his score up to fifty-nine — two more than McCudden. In less than a week he had overcome a seven-kill deficit and was once again recognized as the RAF's deadliest ace. Moreover, he was now the leading Allied scorer because Georges Guynemer, the top French pilot, had been killed in action with fifty-three planes to his credit.

Bishop started his streak on the 30th, when he knocked down a pair of Albatros D-5s and a two-seater. He then closed out the month by downing two planes of a type he had not met before. They were the fast-diving Pfalz D-3 fighters. Although not as handy as the SE5A, they were considerably more dangerous than the old Albatros. Even so, Billy forced a wounded Leutnant Erich Kaus to land and shot a second German down out of control.

June came and he continued to hold a hot hand, scoring perhaps the greatest victory of his career when he shot down high-scoring ace Paul Billik, the commander of Jasta 52. Bishop shot down Billik's black-painted Pfalz during the evening patrol on the first of the month, but the thirty-one-kill ace survived with only a minor wound. A day later, on June 2, Bishop downed a black and white Pfalz.

He continued his pace as the week progressed, sending an Albatros down in flames on the 4th and sending a second D-5 down out of control on the same patrol.

All of this brought his total up to sixty-two. And the Albatros victories were registered in dramatic fashion. Flying over the North Sea, Billy sighted a flight of eight Germans droning along just above the waves between the coastal towns of Ostend and Nieuport. They were on the lookout for DH9s. Bishop stalked them patiently, waiting until one careless fellow strayed a bit behind the others. The ace then struck in a flash and vanished, phantom-like, into a cloud. The crippled Albatros plunged into the water, sending up a huge geyser before disappearing beneath the surface.

Startled by the attack, the other Germans milled about in confusion, looking for an intruder. Bishop seized a quick opportunity and sent a second man plummeting toward the water. It was almost child's play. Popping back into the clouds, he headed for home. It was small wonder that he wrote in a combat report that enemy pilots "seem to be afraid of SE5As."[2]

Perhaps mindful of the mistrust some people had in him during the middle portion of his stay with 60 Squadron, Bishop began sprinkling his victory claims with notations of supportive evidence. On May 31, for instance, he wrote at the bottom of a report: "This enemy aircraft must have been seen by AA batteries of the Second Army as visibility was very good." A couple of days later, in claiming another victory, he wrote: "Lieutenant Springs confirms the EA [enemy aircraft] I shot down." And just a day later, he noted, "This machine was seen and confirmed falling out of control by Lieutenant Callahan." John Grider's diary provides confirmation for another victory during this period. Grider noted that AA batteries confirmed a Bishop kill.

What was it like to be on the receiving end of an SE5A's guns? An inkling of that feeling can be gained by reading the diary of Leutnant Paul Strahle, a courageous Albatros pilot who was stationed in the Dunkirk district directly across the lines from the Flying Foxes. Strahle records being shot down twice in four days in late May. The first time, he came down in a shell-pocked field, slamming his head onto the top wing of his fighter as it flipped over. The plane was a total write-off and Strahle had a mild concussion. But he refused to leave the line. Three days later, he glided home with a dead engine; his Albatros had been hit sixteen times by bullets from an SE5A. He was wounded in the arm and there were oily splotches covering his face and most of his machine.

But if Strahle and the rest of the German fighter pilots in the area were not up to the formidable new challenge, that did not mean the Imperial Air Service's bomber crews couldn't do the job. Petit Synthe suddenly became a popular target for the Gotha and AEG night raiders. Canals in the vicinity made the aerodrome almost as conspicuous by moonlight as in the daytime.

At first, the Flying Foxes did not take the attackers very seriously. They stood around outside the mess on warm June nights and watched with drinks in their hands as the black-crossed planes flew overhead. But one night, Bishop was standing outside a dugout, arguing with a sentry that it wasn't necessary for him to wear a helmet, when a Gotha passed directly overhead. Billy clamped the headgear on just as a bomb exploded. A chunk of shrapnel struck the ace forcefully on the skull, denting the helmet and knocking him over. Although badly shaken, he was unhurt. After that, Grider told his diary, the Foxes swallowed their pride and scurried for cover at the first hint of raiders.

The DH9 crews at Petit Synthe were not so fortunate. A gaggle of Gothas came in low and illuminated the night sky with burning parachute flares. The flares glowed brightly, swinging leisurely on their chutes and washing the drome in green light. One of the twin-engine bombers scored a direct hit on a hangar with a king-sized phosphorous bomb. The big canvas tent burst into flames, lighting up every corner of the field. Another thirty-one bombs came raining down out of the night. When it was all over, the whole place was ravaged and forty men were dead. Few of the DH9s were destroyed because the squadron was out on a mission at the time. But when the planes returned, they found the drome in flames and the field too cratered to land on. Eventually, the machines set down on the beach at Dunkirk.

During these weeks, Bishop's popularity with his men began to suffer. Nothing was said to him but he could sense a change in attitude. He was fully aware of what was bothering them: they weren't getting much action. So far, the squadron had done remarkably well, but almost all the success was a result of Bishop's lone-wolf forays.

The pilots kept a big white scoreboard in the mess with a blood-red number on it to signify the group's kills. Of the first ten victories, no fewer than eight belonged to Bishop. That was not a healthy situation and the major knew it.

"The truth is, he wasn't a particularly good leader of men," said pilot Tommy Williams. "He seldom led a patrol and he did his best work while he was alone. Spencer Horn was the unofficial leader of the squadron. Everyone knew that Bishop should never have been given his own command."[3]

Springs became so frustrated waiting for his commander to show him how the game was played that he took off alone one afternoon and foolishly attacked six Germans by himself. After a ferocious dogfight, he barely escaped with his life, shaking off his determined attackers only by going into a near-suicidal power dive that peeled the canvas off his top wing.

When Springs got back to the aerodrome he was so badly shaken that he piled his SE5A right into Bishop's parked fighter. Both aircraft were wrecked, but the ham-fisted American was unhurt. Bishop, looking on from a hangar, angrily strutted across the field to deliver a stiff reprimand.

"That's three of our planes you've wrecked so far. Don't you think it's time you concentrated on the Huns?" Bishop demanded sarcastically.

Springs, undaunted, ran his fingers across the major's row of colourful ribbons.

"You see these medals? Well, I just want to tell you that you are welcome to them!" With that, he stomped off in a huff.

Bishop's popularity with his men reached its lowest point when he flatly refused to allow them to attend the funeral of Lobo Benbow. Poor Benbow, the man who had dangled headfirst out of a London theatre box, had become the Foxes' first casualty when he boldly tried to take on four Germans singlehanded. They blew him out of the sky in short order, shooting off both his wings. Benbow crashed behind Allied lines and was buried by strangers.

When the pilots argued that Benbow should not go to his grave in such a fashion, Bishop stood his ground, insisting that a funeral might unnerve them.

On June 8, word came through that the Foxes were to move south to St. Omer. During their brief stay at Petit Synthe they had bagged eighteen planes. Their leader registered a dozen of those kills. But now they were headed for a sector where intense fighting with some of Germany's better Jastas was anticipated. Now there would be plenty of opportunity for glory — and danger — for all of them.

Bishop was disappointed. The squadron's new home, located three miles south of St. Omer, was tiny. He was quickly discovering what other RAF flyers had known for years: Filescamp Farm was the best aerodrome in France. It had been a real gem, with a variety of recreational facilities and the longest runway on the Western Front.

This was nothing more than a field, about 300 yards square, cut out of a forest. The runway was lumpy and there was barely enough clearance to set down an SE5A. Fortunately, the quarters were comfortable. They were situated at the top of a lovely treed hill overlooking the flight line. A peaceful glade provided pilots a place to sleep between patrols.

When the Flying Foxes arrived, poor flying weather that restricted operations for several days greeted them. Bishop spent the time painting a red Indian, crawling on all fours, on the side of his plane. When he was done with that, he organized a visit to 60 Squadron, which was stationed nearby. To his shock, he recognized hardly a soul when he got there. He should have known better, but subconsciously he had been expecting to find the old crew that he had left in August 1917. Such was not the case. Most of those men were now dead.

Grider wrote in his diary: "It was a good party. I think we won, as when we left their CO was doing a Highland fling with a couple of table knives for swords."[5]

The Foxes arrived back in St. Omer just in time to be caught in the middle of an air raid. With Bishop and four other pilots all screaming instructions at the top of their lungs, the chauffeur raced down the narrow cobblestone streets with bombs exploding behind the car. Twice he jumped the curb in his panic.

As the foul weather persisted, the Foxes often went swimming in a nearby watering hole. One day, as they frolicked naked in the surf, several explosions shook the earth just 200 yards away. Someone frantically ordered them out of the water, warning of the danger of concussion. Bishop and the others scampered ashore and dashed for shelter. They raced, stark naked, up to a lorry and ordered the driver to take them out of the shellfire. The man laughed and told them nearby French troops was blowing up German mines brought ashore by minesweepers. It wasn't artillery fire at all.

The skies finally cleared on June 15. The Foxes were to patrol a sector from Ypres to Nieppe, and Bishop was ready for another round of dogfights. It was a "hot" area and it did not take him long to find his mark. Flying alone after supper, he stalked a fishtailed Pfalz east of Satires. A quick squirt from both guns gave him his first kill in more than a week. The next day, the 16th, he cut down two pilots, bringing his score up to sixty-five.

But there was shocking news waiting for him as he landed his plane that evening with the setting sun. That night he wrote to Margaret: "Here is the awful news. General Webb-Bowen rang up tonight to say that I had been recalled to England. Unofficially he told me it was at the request of the Canadian government. I have never been so furious in my life."[6]

The government wanted Bishop to survive the war. He was the first internationally famous hero the nation had produced and it would not do to have him killed during the last months of a war that was all but won. His death would be a serious blow to public morale. And someone would have to explain why a man who had done so much had been left at the Front for so long. Besides, he had been in uniform since 1914 and had more than earned a rest. Officially, it was announced that he would work on the formation of a Canadian Air Force. Bishop had been pushing for such a force himself, but he never dreamed that he would be hauled out of action to organize it. In another month, assuming he was not killed, he was sure he could surpass the Red Baron's record of eighty victories. The only consolation was that he was to be promoted again, this time to the rank of lieutenant-colonel. Bishop was under orders to stay on the ground until transfer papers came through. However, when one of the Foxes was killed in action, Bishop stormed into the office of an RAF colonel and announced:

"Mister, I'm flying again!"[7] The officer gave him permission to continue combat operations until formal word of his posting arrived.

Bishop used what few days were left to him to put on one of the bloodiest displays ever witnessed over the Western Front. On June 17, he blew apart an Albatros and a pair of two-seaters, downing five men with just fifty-five rounds of ammo. And he did it in a scant twenty minutes.

The next day, he bagged a pair of Albatros pilots. German Air Force units were highly mobile again, making it difficult to compare their casualty records to Allied victory claims with any degree of accuracy.

But long-suffering Jasta 56 was in the vicinity of 85 Squadron at this time and its records show two pilots lost that day — Leutnant Heins and Vizefeldwebel Kohler. Both were flying Albatros D-5s.

That afternoon a courier brought the official word. Billy was to leave for England the following day at noon. The Foxes gave him a rousing send-off, toasting him with a drinking bash that lasted until 3 A.M. At the height of the festivities he was overheard to moan, "Oh, for one more fight in the air!"[8] There was still time. If he rose early, he could squeeze in a morning patrol before heading back.

It is difficult, looking back now, to understand why Bishop was so anxious to risk a final flight over hostile territory. He had everything to lose and nothing to gain. His title of RAF ace of aces appeared safe and he had already won every honour in the empire. He could go home in one piece, with still another promotion and the prospect of living another forty years.

Why, then, did he sail back into combat? Probably because he realized that nothing he would ever do again would quite match the drama of his life as a fighter pilot. He was only twenty-four years old, yet he knew that whatever years were left to him would be anti-climactic. How would a daredevil ace adjust to life in an office, working behind a desk?

No matter what career he chose it could not match the thrills of his wartime experiences. He would always remember those sometimes-desperate days in France as the period when he felt the most alive. On the Front he was living, not just existing. He wanted to experience, one more time, the danger and undeniable excitement of an aerial duel.

The blue-nosed SE5A climbed through the overcast and headed east in the direction of Ypres.

Bishop was surprised to find that, in the upper sky, visibility was much better than it had been at ground level. He had a hangover from the previous night's bash and he did not really expect to find any enemies up in the wretched weather. But it was his last chance to bag a German or two and he could not pass it up.

Dropping out of the mist to gain his bearings, the ace found himself over the shattered stumps of Ploegsteert Wood. His hawk eyes caught sight of three brown specks moving away from him over to the left.

Pfalz!

Opening the throttle, he tugged back on the joystick, lifting the SE5A into a steep climb. Gaining the necessary altitude, the major paused momentarily to adjust his gun sight and in that instant the tables turned.

The Pfalz formation banked around and all three Germans came charging at the British plane with guns winking. Spandau bullets hacked into the tautly doped wings of the blue-nosed biplane. Bishop squeezed off an ineffectual burst of his own in the split second before the enemy dove under him to avoid a collision.

The reflexes of the most dangerous fighter pilot on the Western Front took over. Bishop's arms and feet worked the controls simultaneously, almost as if he had become part of the machine. He whipped the SE5A smartly around and went straight for the three Germans. Something told him to look behind and a quick glance revealed two more Pfalz fighters dashing out of the mist, their guns pointed in his direction. It was five against one, with three Germans in front of him and two on his tail.

Ignoring the planes to his rear as best he could, the Canadian met the head-on charge of the original three. One deadly burst from his guns raked the rearmost Pfalz, sending it down in a spinning nose-dive. The other two veered quickly out of his line of fire and, in their frozen panic, the Germans brushed together in a sickening mid-air crash. The machines, joined at the wing-tips, hurled into the forest below. Three down, two to go!

Bishop wasted not a moment, looping violently to throw off the aim of his rear antagonists. They flashed underneath and, having witnessed the fate of the other three, decided that discretion was the better part of valour. Both fled with noses well down, for the nearest cloudbank.

But the avenging SE5A was not about to let them get away. Bishop was on their tails in a flash, with his Vickers and Lewis thumping relentlessly from 200 yards out. A fourth Pfalz exploded in flames and crashed into the trees. The last German, who by now must have been whining with terror, barely managed to reach the clouds and safety.

Bishop had downed four men in as many minutes, but he still was not satisfied. He milled about the area for a few minutes and then stumbled onto a two-seater. His single-minded vendetta was paying off. The Germans had not seen him.

Bishop slipped under the reconnaissance machine and closed in for a point-blank shot at its looming fat belly. The crew was totally unaware of the sudden death creeping up on them. The observer's Parbelleum gun pointed idly skyward.

Twenty rounds sliced into the underside of the German plane. Flames instantly shot out from its engine and the plane keeled over, wobbling under only partial control. The wounded pilot struggled to control his burning machine. He fought desperately with the instruments, right up until the moment the plane slammed into a hillside. Bishop circled and watched as fire devoured his seventy-fifth victim.

He scoured the sky for more prey, but saw nothing. Reluctant to go home while he still had bullets in his guns, he dove on German troops below, blazing away until both guns went silent. With ammo exhausted and fuel running low, there was nothing more he could do. Billy Bishop climbed into the clouds and flew west. His war was over.

EPILOGUE

Was Billy Bishop a hero or a liar? That question has plagued aviation historians ever since researchers began matching Bishop's victory claims to German Air Force casualty records.

The cross-checking produced an alarming number of discrepancies and cast doubt upon some of Bishop's most famous exploits. Those doubts were magnified when it became clear that several of Billy's squadron mates were skeptical about the accuracy of some of his claims.

The controversy exploded into the open in 1982 with the release of a National Film Board of Canada documentary that suggested Bishop was a fraud. The film hinted strongly that Bishop lied about many of his victories, including his famed solo raid on a German airfield. A Canadian Senate committee conducted full-blown hearings into the charges in late 1985, in what turned out to be a vain attempt to get to the bottom of the issue. By the time the proceedings had concluded there were those who said that Bishop had actually shot down very few Germans — that his record of kills was highly dubious.

The root of the debate lies in the manner in which the Royal Flying Corps granted victories. Enthusiasts checking Bishop's record lost sight of a vital point. And that is the fact that there were four different victory categories in the RFC, including destroyed, driven down out of control (DOOC), driven down (DD) and forced to land (FTL). An enemy plane listed as destroyed was one seen to crash, fall apart in the air or go down in flames. Those categorized as DOOC were aircraft spotted falling out of control but not actually seen to crash. Such planes were usually considered to be in their death dives, but in reality, that was seldom the case. In fact, to drop into an intentional spin was a favourite tactic of a German pilot in trouble. Most planes claimed as DOOC by

RFC airmen in general were not, in fact, destroyed.

Machines reported as driven down were planes seen to fall, apparently at least under partial control. Such aircraft may have been damaged but in almost no cases were they actually destroyed. Planes listed as FTL were usually damaged and often contained wounded crewmen. But they were definitely not destroyed.

Unfortunately, both during and after the war, most writers (and many air force officials) simply added the four categories together and announced "victory totals." It was impossible for the public to differentiate among the various categories and it has generally been assumed that each "victory" represented a wrecked enemy plane and a dead German pilot. In Bishop's case the War Department helped foster the myth. In awarding Billy the Distinguished Flying Cross in 1918, it very flippantly announced: "The total number of machines destroyed by this distinguished officer is seventy-two (he also downed three balloons for a total of seventy-five aircraft.)"

But while Bishop was credited with seventy-five victories, by no means were all of the planes destroyed. In fact, records from 60 and 85 Squadrons show he claimed fifty planes as destroyed, seventeen down out of control, three forced to land, two driven down and three balloons, one of which was driven down. In other words, while he officially defeated seventy-five German aircraft in combat, only two-thirds of his victims were destroyed for certain.

It should be stated here that Bishop was not alone in this respect. Only twenty-eight of Albert Ball's forty-four victories were officially recorded as destroyed. Mick Mannock's sixty-one conquests included a full twenty as DOOC.

It is hardly surprising, therefore, that many "victories" of all the leading RFC aces cannot be substantiated in German records.

But that does not mean these men were frauds. A good case in point is the two German fighters credited to Bishop on April 22, 1917. German records indicate no aircraft were lost in the fight and it would be easy to accuse Billy of being overly optimistic in his claims — or even of outright lying.

However, the truth is that Bishop never claimed that he destroyed either of the enemy planes that day. This was the famous fight in which he used Jack Scott as a decoy and then swooped down to pick off the two Germans who fell into his trap. In his combat report he made no claim whatsoever of killing his two opponents. The report reads in part: "I fired fifteen rounds at one and he dived steeply, apparently damaged. I then attacked a second one from the flank and fired twenty rounds at him, most of the bullets apparently hitting his machine. He went down through the clouds, apparently out of control."

In this instance, Billy had five Allied witnesses — Scott and four other 60 Squadron pilots flying overhead. But he claimed one as only damaged and the other as DOOC. Squadron records show that Major Scott listed one as driven down and the second as DOOC. Both German planes disappeared into the clouds below and no one saw them crash.

Bishop pulled off the operation brilliantly, defeating two enemy pilots and very probably sending them both home in damaged machines. They had been removed as a threat. And although it is highly doubtful that either German aircraft crashed, Jack Scott was perfectly justified, under RFC rules, in crediting Billy with two "victories." Clearly, those who have questioned Bishop's integrity on that day are simply guilty of sloppy research.

Although Bishop was doubtlessly ambitious, his combat reports are often very modest. There are numerous statements such as: "I fired the remainder of my drum from long range at it, but cannot say whether I hit it or not." Or: "He dived away and I fired about thirty shots at him with no apparent results." Or: "I engaged them and one double-seater went down in a nose-dive but I think partly under control."

The number of witnessed Bishop victories is hotly disputed. Breteron Greenhous has said he could find no more than five written confirmations in Billy's combat reports, including just one for 1918, that being the Pfalz D-3 that Elliott White Springs saw Bishop shoot down on June 1 of that year. But in a combat report written the very next day, Bishop claimed another witnessed victory. The document, which is on file at the University of Western Ontario, reads as follows:

> I led Lt. Callahan and Lt. Thomson diving on eight E.A. I
> fired at four different E.A., one of which fell out of control
> for 1,500 feet, then broke up in pieces. This machine was
> seen and confirmed falling out of ocntrol by Lt. Callahan.

British researcher Timothy Graves is quoted in the October 30, 1988 edition of the *Toronto Star* as saying he found evidence that thirteen of Bishop's victories were witnessed.

In October 1984, Joe Warne, the official historian of 60 Squadron, sent the author a list of Bishop's 1917 victories claims that included ten which he believed were "confirmed by witness." The same document listed eight other claims in which, he said, "I deduce that others confirmed the action because Bishop was flying as a member of a patrol." In those cases, however, he could find no specific evidence of witnesses. He came to his conclusions after poring over "my huge collection of data for WW1."

I do not wish to misrepresent Warne's position on Bishop. He believed the Canadian received credit for many victories for which there was not a shred of evidence, including the three for which he won the VC. An honest and able researcher, Warne wrote "all air fighting claims have been proven over-optimistic, WW1, WW2 and Falklands included, and few aces' records can be satisfactorily matched, but BB's case appears to be disproportionately out of scale, particularly when compared with Ball and von Richthofen." Warne came to the reluctant conclusion that the majority of Bishop's claims were impossible to substantiate. But the very fact that Warne cannot be accused of being 'pro-Bishop' makes his conclusion that Billy had ten to eighteen witnessed victories in 1917 all the more credible.

My own opinion is that there were witnesses for at least twenty-three of Bishop's victories, including eighteen for 1917 and five for 1918. Some of the confirmations I uncovered are not to be found in official records. For example, William Molesworth of 60 Squadron mentions seeing Bishop shoot down an Albatros D-3 in flames in a letter he wrote home on the evening of August 5, 1917. He described the fight in detail, saying Bishop turned the German plane into "a flaming mass."

Another confirmation can be found in the diary of John Grider. Writing an entry for May 31, 1918, Grider noted:

> They are changing the score now as the major has just come down and has shot down two more Huns – a scout and a two-seater. Archie [the crew of an Allied anti-aircraft battery] saw one of them go down and another one broke up in the air.

In his combat report, Bishop made no mention of the fact that one of his victories had been witnessed. Had Grider not gone to the trouble of mentioning it in his diary, there would be no written record of it today. Nor was this the only time that happened. Authur Bishop inadvertently made that clear in his book, when he described his father's attack on two Albatros D-3s on the evening of May 30, 1918. He wrote:

> The sun was too low for Bishop to use as cover. So he dived under them and attacked from the rear. Both went down, billowing smoke. The second plane disappeared into a cloud bank and Bishop did not see it crash. When he landed he learned that the nearest anti-aircraft battery had reported seeing only one plane crash in flames. Although he was sure he had killed the pilot of the second plane with a double burst of machine gun fire at twenty yards range Bishop philosophically accepted the verdict: three confirmed kills in one day wasn't bad hunting, his squadron mates pointed out not without irony.

This passage is interesting on a number of fronts. Billy does not mention in his combat report that one of his victories on the evening patrol had been witnessed. We only find out about it because Arthur

Bishop records his father's verbal complaint about one of the kills not being confirmed. The paragraph also shows that, contrary to what some of Bishop's critics have claimed, Billy's victories were not automatically accepted by higher authority. Finally, one has to ask whether Billy's other two confirmed victories for that day had been witnessed, even if there's no written record of it.

Arthur, it should be noted, wrote his book 17 years before there was any controversy about Bishop's record, so he could hardly be accused of covering for his father.

Other respected researchers provided me with still more confirmations. British historian Dennis Hylands, for one, supplied documentation that proves a certain Lt. Barnett of 11 Squadron witnessed a Bishop victory on July 17, 1917. Joe Warne also listed this as a witnessed victory, although his letter did not provide the name of the witness. Warne did, however, note that the Bristol Fighter crew of Capt. Clement and Lt. Carter of 11 Squadron were likely witnesses for Bishop's claim for August 6, 1917.

In their authoritative book *Above the Trenches*, authors Christopher Shores, Norman Franks and Russell Guest list a Bishop victory for April 8, 1917, as being "shared" with Jack Scott, thus providing evidence of another witnessed Bishop victory that is not acknowledged by some of his critics.

Yet another confirmation that the critics have overlooked is contained at the bottom of an undated Bishop combat report. The document, which the late historian F.H. Hitchen believed was written on June 24, 1917, reads as follow:

> While escorting FEEs one HA attacked one FEE and another was flying in towards it. I dived and fired at the last one from long range and it flew away. I then attacked the HA fighting with the FEE. I fired 10 rounds and he turned on me. I dived and held my tracers in front of him. He ran into them and flew for about 300 yards seemingly only partly under control.

Attached to the report is a note, presumably written by Jack Scott, that states "an observer in 11 Squadron saw a M/C land under control." In this case, it would appear that Bishop had a witnessed FTL victory.

Greenhous concedes in his book that there may have been some Bishop confirmations that he doesn't know about. He writes:

> Of course there is always the theoretical possibility that Bishop's colleagues did see his opponent fall and that, after those first two victories (which were witnessed), Bishop did not bother to record their evidence since it was clear to him that his superiors would support all his claims, witnessed or not.

When he wrote that passage Greenhous didn't realize how on the mark he was. The late Tim Hervey, who flew with 60 Squadron in 1917, told me the victories Bishop scored while flying as a member of a patrol were almost always witnessed by his mates. "As leader of the flight he'd dive down and make the kill while the others looked on from above, with a bird's-eye view of the action," he said. Hervey made specific reference to the two victories Bishop was credited with winning on April 22, 1917, saying they'd been witnessed by no less than five 60 Squadron pilots, including Major Scott. Hervey, who was a prisoner at the time, said he heard about the fight from some of the participants after the war. "The pilots I talked to all marvelled at how Bishop pulled off that ambush," he said. He added Major Scott did not always bother to record in writing verbal confirmations of kills that had been phoned in by airmen from other squadrons.

In fairness to Greenhous, he wrote his book after Bishop's flying mates were all dead, making it impossible for him to find some of the confirmations I was able to uncover. He could not have known, for instance, that Spencer Horn once told Tommy Williams that he had seen Bishop shoot down a total of three planes.

Still, there can be no doubt that most of Bishop's victories were unwitnessed. But does that make him a liar? And more to the point, did he win the Victoria Cross, the empire's highest gallantry award, by making up a story? Did he, as some say, simply land behind his own lines and riddle his plane with his own gun before flying home with a false tale of having destroyed three planes over a German aerodrome?

Certainly, the doubts expressed by some of his contemporaries about the raid are difficult to dismiss. Men such as Caldwell, Horn and Fry were decorated aces in their own right and it is preposterous to suggest that they could have been motivated by petty jealousy. Caldwell, in fact, was the top scoring New Zealand pilot by the war's end. And, as we have seen, they were not alone in their suspicions. But could these undeniably courageous men have been honestly mistaken?

Their doubts were based on five key points:
- Bishop returned from the raid without his machine gun.
- He admitted being on the ground behind Allied lines before returning to base.
- The bullet holes in his plane were in close groups, indicating that the aircraft may not have been moving when it was hit.
- Damage to his Nieuport was not as extensive as has often been claimed.
- German records make no mention of any such raid.

On the surface, the evidence is extremely damaging. It would appear that there is strong reason to doubt that the attack ever took place.

But the evidence is misleading.

The fact that he came home without his gun can be explained easily enough. It has been widely reported that Billy threw the Lewis overboard to reduce weight and thus facilitate his escape. But such a move would have been absurd. The gun did not weigh much and it provided very little extra drag. It would have been difficult to dismantle the gun and fly the plane at the same time anyway. No pilot trying to out run a swarm of enemy fighters would spend the time and effort needed to perform such an arduous task. But there is no record anywhere of Bishop saying he tossed the weapon for that reason. The only recorded explanation is found in Fry's autobiography. The Englishman quoted Bishop as saying he threw the gun overboard because it had become

stuck in a downward position on its Foster mount while he was changing ammo drums and he was unable to get it back on the top wing.

Certainly a gun in that position would block a pilot's vision as well
as presenting a very real safety hazard in the event of a heavy landing.
So there was good reason to throw it away. Of course, it would have
been difficult to disconnect the gun from its Foster mounting and the
trigger cable from the control column while being pursued by four
adversaries, but there is nothing to say that Bishop did not conduct the
chore after crossing the safety of Allied lines — where he would have
had ample time to do the job before landing.

As for being on the ground before returning to base, there is nothing mysterious about that. Any pilot will admit it was easy to become
lost — even flying over familiar territory —if you skim the treetops for
any length of time. Bishop's explanation that he landed in a field to ask
farm workers for directions is entirely credible.

Regarding damage to the Nieuport, the evidence is inconclusive.
Some say it was in tatters but that would appear to be gross exaggeration as Bishop flew it again later that day. Stories that it contained 100
bullet holes cannot be backed up by any damage report on file with 60
Squadron. But undoubtedly, there were several punctures in the plane.
Jack Scott, at the bottom of Bishop's combat report, wrote: "His
machine is full of holes caused by machine gun fire from the ground."

The key question, obviously, is how closely grouped were the holes?
Men like Caldwell and Fry apparently felt they were so close that the
Nieuport could not possibly have been moving at the time it was hit. Fry,
for one, counted a "group of about five bullet holes in the rear half of his
tailplane, the elevator, within a circle of not more than six inches diameter at the most." The Englishman wrote the remark six decades after the
war and the holes may not have been as tightly grouped as he remembered. But there is little doubt but that they were close because squadron
mechanic A.A. Nicod, who was also on the scene, counted a dozen tears
— all compacted together — in the fuselage behind the cockpit.

Still, that hardly proves that the Nieuport was not in flight when it was
hit. Canadian Sopwith Pup ace Joe Fall once reported placing three trac-

ers into the moving head of an enemy aviator. Because only one slug in three was normally a tracer, it is probable that Fall managed to put nine bullets into his opponent's skull — an extremely small target indeed.

And Bishop, it should be noted, reported flying at treetop level while executing stall turns directly over the heads of German ground gunners. In addition, at least one Albatros pilot got behind Billy briefly in a close-quarter dogfight above the aerodrome. The D-3 pilot did, in fact, fire a burst at Bishop from that position before the ace was able to gain the upper hand. Under such conditions, hits could be expected to be closely bunched.

Aside from all that, critics have overlooked other evidence provided by Nicod who, as the squadron's chief mechanic, must be considered an expert witness when it comes to aircraft battle damage. Nicod, in his writings, made it clear that the bluenose had more than just a dozen closely grouped bullet holes near the cockpit. He said the machine was "badly damaged by anti-aircraft guns and machine gun fire." The statement is significant because it proved that Bishop crossed into enemy territory that morning. It is possible that Billy could have inflicted bullet holes on his own plane using his Lewis machine gun, but he obviously could not have produced the shrapnel damage caused by anti-aircraft cannons.

Finally, it must be pointed out that not every 60 Squadron airman who saw the machine gun marks voiced concern about the tightness of the holes. The writings of Scott and Molesworth, for example, express no such doubts. Nicod definitely believed Bishop, describing the raid as a "stupendous feat." In any case, with the absence of photographic evidence, it is impossible to say anything conclusive about the damage that the Nieuport B1566 sustained that morning. About all that can be said is that the majority of witnesses did not become suspicious of Bishop's claim by what they saw.

What has been overlooked throughout the whole controversy is the evidence provided by American aviation historian and First World War pilot Arch Whitehouse. As far back as 1962, Whitehouse, who knew many former German and Allied airmen personally, quoted German aviation authorities as admitting that Bishop had attacked one of their aerodromes. They denied, however, that he destroyed three planes, insisting that he came in low, made one firing pass and then retreated when the Albatroses took off after him.

There is yet another reason to believe that Bishop carried out the raid. And that is contained in Willie Fry's book. The old pilot relates that Bishop asked him to come along on the mission twice — once the night before in the squadron mess and again at dawn on June 2. Surely a man planning a fake attack would not be inviting others to come with him — right up to the point of take-off.

There can be no question, therefore, but that Bishop honestly planned to carry out the raid. And, based on Whitehouse's long forgotten evidence, there is no doubt that Bishop raided the enemy camp that morning.

That leaves only the question of how much damage he inflicted. Are we to believe Bishop's claim that he shot down three planes or the assertions of German authorities that he caused very little damage?

Fortunately, the choice is simple because there was a third set of witnesses to the affair. French civilians living in the Estourmel/Esnes area saw the whole thing. Two German airfields were located in the area, a permanent facility at Estourmel and a temporary field a scant four miles away at Esnes. In between lay nothing but flat farmland, giving farmers working in nearby fields ringside seats to the fight. They not only saw what happened, they remembered it very well and told their story to a group of British pilots from 12 Squadron in the autumn of 1918. Lieutenant Phil B. Townsend, an RE8 two-seater pilot with 12 Squadron, helped unlock the Bishop VC mystery in a 1985 letter to a British magazine, providing important new evidence. He wrote:

> As an active pilot in 12 Squadron in 1918 when we moved from Vaux Vrancourt (Somme) to the ex-German aerodrome at Estourmel, we were told that a British scout had attacked the German aircraft one morning in 1917 and had shot down three Huns. At that time no one seemed to know

who it was. Later, years after World War One, we realized
that such a feat was achieved by Billy Bishop and therefore
I for one can believe him.[2]

Contacted by the author in early 1986, Townsend said that the information was "learnt from local French people," who reported the raid
took place during the spring (which coincides with Bishop's claim).[3]

Two years later, Townsend qualified his statement, saying he hadn't
talked directly to the civilians. His squadron mates had talked to them
and relayed the news to him, he said. Still, as historian David Bashow
points out, Townsend's testimony is "interesting, since it appears that
farmers near Estourmel were aware of an attack on an airfield somewhere in the vicinity at the appropriate time."

Further evidence that French farmers had seen the fight surfaced on
April 17, 2002, when Group Capt. Arnie Bauer, who had visited Esnes
eighteen years earlier, told the Toronto Sun "I spoke with an elderly man
in 1984 who grew up on a farm there and witnessed the raid."

Bashow believes the airfield Bishop attacked was located at Esnes,
which was occupied on the morning of June 2, 1917 by Jasta 20. In his
book Knights of the Air, he makes a convincing case, pointing out the
names of three Jasta 20 pilots mysteriously disappeared from the unit's
roster around the time of the raid.

As for the French civilians telling 12 Squadron pilots that they'd seen
an attack on Estourmel, Bashow speculated they were referring to the
Estourmel area, not the exact airfield location. With two airfields so
close together, that was certainly possible. Quite possibly something
was lost in the translation from French to English. In any case, there are
two independent reports that farmers witnessed an airfield attack in
the Estourmel/Esnes area.

Still more proof to confirm Bishop's exploit was provided to the
author by Canadian Cavalry Captain George Stirrett. Stirrett was with a
group of Allied soldiers who took prisoner the crew of a German two-
seater. Recalling the incident in a 1981 interview, he said: "The observer
spoke fairly good English and I talked to him for quite awhile before he

was taken away. The Germans always made the observer an officer you know — he was the man in charge of the plane. The pilot was considered more or less just a chauffeur. Anyway, I had applied to get into the RFC earlier in the war and had been turned down, but still had a real interest in flying. Billy Bishop was, at this time, quite famous and I bragged to the German that he was a friend of mine, that we'd served together in the cavalry and gone overseas together — the whole works. He told me Bishop was well known to the German airmen and that his airfield attack had been the talk of the whole German air force. He said Bishop had shot down three planes and that two of the pilots had been badly shaken up. It created a real stir because the squadron that Bishop beat up was commanded by Werner Voss, who he said was considered by a lot of Germans to be their greatest pilot, even greater than Richthofen."[4]

It's important to note that Stirrett made his remarks a year before the Bishop controversy became public. He knew nothing about the doubts about the ace's record and could not be accused of attempting to cover for an old friend.

And his testimony corroborated, for the first time, rumours that were circulating during the war that the VC raid had been confirmed by German prisoners. Historian George Drew reported in the 1930s that enemy POWs had backed up Bishop's story, but he provided no evidence that such was actually the case.

In 1993 former Rumpler two-seater pilot Otto Roosen provided the first solid confirmation from the German side. Roosen, who was ninety-seven years old at the time, told the author he knew all about the raid. Asked specifically if he learned about it during the war, he said, "oh yes, we all knew about it. Our pilots talked about it for weeks. I talked to pilots who were there, but I can no longer remember their names."

In sum, the bombshell revelations of Townsend, Stirrett, Bauer and Roosen make it clear that Bishop did shoot down three planes that morning. So why don't German records show the losses? Probably because none of the three pilots were killed or wounded by the

Canadian's fire. Perhaps their planes were not even that badly damaged. Bishop's combat report states that the first two Albatroses were hit while flying extremely low to the ground. They were travelling slowly —just beginning to pick up speed as they lifted off the runway— when they were pounced upon. One fell fifty feet and the second just twenty-five. Even the third, shot down in a dogfight, was only 200 feet up. It was not at all uncommon for pilots to walk away from low level crashes in those days. Nor was it abnormal to repair a plane that had simply crash-landed from low altitude — especially in instances like this one, where no fire was involved. If there is no official German record of losses it is because Jasta commanders often did not note a loss unless a pilot had become a casualty.

In any case, the evidence of Whitehouse, Townsend, Bauer, Roosen and Stirrett provides a mountain of circumstantial confirmation that Bishop attacked a German aerodrome. And regardless of how much damage he inflicted, any pilot who had the courage to come in low, seventeen miles behind enemy lines, to attack an enemy squadron by himself, deserved the Victoria Cross.

Those who use German records to question the legitimacy of Bishop's VC should take a look at what those same documents say about other Victoria Cross winners. Consider the following:

- Canadian William Barker won the VC for shooting down four planes before being shot down and seriously wounded in a battle that was witnessed by thousands of frontline troops, including a general. Curiously, there's no German record of any fighter losses that match Barker's victories. Nor is there a record of any German pilot claiming to have shot Barker down.
- Canadian two-seater pilot Alan McLeod won the VC for a fight in which his gunner claimed three victories, none of which can be substantiated through German records.
- British ace Albert Ball won the VC for downing a dozen planes in two weeks, but only three of those kills might be substantiated through German records and only one appears to be a definite match.
- No more than twenty-one, and possibly as few as fifteen of the

sixty-one victories claimed by VC-winner Mick Mannock are confirmed in German documents.

- Only one of the seven victories claimed by VC-winning British ace
  Lanoe Hawker is supported by German records.
- British pilot Alan Jerrard won the VC for downing three planes
  over an Austrian airfield. Although his victories were witnessed by
  two decorated aces, they do not show up in enemy records.

Nor are British Empire pilots the only ones to come into doubt in this
regard. For example, there's no German confirmation of the exploit for
which American ace Eddie Rickenbacker won the Congressional Medal
of Honor, and very few of the seventy-five victories claimed by French
ace Rene Fonck are confirmed in German documents. The records of
literally dozens of other Allied aces would also be gutted if we relied on
notoriously piecemeal German records. Indeed, most historians now
accept that German records are so incomplete that it's virtually impossible to use them to prove much of anything.

Otto Roosen agreed with that assessment. In fact, he was openly con-
temptuous of German casualty records. "Our leaders didn't want to
admit that sort of thing," he said. "If they could salvage a compass from
the cockpit they'd say the plane was only damaged. It wouldn't go into
the records as having been shot down."

British ace Ira Jones was another who had little faith in German documents and he had good reason for his doubts, as he outlined in his
1954 book, *Tiger Squadron.* Jones wrote:

> "On June 19, 1918, Major (later Colonel) Billy Bishop, VC,
> DSO, MC, DFC, who was commanding 85 Squadron, shot
> down five Huns before breakfast, and Captain Cobby, DSO,
> MC, DFC, Number 1 Australian Squadron, shot down one
> Hun after tea. These were the only victories claimed by the
> Royal Air Force. In reply to our query, the German Air
> Ministry said (after the war) that they had lost neither
> pilots nor aircraft on June 19th. I know for a fact that that

statement was a lie. Captain Cobby's victim was lying, riddled with bullets, in my hangar at Clamarais North aerodrome, near Saint Omer, on the evening in question."

Jones's story lends credibility to claims in some quarters that German
commanders sometimes shamelessly disguised battle casualties as accidental losses in order to keep their combat records more impressive.

As for the claim of former RFC pilot Archibald James that "everybody" in the corps knew that Bishop was lying about victories, that just
isn't true. Canadian ace William Stephenson, who flew on the same section of the Front as Bishop, wrote in 1985: "I never heard a whisper of
criticism against him, and it is nonsense to suggest that it 'was common
knowledge he exaggerated.'" [6]

Pilot Cecil Knight, who flew with Billy in 21 Squadron in 1916, was
even more blunt. Asked in an interview if he had ever heard rumours
that Bishop was a fraud, the old flyer declared emphatically: "Never! I
would doubt it! It was not in the character of Bishop as I knew him to
do a thing like that."[7]

Historian Stewart Taylor, speaking to a Canadian senate committee
in 1985, said when he spoke to 60 Squadron pilot J. B. Crompton in
1968, Crompton "could not say enough about Bishop." Crompton also
provided confirmation of a Bishop victory, although which one is not
clear. "On his third patrol over the lines," Taylor said, "they ran into
some enemy machines. Crompton said he never saw a flight commander — Bishop obviously had fantastic eyesight — spot something
so quickly that no one else had seen — not even his deputy flight commander; but Bishop went down on this machine and shot it down and
returned to the flight. Crompton said he never felt so comfortable as
being posted to a flight with such a capable flight commander."

The Canadian ace also comes in for praise in both the public and
private writings of many pilots, including several who flew with him.
The names of Molesworth, Percival, Scott, Springs, Hervey, Neville,
Rutherford and Grider come immediately to mind. In fact, when
Bishop was given command of his own squadron in 1918, the War

Office was swamped with applications from 200 pilots who wanted to join the new outfit. That statistic, more than anything else, should refute the claim that it was an open secret among RFC airmen that Billy was a fraud. And while it is true that three former 60 Squadron pilots refused to sign a British RAF Museum 'flown cover' commemorating Bishop's raid when asked to do so in 1977, it is also a fact that another squadron member, Edgar Percival, did put his signature to the cover. And squadron member Tim Hervey indicated that he, too, would have signed, had he been asked.

Percival died just before the author could contact him, but his brother, Robert, did respond to a letter. He wrote: "I feel Edgar must have respected Bishop for I have never heard Edgar criticize him. Edgar was one who always expected the highest standards to be kept and I feel sure that if Bishop had fallen short in this respect one would have heard it from Edgar."[8]

It would appear that the main reason why only one of four pilots would sign the cover was that Bishop's critics simply outlived his supporters.

When all is said and done, it would seem that about two dozen of Billy's victories, although claimed in good faith as down out of control, driven down or forced to land, should be subtracted from his total because they were not true "kills."

What of the rest? It is possible that, on a few isolated occasions, he was overly optimistic in his claims. No one will ever know. But it is known that Bishop wanted very badly to be the leading ace. He made no bones about it, making constant reference to his score in letters home and in his autobiography, which was written mid-way through his career as a fighter pilot. He knew what fame could do for him because, after his initial successes, society showered him with awards.

There is no doubt he was ambitious. He coveted decorations as well. He said in one letter, written home before word came through that he had won the Victoria Cross, that he thought he deserved the VC.

But Billy was hardly to be blamed totally if he got caught up in the wartime atmosphere. Once he became the top scoring ace, there was enormous pressure on him to add to his score. And the authorities, eager to present the public with a new hero, were not afraid to grant him credit for victories even in cases where he had no witnesses. Perhaps it was the climate of the time, more than anything else, that explains why some of the victory claims of all of the war's greatest aces are in doubt.

Certainly, wartime stories were sometimes embellished. Bishop himself may have been subconsciously hinting at as much during a newspaper interview later in life in which he was asked to comment on his 1917 book *Winged Warfare*. "It is so terrible that I cannot read it today," Billy said. "It turns my stomach. It was headline stuff, whoop-de-doo, red-hot, hurray-for-our-side stuff. Yet the public loved it."

Of course, for the hero worshippers none of this will do. They want their legends left completely intact, regardless of what the facts may be.

In the final analysis what are we to make of Billy Bishop? Clearly there are enough confirmations of his deeds to state that he was an extremely high-scoring ace, even if his more controversial victories are subtracted. And the world will not soon forget that, during the terrible month of April 1917, flying his outgunned Nieuport, he was virtually the only pilot in the Allied forces who was able to take on the Germans and beat them time and again.

He was a hero — of that there can be no doubt. An imperfect hero, possibly, but that only proves that he was human.

A P P E N D I X   A

Billy Bishop's Victory Log

The following list of Billy Bishop's seventy-five confirmed victories was assembled from a number of sources, including official records, the letters and diaries of men who flew with him and from interviews I conducted with Bishop contemporaries. It differs in several respects from other published versions of his tally sheet, including, as it does, his balloons and identities of many Allied servicemen who confirmed his kills.

In some cases I have provided names of German airmen who appear to have been his victims, but most of these should not be considered conclusive because German records are woefully incomplete. I have dropped some of the German names I included when this book first appeared fourteen years ago, because new evidence has since cropped up.

Likewise, I have dropped John Gurdon and J.J. Scarmanga as witnesses for a pair of victories Bishop was credited with after two enemy fighters collided on June 19, 1918. Gurdon and Scarmanga reported seeing such a collision that day in the same sector of the front that Bishop was operating over. However, I have since learned that the time they gave in their report does not match Bishop's claim and it would be less than honest of me not to acknowledge the mistake.

It should be noted that, although Bishop scored the majority of his kills on solo flights, he by no means made victory claims every time he went out alone. Indeed, his logbook shows he made seventy-two solo missions without registering a claim.

ABBREVIATIONS USED:

DOOC — Down out of control

DD — Driven Down

FTL — Forced to land

KIA — Killed in action

WIA — Wounded in action

AA — British anti-aircraft battery

1917

(1) Albatros D-3. March 25, 1917. Crashed near Arras. Witnessed by Lieutenants Binnie and Bower, 60 Squadron, RFC, and by AA.

(2) Albatros D-3. March 31, 1917. Crashed near Gavrelle. Witnessed by AA and Lieutenant Leckie, 60 Squadron, RFC.

(3) Albatros D-3. April 7, 1917. DD near Arras. Solo flight.

(4) Balloon. April 7, 1917. Flamer near Arras. Solo flight.

(5) Albatros C-5 two-seater. April 8, 1917. DOOC near Arras. Shared and witnessed by Major Scott, 60 Squadron, RFC.

(6) Balloon. April 8, 1917. DD. Near Arras. Some sources list this as an unconfirmed victory.

(7) Albatros D-3. April 8, 1917. DOOC near Vitry. Possibly Leutnant Wilhelm Frankl, KIA

(8) Albatros D-3. April 8, 1917. DOOC near Douai. Vizefeldwebel Sebastian Festner.

(9) Aviatik two-seater. April 20, 1917. Flamer near Biache. Solo flight.

(10) Albatros D-3. April 22, 1917. DD near Vis-en-Artois. Witnessed by Lieutenants Young, Horn, Fry and Rutherford and Major Scoff, all of 60 Squadron, RFC.

(11) Albatros D-3. April 22,, 1917. DOOC near Vis-en-Artois. Witnessed by Lieutenants Young, Horn, Fry and Rutherford and Major Scoff, all of 60 Squadron, RFC.

(12) Albatros C-3 two-seater April 23, 1917. FTL . Solo flight.

(13) Albatros D-3. April 23, 1917. Crashed near Vitry. Witnessed by Nieuport pilot from 40 Squadron, RFC

(14) Balloon. April 27, 1917. Flamer near Vitry. Solo flight.

(15) Halberstadt D-3. April 29, 1917. Flamer near Baralle. Witnessed by FE2B crew, 11 Squadron, RFC.

(16) Aviatik two-seater. April 30, 1917. Crashed near Lens. Solo flight.

(17) Albatros C-3 two-seater April 30, 1917. FTL near Monchy. Solo flight.

(18) Albatros C-3 two-seater. May 2, 1917. Crashed near Epinoy. Possibly Unteroffizier Niese, KIA, Vizefeldwebel Seifert, WIA. Solo flight.

(19) Albatros C-3 two-seater. May 2, 1917. DOOC near Epinoy. Solo flight.

(20) AEG C-4 two-seater. May 4, 1917. Crashed near Brebieres. Witnessed and shared by Lieutenant Fry, 60 Squadron, RFC, and by AA.

(21) Albatros D-3. May 7, 1917. DOOC near Vitry. Solo flight.

(22) Albatros D-3. May 7, 1917. DOOC near Vitry. Witnessed by Lieutenant Lloyd, 60 Squadron, RFC.

(23) Albatros D-3. May 26, 1917. DOOC near Izel-les-Epeurchin. Solo flight.

(24) Rumpler two-seater. May 27, 1917. Crashed near Monchy. Possibly Vizefeldwebel Fritz Johanntges, KIA, Oberleutnant Gerd von Roedern, KIA. Solo flight.

(25) Albatros D-3. May 31, 1917. Crashed near Phalempin Aerodrome. Solo flight.

(26) Albatros D-3. June 2, 1917. Crashed over enemy airfield in Esnes/Estourmel area. Solo flight.

(27) Albatros D-3. June 2, 1917. Crashed over enemy airfield in Esnes/Estourmel area. Solo flight.

(28) Albatros D-3. June 2, 1917. Crashed over enemy airfield in Esnes/Estourmel area. Solo flight.

(29) Albatros D-3. June 8, 1917. Crashed near Lille. Solo flight.

(30) Albatros D-3. June 24, 1917. Flamer near Beaumont. Witnessed by FE2B crew, 11 Squadron, RFC.

(31) Albatros D-3. June 25, 1917. DOOC near Dury. Witnessed by Lieutenants Rutherford, Young and Soden, 60 Squadron, RFC.

(32) Albatros D-3. June 26, 1917. Flamer near Etaing. Solo flight.

(33) Albatros D-3. 26 June, 1917. DOOC near Etaing. Solo flight.

(34) Albatros D-3. June 28, 1917. DOOC near Drocourt. Solo flight.

(35) Albatros D-3. July 10, 1917. DOOC near Vitry. Witnessed by

Major Scott, 60 Squadron, RFC.

(36) Albatros D-3. July 12, 1917. Flamer near Vitry. Witnessed by Lieutenant Robert Little, RNAS Squadron 8.

(37) Albatros D-3. July, 17 1917. Crashed near Havringcourt. Solo flight.

(38) Albatros D-3. July 17, 1917. Crashed near Marquion. Solo flight. Witnessed by Lieutenant Barnett, 11 Squadron, RFC.

(39) Albatros D-3. July 20, 1917. DOOC near Havringcourt. Solo flight.

(40) Albatros D-3. July 28, 1917. Flamer near Phalempin. Solo flight.

(41) Albatros D-3. July 29, 1917. DOOC near Beaumont Witnessed by Captain Caldwell, 60 Squadron, RFC.

(42) Albatros D-3 (Jasta 12). August 5, 1917. Flamer near Monchy. Leutnant Burkhard Lehmann, KIA. Witnessed by Lieutenant Molesworth, 60 Squadron, RFC.

(43) Albatros D-5. August 5, 1917. DOOC near Monchy. Witnessed by Lieutenant Molesworth, 60 Squadron, RFC.

(44) Albatros D-3. August 6, 1917. Crashed near Brebieres. Witnessed by Lieutenants Clement and Carter, 11 Squadron, RFC.

(45) Albatros C-5 two-seater. August 9, 1917. Crashed near Ecourt. Solo flight.

(46) Albatros D-3. August 13, 1917. Flamer near Douai. Solo flight.

(47) Albatros D-3. August 13, 1917. Flamer near Douai. Solo flight.

(48) Albatros C-5 two-seater. August 15, 1917. DOOC near Henin. Solo flight.

(49) Aviatik two-seater. August 16, 1917. Crashed near Harnes. Solo flight.

(50) Albatros D-3. August 16, 1917. Crashed near Carvin. Solo flight.

1918

(51) C-type two-seater. May 27, 1918. Crashed near Houthulst. Flieger Kark Andreison, KIA, Leutnant Keil, WIA. Witnessed by AA.

(52) Albatros D-5. May 28, 1918. Crashed near Cortemarck. Unteroffizier Siche, WIA. Solo flight

(53) Albatros D-5 May 28, 1918. Crash-landed near Cortemarck. Unteroffizier Peisker, WIA. Solo flight.

(54) C-type two-seater. May 30, 1918. Crashed near Roulers.

(55) Albatros D-5 . May 30, 1918. Flamer near Roulers. Solo flight.

(56) Albatros D-5. May 30, 1918. Crashed near Armentieres. Solo flight. Witnessed by AA.

(57) Pfalz D-3. May 31, 1918. FTL near Quesnoy. Witnessed by Lieutenant Horn, 85 Squadron, RFC

(58) Pfalz D-3. May 31, 1918. DOOC near Lille. Possibly Leutnant Erich Kaus, WIA. Solo flight

(59) Pfalz D-3 June 1, 1918. Crashed near Estaires. Leutnant Paul Billik, WIA. Witnessed by Lieutenant Springs, 85 Squadron, RAF.

(60) Pfalz D-3. June 2, 1918. Crashed near Armentieres. Witnessed by Lieutenant Callahan, 85 Squadron, RAF.

(61) Albatros D-5. June 4, 1918. Flamer off Ostend. Solo flight.

(62) Albatros D-5. June 4, 1918. DOOC near Leffinghe. Solo flight.

(63) Pfalz D-3. June 15, 1918. Crashed near Estaires. Solo flight.

(64) C-type two-seater. June 16, 1918. Crashed near Armentieres. Solo flight.

(65) Albatros D-5. June 16, 1918. Crashed near Armentieres. Solo flight.

(66) C-type two-seater. June 17, 1918. Flamer near Staden. Solo flight.

(67) C-type two-seater. June 17, 1918. Crashed near Sailly-sur-Lys. Solo flight.

(68) Albatros D-5 June 17, 1918. Flamer near Laventie. Solo flight.

(69) Albatros D-5 June 18, 1918. Crashed near Ypres. Possibly Leutnant Rudolph Heins, WIA. Solo flight.

(70) Albatros D-5. June 18, 1918. Crashed near Ypres. Possibly Unteroffizier Kohler, WIA. Solo flight.

(71) Pfalz D-3. June 19, 1918. Crashed near Ploegsteert. Solo flight.

(72) Pfalz D-3. June 19, 1918. Crashed near Ploegsteert. Solo flight.

(73) Pfalz D-3. June 19, 1918. Crashed near Ploegsteert. RAP. Solo flight.

(74) Pfalz D-3. June 19, 1918. Crashed near Ploegsteert, Solo flight.

(75) C-type two-seater. June 19, 1918. Flamer near Neuve Eglise. Solo flight.

Following is a list of Bishop's five unconfirmed victories. Had these claims been accepted by authorities, he would have had eighty kills — the same number as credited to the war's greatest ace, Baron Manfred von Richthofen.

(1) Albatros D-3. April 6, 1917. Near Cherisy. Pilot Eicholz, KIA. Solo flight.
(2) AEG C-4 two-seater. April 8, 1917. DD near Vitry. Some sources
   list this as a confirmed victory.
(3) Albatros C-3 two-seater. April 30, 1917. FTL
(4) Albatros C-3 two-seater. May 2, 1917. FTL near Lens. Solo flight.
(5) Albatros D-5. May 30, 1918. DD smoking near Armentieres. Solo flight.

BIBLIOGRAPHY

BOOKS

Baker, David. *Billy Bishop: The man and the aircraft he flew*. London. Outline Press. 1990.

Bashow, David. *Knights of the Air: Canadian Fighter Pilots in the First World War*. Toronto. McArthur and Co. 2000.

Bishop, Arthur. *The Courage of the Early Morning*. Toronto: McClelland and Stewart Limited, 1965.

Bishop, William. *Winged Warfare*. Toronto: A Totem Book, 1976.

Bishop, William. *Winged Peace*. Toronto: MacMillan Company of Canada Ltd., 1944.

Cosgrove, Edmund. *Canada's Fighting Pilots*. Toronto: Clarke, Irwin and Company, 1965.

Dodds, Ronald. *The Brave Young Wings*. Stittsville: Canada's Wings, Inc., 1980.

Douglas, Sholto. *Years of Combat*. London: Collins, 1963.

Drew, George. *Canada's Fighting Airmen*. Toronto: The MacLean Publishing Company Ltd., 1931.

Fry, William. *Air of Battle*. London: William-Kimber and Company, 1974.

Greenhous, Brereton. *A Rattle of Pebbles: The First World War Diaries of Two Canadian Airmen, Don Brophy and Harold Price*. Canada: Ministry of Supplies and Services, 1987.

Greenhous, Brereton. *The Making of Billy Bishop*. Toronto. The Dundurn Group. 2002.

Harris, Norman. *The Knights of the Air*. Toronto: The MacMillan Company, 1958.

Jones, Ira. *Tiger Squadron*. London: W.H. Allen and Company, 1954.

Lewis, Cecil. *Sagittarius Rising*. London: Peter Davies Limited, 1936.

Longstreet, Stephen. *The Canvas Falcons*. New York: Ballantine Books, 1972.

Morris, Alan. *Bloody April.* London: Jarrolds Publishers, 1967.

Morris, Alan. *The First of the Many.* London: Jarrolds Publishers Limited.

Moynihan, Michael. *A Place Called Armageddon.* North Vancouver: Douglas David and Charles Limited, 1975.

Norton, Graham. *London Before the Blitz: 1906 – 1940.* London: Macdonald and Company, 1970.

Nowarra, H.J. and Kimbrough Brown. *Von Richthofen and the Flying Circus.* Los Angeles: Aero Publishers, 1964.

Oughton, Frederick and Vernon Smyth. *Ace With One Eye.* London: Frederick Muller Ltd., 1963.

Platt, Frank. *Great Battles of World War One: In The Air.* Toronto: A Signet Book, 1966.

Preston, Arthur. *Canada's RMC.* Toronto: University of Toronto Press, 1969.

Reid, Gordon. *Poor Bloody Murder.* Oakville: Mosaic Press, 1980.

Reynolds, Quentin. *They Fought for the Sky.* Clarke Irwin and Company, 1958.

Richthofen, Manfred von. *The Red Baron.* New York: Ace Books, 1969.

Santor, Donald. *Canadians at War: 1914-1918.* Scarborough: Prentice-Hall of Canada Limited, 1978.

Scott, Jack. *The History of 60 Squadron, RAF.* London: Heinemann Publishers, 1919.

Smithers, A.J. *Wonder Aces of the Air.* London: Gordon and Cremonesi, 1980.

Shores, Christopher. *Air Aces.* Greenwich, Connecticut: Bison Books Corporation, 1982.

Sims, Edward. *Fighter Tactics and Strategy, 1914–1918.* Harper and Row Publishers, 1972.

Springs, Elliott White. *War Birds: The Diary of an Unknown Aviator.* London: Temple Press, 1966.

Titler, Dale. *The Day the Red Baron Died.* New York: Ballantine Books, Inc., 1970.

Whitehouse, Arch. *Decisive Air Battles of the First World War.* New York: Duel, Sloan and Pierce, 1963.

Whitehouse, Arch. *The Years of the Sky Kings.* Garden City, New York: Doubleday and Company Inc., 1959.

Willems, John. *The Other Battleground, The Home Fronts: Britain, France and Germany, 1914 – 1918.* Chicago: Henry Regnery Company, 1972.

Winter, Denis. *The First of the Few.* London: Penguin Books Limited, 1982.

Wise, Sydney. *Canadian Airmen and the First World War.* Toronto: University of Toronto Press, 1980.

JOURNALS, MAGAZINES AND DIGESTS

Cross and Cockade Journal (USA) 1960–1973
Cross and Cockade Journal (UK) 1983–1987
Liberty Magazine
Popular Flying
Air Classics
Airforce Magazine
Hanging a Legend, a digest published by Clifford Chadderton and the War Amputees of Canada, 1986

NEWSPAPERS

Owen Sound *Sun*
Toronto *Globe*
Toronto *Star*
Toronto *Globe and Mail*
London *Daily Mail*
Ottawa *Citizen*
London *Times*
Vancouver *Sun*

AUDIO VISUAL

The Kid Who Couldn't Miss. National Film Board of Canada, 1982.

NOTES

Abbreviations Used:

AI	author interview
AC	author correspondence
Bish file	Bishop file, Directorate of History, Department of National Defence.
Hitchens	Beatrice Hitchens Memorial Aviation Collection, University of Western Ontario.
CCUSA	*Cross and Cockade Journal*, USA
ICCUK	*International Cross and Cockade Journal*, UK
TCEM	*The Courage of the Early Morning*
War Birds	*War Birds: The Diary of an Unknown Aviator*
History	*The History of Sixty Squadron*
GBWW1	*Great Air Battles of World War One: In the Air*
The Kid	*The Kid Who Couldn't Miss*
WW	*Winged Warfare*
WP	*Winged Peace*
YSK	*Years of the Sky Kings*

CHAPTER ONE

1 *The Brave Young Wings*, p. 44

2 *Globe and Mail*, Sept. 12, 1956

3 TCEM., p. 103

4 AI

5 AI

6 *Canada's RMC*, p. 195

7 *Canada's RMC*, p. 195

8 TCEM, p. 18

9 unidentified newspaper clipping, Bish file

10 GBWW1, p. 28

11 GBWW1, p. 28

CHAPTER TWO

1 AI
2 *Poor Bloody Murder*, p. 13
3 Bish file
4 AI
5 Bish file
6 AI
7 Bish file
8 AI
9 AI
10 AI
11 AI
12 Bish file
13 Bish file
14 Bish file
15 AI
16 AI
17 AI
18 Bish file
19 Bish file
20 *Poor Bloody Murder*, p. 98
21 Bish file
22 AI
23 AI
24 WP, p. 32
25 Bish file
26 WP, p. 33
27 AC
28 Bish file
29 AC

CHAPTER THREE

1 AC
2 AC

3 TCEM, p. 35
4 Bish file
5 *Air of Battle*, p. 24
6 GBWW1, p.58
7 Bish file
8 AC
9 AC
10 AC
11 AC
12 AC
13 AC
14 AC
15 AI
16 AC
17 *The Kid*
18 TCEM, p. 41
19 TCEM, P. 41
20 TCEM, p. 41
21 TCEM, p. 41
22 *The Kid*
23 Bish file
24 WP, p. 40
25 YSK, p. 186
26 YSK. p. 186
27 YSK p. 186

CHAPTER FOUR

1 CCUSA Vol. 1, No. 1, 1960
2 AC
3 AC
4 AC
5 AI
6 *Popular Flying*, Dec. 1934
7 AC

8 *Air of Battle*, p. 116
9 AI

CHAPTER FIVE
1 Hitchens
2 Bish file
3 Bish file
4 *History*
5 *History*
6 AI
7 Hitchens
8 WW, p. 111
9 *History*
10 WW, p. 47
11 WW, p. 47
12 Bish file

CHAPTER SIX
1 AC
2 *They Fought for the Sky*, p. 217
3 Hitchens
4 WW, p. 82
5 *The Canvas Falcons*, p. 310
6 *The Canvas Falcons*, p. 310
7 AC
8 AC
9 GBWW1, p. 39
10 *A Place Called Armageddon*,
   p. 144
11 *History*, p. 24
12 *History*, p. 95
13 *History*, p. 96
14 *History*, p. 95
15 AI

16 AI
17 *History*, p. 32

CHAPTER SEVEN
1 AI
2 TCEM, p. 87
3 Bish file
4 Bish file
5 WW, p. 89
6 WW, p. 89
7 Hitchens
8 *Ace With One Eye*, p. 186
9 *History*, p. 44
10 *History*, p. 95
11 *Popular Flying*, Dec. 1934
12 *Air of Battle*, p. 131
13 *Air of Battle*, p. 131
14 *Air of Battle*, p. 137
15 AI
16 *Years of Combat*, p. 252
17 *History*, pg. 46

CHAPTER EIGHT
1 *History*
2 *Globe and Mail*, Sept. 12, 1956
3 *Popular Flying*, May 1935
4 CCUSA, Vol. 9, No. 3, 1968
5 CCUSA, Vol. 9, No. 3 1968
6 *Popular Flying*, October 1934

CHAPTER NINE
1 *Globe*, Sept. 3, 1917
2 AI
3 WW. p. 149

4 Bish file

5 *Air of Battle*, p. 135

6 YSK, p. 189

7 YSK, p. 189

8 TCEM

CHAPTER TEN

1 *Air of Battle*, p. 135

2 *Hitchens*

3 Minutes, Veterans Affairs sub-
   committee, Senate, Nov. 28,
   1985

4 Minutes, Veterans Affairs sub-
   committee, Senate, Nov. 28,
   1985

5 AC

6 AC

7 AC

8 *Years of Combat*, p. 195

9 GBWWI, p. 195

10 *Air of Battle*, p. 137

11 AC

12 AC

13 AC

14 GBWW1, p. 63

15 YSK, p. 188

16 YSK, p. 188

17 AI

CHAPTER ELEVEN

1 Bish file

2 *Owen Sound Sun*, October 1917

3 AI

4 *The Red Baron*, p. 111

5 Bish file

6 AI

7 GBWW1, p. 68

8 *Knights of the Air* (Harris),
   p. 129

CHAPTER TWELVE

Main sources are the Owen
   Sound *Sun* and the Toronto
   Globe, October and November
   1917

CHAPTER THIRTEEN

1 *War Birds*, p. 56

2 *War Birds*, p. 81

3 *War Birds*, p. 81

4 *War Birds*, p. 84

5 *War Birds*, p. 89

6 *War Birds*, p. 8

7 *The Day the Red Baron Died*,
   p. 259

8 TCEM, p. 145

9 *War Birds*, p. 91

10 AI

CHAPTER FOURTEEN

1 *War Birds*, p. 96

2 Hitchens

3 AI

4 *Fighter Tactics and Stategy*,
   1914-1970, p. 74

5 *War Birds*, p. 120

6 Bish file

7 *Liberty Magazine*, January 1940

EPILOGUE

1 *Decisive Air Battles of the First World War*, p. 344

2 ICCUK, Vol. 16, No. 4, 1985

3 AC

4 AI

5 *Tiger Squadron*, p. 255

6 *Hanging a Legend*, p. 72

7 *The Kid*

8 AI

9 *Globe and Mail*, Sept. 12, 1956

INDEX